FLIP THE
FUNNEL

FLIP THE FUNNEL

How to Use Existing Customers
to Gain New Ones

JOSEPH JAFFE

WILEY

John Wiley & Sons, Inc.

Published by John Wiley & Sons, Inc., Hoboken, New Jersey.
Published simultaneously in Canada.

For general information on our other products and services or for technical support, please contact our Customer Care Department within the United States at (800) 762-2974, outside the United States at (317) 572-3993 or fax (317) 572-4002.

Wiley also publishes its books in a variety of electronic formats. Some content that appears in print may not be available in electronic books. For more information about Wiley products, visit our web site at www.wiley.com.

ISBN 978-0-470-48785-3

Printed in the United States of America.

10 9 8 7 6 5 4 3 2 1

My dearest Terri, Amber, Aaron, and Jack.
I love you all so much.

Contents

      Conversation, Commendations   217

15   The Economic Benefits of Customer Experience   237

16   Cultural Sell-through and Organizational Sign-off   247

17   Flip the Funnel for Your Personal Life   263

18   I Had a Great Experience—How about You?   269

      Resources   275

      Index   277

Foreword

I had a simple question for eBay about one of their policies. A simple, specific question. So I sent them an e-mail. They sent me back an e-mail. It was obviously preforumulated, although it started with my name. That's great. Awesome! They know my name! How did they do that? And it was a pretty great-looking e-mail. High-fives around the conference room when they banged that one out. It was chock-full of helpful information, and there were so many different questions it could have answered. They probably thought it was super efficient, because you have one thing that does all these different things. Unfortunately, out of all the questions it answered, none of them was mine. I asked for an apple, they gave me an orange, and I'm supposed to be happy because it's a fruit. Now, to make matters worse, after getting this non-helpful e-mail, I wrote back to say hey, you didn't answer my question. They didn't respond to this second e-mail, but they did send me a survey. They wanted me to rate my interaction. And I'm like, awesome. So I'm going through this survey, checking off every box to say, "You guys suck, and you suck, and you suck and you suck." And in the middle of the survey, it malfunctions. Their customer service is so bad that it even gets wrong me telling it how bad it is.

Processing is not solving. If a supposed solution uses automation to get through more of your customer input faster while fixing fewer problems, it's not a solution, it's a failure.

The reason why customer service is so horrible these days is that it is not a machine for making widgets. This hasn't stopped businesses from judging it like it is. Companies see customer service as debit on the balance sheets. A call center is a cost center. Instead of seeing the future profits that can accrue from happy customers, companies want to cut cut cut. In the name of efficiency, people who can't even understand the English words they're speaking are representing brands in crucial customer engagements. Are you really going to abdicate the last mile of customer interaction, the one where most problems, and stories for Consumerist.com, of which I'm the co-Managing Editor, arise to a population of low-paid, disenfranchised workers with zero career potential within the company, no stake in the brand, and an average turnover rate of just a few months? In the pursuit of next-quarter profits, too many companies have said "yes."

If you bought what you thought was a new microwave and came home to find the box full of wet towels instead of a microwave, you could easily say, "This is a rip-off." It gets harder when you're evaluating business practices. They come with bubbly corners, everything looks so pleasing and professional, everyone wears a tie, and all the "policies" are clearly explained in nanoscopic print. That doesn't change what lies there once you cut away all the fat and gristle. We call it a scam. They call it a business plan.

The worst thing about the edicts of the Church of Churn and Burn isn't that they're "mean" or violate some whitepaper's thumb suck on "best practices"; it's that it makes less money. Their avowed justification for being a jerk, profits, doesn't even hold its own water. This notion of get the customers in the door, get as much money as you can from them, then toss them out the back and launch your next marketing campaign to get the next batch of suckers, is dead. It might have worked when you could just bombard consumers into submission with enough repetitions of your 30-second spot, but consumers are getting the real scoop from each other with unprecedented ease, breadth, and depth. The Internet has accelerated word-of-mouth to the degree that one reader's customer-service horror story can go from Consumerist.com to the tops of social news networks to major news outlets in just a few days. How cost-effective did you say was the idea of firing all your experienced floor employees and replacing them with raw recruits, Circuit City, R.I.P.?

You're probably being ripped off at this very moment and you don't even know it. Have you seen what your frequent flyer miles are worth lately? Probably a lot less than when you signed up. Everywhere we turn, companies are pulling back from the value they offered when you signed the contract and handed over your payment, and leaving fees and restrictions in their wake. Gift cards whose value dwindles over time. Credit-card payment due dates getting shorter and shorter. Customers with one late payment on their credit card having their interest rates shoot up to the highest the law allows. Impossible-to-fulfill warranty repairs. Overdraft fees completely disproportionate to their cost. Health insurance coverage denied for the flimsiest of reasons. The list goes on.

A number of false prophets say they have the answer. It's almost rote that each iteration of "new marketing 2.0 get jiggy with the Internets" advice uses as its proof of concept some story about how there was this one guy who absolutely loved this company's – let's say hats – and every time he got on the plane he would tell people how these hats rock. He sent in his ideas on how to make hats even better and rather than not even reading what he wrote or responding with a form letter and some free coupons, the hat company sent him more free hats and incorporated some of his suggestions in their future designs. Yay, see how treating your customers nicely and using their feedback works. This is ground-breaking research? I always thought the secret of business was figuring out what people need and selling it to them. Apparently, others hold different opinions. They've opted to build entire empires based on telling people what they want and then selling it to them. It works, until people stop listening. You can't tell people what to do if they're not listening. Well, it's not that they're not listening; they're just getting their information from a lot more sources. Sources that are faster, better, and independent. In this new environment where customers demand instant accountability, your street cred is priceless.

Surely there must be a way to bridge the gap between us and our customers. Jaffe's book seems a pretty good place to start. He gets that customer service is marketing, and that marketing is listening. As he details, it might take under a minute to ruin a customer's opinion of your company, but Google will remember their blog post forever. Crisis mitigation is but just the first step, though. Using social media to put out PR forest fires is one thing, but can you cultivate bonfires of customer joy?

Through success stories like USAA, Zappos, and the Obama campaign, *Flip the Funnel* demonstrates how leading-edge marketers are authentically engaging with their customers and building long-term relationships, relationships that can live through and beyond economic downturns. With insight, enthusiasm, and real-world examples, Jaffe illuminates the philosophies and techniques marketers need to be using to survive in a world where the communications playing field is flattening and average citizens are seizing power and dictating the terms of what gets paid attention. Not only is marketing no longer one-way, it's not even two-way. It's a conversation between you, me, and everyone I'm talking to about what we're talking about. Sure, social media is a huge part of the equation, but you can't just slap your company on Facebook and expect to start a revolution. As Jaffe shows, it's not which tools you use, it's how you use them, and why.

In this book, Jaffe proves how by making customer experience paramount, retention becomes the new acquisition. This is the "flip" of the traditional "marketing funnel" that forms the basis for this book's title. Within he reveals how some of the most exciting and inspiring organizations are shifting the marketing model so that they start with the sale rather than ending with it. After all, if activated brand advocates are your best form of advertising, do you really need more advertising? Or do you just need a better way of relating to your customers?

—Ben Popkin
Co-Managing Editor, Consumerist.com

Acknowledgments

I want to thank my fellow crayonistas, in particular Amadeo Plaza for his contributions toward this book. In addition, I want to thank Greg Verdino for his ongoing counsel and also because I didn't thank him in *Join the Conversation.*

A number of organizations helped make this book possible, but in particular Forrester Research and Satmetrix gave me access to key research, data, and insights.

To Seth Godin, who (unbeknownst to me) authored an e-book several years back titled *Flipping the Funnel.* When I found out about it, I asked him how he felt about my book concept, which admittedly was different enough from his specific take. Being the gentleman he is, he told me to venture forth, be fruitful and multiply, which I found strange but uplifting nonetheless. Thanks, Seth.

This book is all about customers and so to *my* customers, both crayon clients who have allowed me the incredible opportunity to work with their esteemed brands and put all this theory into practice, and to the countless companies that put their money where my mouth is and bring me out to speak to audiences in every major continent on this planet—thank you all for your business, friendship, and continued support.

To my community of readers, listeners, viewers, friends, fans, and followers, thank you for all your wisdom and for making me look smart.

As always, to my Mother. Do I even need to give a reason?

Preface

What if we got it all wrong? What if everything we held about doing business was backwards? What if all our theories, assumptions, and best practices were, in fact, flawed?

Those are some of the questions I hope to answer — or, at the very minimum, stress test — in this book. And in doing so, I hope I'm able to offer up a few paths less traveled for you to explore and ultimately venture down when it comes to building businesses, brands, and relationships.

In many respects, *Flip the Funnel* is a logical evolution and inevitable conclusion of sorts from my first book, *Life after the 30-Second Spot,* through my second, *Join the Conversation,* to "this." In all three books, I've done my utmost to debunk some of the worst-kept secrets in the business and marketing worlds. In all three books, I essentially take *aim* at dirty little secrets, unafraid to say the things most dare not, and am prepared to ask the questions that many wish were put out there yet that remain relegated to back-office conversations.

Starting with *Life after the 30-Second Spot* (which is slowly but surely becoming required reading across university campuses), I focused on the three primary colors of red, yellow, and blue — or television, radio, and print — and claimed that *in its existing form,* the 30-second spot (as a metaphor for a certain way of doing business) is either dead, dying, or has outlived its usefulness. I essentially interrogated what we call paid media as nothing more than an unnecessary evil, a traditional and therefore predictable, staid, and decreasingly impactful blunt object. In its place, I introduced the concept of nontraditional — that is, emerging or alternative — approaches, or new marketing, the *other* 93 colors in the box of crayons. I outlined ten of these new approaches: interactive, gaming, on-demand consumption, long-form content, communal marketing, experiential marketing, consumer-generated content, mobile, search, and branded entertainment.

Next came *Join the Conversation,* where I took a broad-based view that *all* the communication in the world can get you only so far — after which conversation takes over. Think about it this way: Communication — defined as *us* talking at, to, or down to *them* — gets our foot in the door, while conversation is our consumers' opening the door—as opposed to breaking our feet by repeatedly slamming that door on us—and inviting us into their homes, living rooms, and lives. I made the case that there are literally millions of conversations (alive, real, flawed, authentic, persuasive, human) going on around us at this very moment, so isn't it time we joined in? I asserted the hypothesis that marketing *can* be a conversation, as opposed to an unwelcome guest.

And now here we are: living in a world of transparency, operating on a level playing field where there has been an acute democratization of control. We're doing business amid a rapidly shrinking, flat world where a collective consciousness throbs with a passionate sense of purpose, a global orb of integrity governed by communities or wise crowds, where the four Cs—communication, collaboration, connectivity, and creation (creativity)—fuel social fusion.

Oh and yes, there's that social media thingy: the Web 2.0 phenomenon, the new world, the new order, the antidote or cure to the common cold. Though I live in this world, I'm not governed or brainwashed by it. I live, breathe, and sleep this world, but I'm not reliant on it. And so, if you're expecting a social media handbook—a how-to tactical guide to help you get your blog deployed, friends acquired or influenced, or your tweet stream initiated—quickly return to the store and get your money back.

In contrast, this book is probably the closest I've come to returning to my roots or, arguably, the roots of marketing itself. It's all about finding a balance between the very fundamentals of marketing and business theory and intertwining them with new ideas, uses, stories, and approaches. Think of it as the best of the old combined with the best of the new. Case in point: I'll spend a lot of time talking about customer service, but not the way you usually think about it. Instead, I'll show you how it's not a reactive means of helping customers with problems, but rather a key—perhaps THE key—strategic differentiator that could quite possibly transform your business. I'll cover relationship marketing but, again, not as you've ever thought about it. I'll allude to permission, opting in, e-mail, and CRM (customer relationship marketing or management) without forgetting about the *who* on the other end of the spectrum. In other words, *keeping it real*, having honest, open, and dynamic conversations with the human beings we call customers.

As the title of this book intimates, I'll introduce an entirely new customer behavioral framework that mirrors, counterbalances, or continues where the traditional consumer behavior model leaves off. I'll also put forward several new ideas that will layer neatly on top of the running themes in this book. For example, how does word of mouth combine with customer experience? What is the real role of social media? Is it possible to grow a business from the inside out? What happens when customer evangelists become effective salespeople? Is it possible to incentivize existing customers to spread the good word about you, your company, and your goods and services *without* muddying the waters in the process? Some refer to it as "sponsored conversations"; I call it customer activation or Affiliate 2.0, a new kind of referral-based marketing that works from the inside out.

I'll challenge you to flip everything you knew to be true on its head. I'll encourage you to flip the funnel—and to do so *now*. I'll urge you to focus on retention instead of acquisition to the point where retention *becomes* the new acquisition. As always, I won't expect you to agree with everything I say, but I don't need you to. If you can take away just one actionable insight or idea and put it into practice in a way that saves and/ or earns your company millions of dollars—or your currency of choice— then I will have done my job a million times over.

THE MILE HIGH CLUB

I noticed that the airline industry seemed to come up an awful lot during the writing of this book. And it is fitting that as I write this particular paragraph, I'm actually *on* a flight. So I came up with two reasons as to why flying seemed to contribute so many case studies to this book:

1. More and more airlines are now outfitted with wireless high-speed Internet access. This real-time connectivity is rapidly compressing the speed at which a complaint hits the conversational or social stratosphere.
2. Airlines are famous—or perhaps I should say infamous—for providing poor customer service. Many consumers resign themselves to the fact that they all suck equally. And yet there are stellar examples of how this could—and should—be corrected. The lesson here is simple: Every business in every sector is capable of flipping the funnel.

Every industry has a similar story to tell. What about yours? Will your company flip the funnel by doing what Virgin, Jet Blue, or

SouthWest did to their industry, or litter the trash heap alongside the countless airlines that failed to triumph over mediocrity, convention, and the status quo?

TICK. TOCK.

As with my first two books, this book is an elaborate opinion piece. It's based on my personal vision and unique perspective on where the puck is heading. If I'm even remotely right about what I say, then the ideas, strategies, and recommendations in this book can be truly transformational for business in general—perhaps even *your* business. And I'm not talking about business as usual. I slay sacred cows, even purple ones. I've found that people play it safe too often. They don't make a decision. They're afraid to stick their necks out. I'm not like that, and I hope you appreciate it.

The preceding paragraph is also my way of saying that I'm not professing to be any kind of CRM, one-to-one, loyalty, retention, customer, service, or e-mail marketing expert per se. That just might be a good thing; it allows me to come into this discovery process or journey without prejudice, bias, or baggage. As with marketing in general (ever heard the line "advertising isn't rocket science?"), I believe that treating customers well, remembering their names, respecting their loyalty, rewarding and recognizing their repeat business, and finally, harnessing their untapped potential as advocates, salespeople, and affiliates are all COMMON SENSE. So while I won't elaborate on the various technologies, systems, and convoluted so-called solutions in this space, I will offer strategic guidance and frameworks that I think need to be in place to support any subsequent investment thereafter.

I should also mention that my writing style is unique. It's not for everyone. I write as I speak, and I speak as I write. I use "quotes" a lot and (even) (more) (parentheses) than are sometimes bearable. Perhaps it's a written visualization of how I think; call it nonlinear or ADD, depending on whether you're feeling generous. I hope it doesn't put you off.

One more thing. As you read this book, feel free to reach out to me with questions, comments, or ideas. You can contact me in a variety of ways (see the back of the book), visit the book's web site (www.flipthefunnelnow. com), e-mail me at jaffe@getthejuice.com, or send me a public or private message via @jaffejuice (my primary account) or @flipthefunnel (with specific book-related questions) on Twitter.

Section I

Getting Priorities Straight

1

The Theory behind Flipping the Funnel

It's time to go back to school and open up your Principles of Marketing textbooks, where you'll read about S.T.P. (Segmenting, Targeting, and Positioning), the three key roles for communication (informing, persuading, and reminding), and ultimately, the four pillars of marketing strategy: the four Ps of Product, Price, Place, and Promotion.

Now I'd like you to tear up those textbooks, forget those theories, and start anew with a blank sheet of paper.

Stereotypical demographics are no longer enough to paint a sufficiently rich picture of a prospective customer beyond a superficial outer layer of basic variables. Top-of-mind positioning has been replaced with top-of-page positioning (in other words, search-engine results). The advertising-biased roles of informing, persuading, and reminding are being usurped by involvement, demonstration, and empowerment. The commoditized four Ps have been updated with a new model: the six Cs of Content, Commerce, Community, Context, Customization, and Conversation (per *Join the Conversation*, which I'll reprise a little later in this book).

And now it's time to set our sights on the very foundation of consumer behavior itself: the marketing funnel, aka, A.I.D.A. (the theory, not the opera). A.I.D.A. stands for Awareness, Interest, Desire, and Action. It is widely held to be the simplest and most accurate way of describing the four states or behaviors that almost all consumers experience — from being blissfully unaware of a product, service, offer, or idea that they never knew they needed to the point at which they actually make some kind of commitment (usually monetary) to purchase, invest in, or acquire that item.

Allow me to delve into each stage in a bit more detail.

AWARENESS

Perhaps *A* should stand for alpha male when it comes to the unrelenting hold that awareness has over us, the dominance it exhibits over our attention, and more important, our investment in awareness-led initiatives relative to the other three components. *A* could also stand for Advertising, because it is predominantly this — or, more specifically, paid media — that is deployed in order to deliver on an arbitrary awareness objective.

I'm still not quite sure where it is written that telling and selling[1] should eclipse all other steps in marketing acquisition to the point of dwarfing them in the process. To this day, there are still way too many companies that invest way too much money in efforts that have nothing more than a singular goal: create awareness. Don't take my word for it — take the test yourselves. Divide your marketing dollars into the following four buckets:

Budget Breakdown Against A.I.D.A.

	Investment Dollars	Percentage of Total
Awareness (e.g. advertising)	$	%
Interest (e.g. search)	$	%
Desire (e.g. promotions)	$	%
Action (e.g. e-commerce, POS, in-store)	$	%
		100%

I wonder if it's nothing more than desperation — or perhaps I should say resignation — that motivates otherwise smart people to set a bar so unbelievably low that their entire success or failure hinges on a binary state of being aware or unaware. To be sure, if people don't know about you, your products, their benefits, and what makes them different and/or better than competing products, the odds are much lower that they'll actually purchase your product. Other than serendipitous or accidental encounters at the store, the bus stop, or the watercooler, there has to be some kind of formalized structure or process in place designed to seed, guide, or migrate customers from ignorance to enlightenment.

There *is*, actually. Read on.

---

[1] A phrase introduced by former Procter & Gamble Global Chief Marketing Officer Jim Stengel.

Knowing, however, is not the same as doing. Merely putting something out there in the hope that it will stick is naive, futile, and exceptionallyunrealistic in today's fragmented, cluttered, and brand-wary world. Avinash Kaushik, author of *Web Analytics* and analytics evangelist for Google, refers to much of media communications as "faith-based initiatives." In other words, they are often futile attempts to bridge or reconcile the vast chasm between the two ends of the funnel—exposure and conversion—in order to prove the causal link and proportional relationship between communication (awareness) and commerce (action).

INTEREST

Getting people to care these days is like climbing Mount Everest. People today are skeptical, jaded, cynical, and wary—and increasingly so, due to the hardships and hangover of the recession. And those are the good ones! The rest are apathetic, uninterested, indifferent, and detached. Most messages don't make it through the multiple layers of consumers' near-impenetrable defenses, and the ones that do are greeted with either a pitchfork or a pillow. It's a catch-22 of dire proportions.

As the funnel begins to narrow, what's left is a group of people who have some kind of reaction—positive or negative—toward a promise, value, or selling proposition. It's not guaranteed that they'll remain on the path toward purchase; they're not necessarily motivated to do anything about their raised eyebrow, chuckle, or head nod; and even if they are dead set on getting to the next level, there's no assurance of success, because of a variety of logistical curveballs, such as crashed browsers, closed stores, human error, or other uncontrollable forces.

The one-two punch of Awareness-Interest is a good start, but it falls painfully short of being able to completely close the gap between exposure and conversation. To get to the next phase of the funnel, companies need more follow-through and staying power. However, they typically run out of steam (or budget) in the graveyard of wasted and/or ignored impressions that bleed them dry as they attempt to repeatedly hammer home their message in order to get this far in the first place.

That's where search came to the rescue, hitting the ground running with a presupposition of some kind of qualification of relevance, resonance, and/or interest. With search, consumers travel a two-way street, often initiating a journey or dialogue with a potential brand suitor as opposed to the other way around. Science trumps faith—especially when performance-based pricing ensures that marketers get what they paid for in a transparent package of perfect information.

But search has its shortcomings as well; it cannot exist in a vacuum. For starters, it presupposes baseline knowledge or, dare I say, awareness. Put differently, people don't know what they don't know. Furthermore, as efficient as it might be, search—like awareness—is not a guaranteed direct path to the checkout counter.

Interest is essentially a road sign that says, "You're in the right place" or "You're on the right track." It's the refreshment stand in a marathon race, but it's not a guarantee of a medal, or even an assurance of finishing the race at all.

DESIRE

Brand messaging teaches us that there needs to be a reason to believe, whereas a tactical hook offers a reason to behave. If the former answers the question, "why should I care?" the latter addresses the "what's in it for me?" part of the equation. And don't underestimate the power of "intent" on the part of our consumers or "incent" on the part of ourselves (as sellers), because it's huge. There's simply too much choice in the marketplace for us to foolishly believe that our special brand of secret sauce is so good that all other options pale into obscurity. When the funnel narrows even further at the desire phase, everybody left in the running has some kind of varying state of readiness to make a financial commitment—that is, purchase.

Intent to purchase is 95 percent of the battle won. Being motivated (or even self-motivated) to satisfy a want, need, or desire to purchase a product or service implies a sense of pull that needs to be helped with a final nudge or push to help a consumer get over the hump of best-laid plans. Promotions are probably the best tactic in our marketing toolbox for allowing us to offer up an incentive for consumers to get to that 95 percent mark.

That said: wanting to buy and actually *buying* can be worlds apart. As the saying goes in golf, "99 percent of all short putts never go in the hole." Customized offers and calls to action, incentives to act (now!), and packaging redesigns or modifications—including (but not limited to) *"now with 20 percent more toothpaste"*—are all designed to help overcome the final hurdle that separates consumers from customers.

ACTION

There is light at the end of the tunnel (or rather, funnel.) Where was once a sea of suspects or an army of prospects, we now have a fraction of the mob that made it to the store—physical or online—and committed a portion of their hard-earned salary in exchange for our wares. At the point of purchase (what is referred to in retail as the "final three feet"), the ink is pretty much dry, and there's really not much marketers can do to change a consumer's mind.

Or can they?

With point of sale, couponing, digital signage, and in-store television networks—and on the not-too-distant horizon, RFID, GPS, mobile social networking, and Wi-Fi—the storefront is going to become the new battlefront. For some it will be the last stand, and for others a second chance at (coupon) redemption.

The final few steps of the marketing funnel may seem like a *fait accompli*, but it's a lot harder than it sounds. Walls of competing SKUs, diversions and distractions from in-store displays, and gondola ends designed for that change of heart (a place to dump your unwanted goods) or to make an impulse purchase are all difference makers. It's exponentially magnified online, where pretty much anything and everything is only a click away, and where self-imposed ADD in the form of a Twitter chirp, Outlook ding, or IM ping is enough to reverse several carefully constructed steps of migration from one side of the funnel to the other.

Warts and all, this is the marketing funnel in its simplest terms and definitions: a linear, standardized, and otherwise predictable process of defining, segmenting, and describing consumer behavior from marketing management, communications, and even sales perspectives.

It is a funnel that has stood the test of the time . . . or has it?

Today, the once-shiny funnel is dinged and dented, rusted and dusted. It relies on masses of quantity in order to arrive at a manageable end point of quality; it is a methodology that takes protracted time, endless reserves of energy, and (though not endless) a ton of money. The marketing funnel is synonymous with—and probably should just be called—an acquisition funnel, and it is a funnel of futility when it is an end unto itself.

WHAT'S WRONG WITH THE FUNNEL?

This book hypothesizes that there's something inherently out of whack with the traditional marketing funnel and that there are better ways to optimize it. Most of this book concentrates on the latter approach, the "flipping" part. However, it is worthwhile to spend a little bit of time calling out several shortcomings associated with the incumbent theory in order to provide a base level of context for the suggested alternative.

It's Out of Date

Come on; people aren't predictable, linear, rational, or sequential beings. They probably never were. Though the four steps make sense in theory from a logical or even chronological standpoint, the buying game is very different in reality. In a word-of-mouth and word-of-mouse led world, the process of researching and buying is decidedly *non*linear, and it's likely that some steps are skipped altogether in an always-correcting, efficient, and evolving marketplace.

It's Lopsided or Out of Proportion

The reason the funnel is wider at one end and narrower at the other is not *only* because of the number of people that are theoretically present at each step but arguably because of the amount of money spent or available at each step. If you think about it, shouldn't we be spending more money against qualified prospective buyers versus shots in the dark at bagging a random stranger? Of course we should. It's a complete no-brainer.

It's Oversimplified

There's a fine line between simplifying something complex down to a root or core state and *over*simplifying it to a fault. The marketing funnel does not factor in at least three critical components associated with the qualification process, and even more intriguing is that all three are consumer driven or initiated, starkly contrasting against the incumbent steps, which are all marketing-centric or oriented. These steps are as follows:

1. **Research**—Search is just the tip of the iceberg, a portal into an aggressive and proactive due-diligence process. Consumers today are indefatigable researchers; they will do what they can to make informed decisions that disintermediate marketing mis-direction, hyperbole, overpromise, and hype. They'll also spend

increasing amounts of time talking with peers, colleagues, friends, and family members, as well as interacting with newly formed acquaintances in the social networking and digital community arenas.

2. **Trial** — *Try before you buy* is a crucial solution to hesitation, inability to commit, or indecision. And just like search was the tip of the research iceberg, so, too, is couponing or sampling the tip of the trial step. Oftentimes, trial is indirect or inferred; for example, a movie review today is independently and representatively vetted, endorsed, and validated by a community of "me's" and "you's." When trial becomes an existential experience, there's no danger in seeing a bad movie anymore.

3. **Satisfaction** — Interestingly enough (if we're using Wikipedia[2] as the gold standard), "satisfaction" is the only missing component of A.I.D.A. that tends to make it into conversations about the consumer-qualification process. Perhaps it's because it slots neatly into an acronym (A.I.D.A.S.), and who doesn't love the convenience of a neat-sounding acronym? Satisfaction is the one clue that the funnel is not quite done yet.

It's Linear

Human beings are increasingly unpredictable mammals. Expecting them to go through any kind of process (especially one WE created for THEM) with a degree of standardization and/or certainty is a dangerous assumption to make. With incessant distractions, constantly new propositions, and exciting ways of transacting with a company, it's no longer valid to bank on a predictable path to purchase. Instead, witness a more realistic behavior, mixed with accelerated, skipped, and even repeated steps or pathways to purchase.

It's Open

What happens to the chosen few who make it through to the other end of the funnel? They fall to their grisly deaths in the vertical drop of attrition. Put less grandiosely and more pragmatically, the funnel is purely an acquisition process and does not continue to retention. Perhaps if there were a bucket underneath, we'd be a little more

---

[2] http://en.wikipedia.org/wiki/AIDA_(marketing).

reassured that there was some kind of safety net built into an incredibly costly (or risky) game of conquesting.

It's Incomplete

Even if the funnel were closed insofar as there was a destination or goal, it would still be *incomplete;* the end point would still be a dead end. The marketing funnel produces customers—but then does nothing with them. With so much effort expended to produce a priceless transaction, it is almost inconceivable that we all but abandon our intensity thereafter. Perhaps we're locked into a cruel version of *Groundhog Day,* when we immediately are taken back to the beginning, only to have to repeat our entire marketing mating dance with (as history has shown us) barely any new lessons learned and diminishing success rates.

2

What the Recession Taught Us
(AKA Returning to Basics)

We are living through challenging times. I don't have to tell you that. In the blue corner, we have the worst recession since the Great Depression. In the red corner, we have increasing demands to produce "more from less." This is not exactly the kind of motivation that gets you out of bed in the morning, but it's certainly the kind that keeps you up in bed at night. So what's a self-respecting businessperson to do about it—especially when *your* job might not be there in the morning?

We must understand the past to plan for the future, and when it comes to operating during challenging times, there is good news. Study after study clearly show that companies that continue to invest—and market—during recessionary times almost always reap the rewards of doing so when the economic climate stabilizes. In fact, they don't just do *okay;* they do better than their competitors. Whether it's priming the pump, setting the stage, or just continuing to keep the lights on to brighten an otherwise dim atmosphere, keeping the wheels turning makes sense.

There are probably several reasons or explanations as to why this is the case. Here are three:

1. Attitude (positive)
2. Boldness (risk taking)
3. Continuity

ATTITUDE

The power of positive thinking might sound trite, but when last I checked, entire industries have been built around this simple notion.

Just ask Rhonda Byrne, author of *The Secret,* if "glass half full" trumps or surrenders to a "glass half empty" perspective.

To be clear, I'm talking less about blind hope and more about healthy pragmatism with respect to the rational belief that things will return to how they once were. People drive, eat, and consume; they spend, shop, and buy. These are not up for debate. They're universal truths. Sure, there are times when they might do less of these things than they used to—such as business or personal travel—but for every door that closes, another opens. Case in point: videoconferencing, like Cisco's Telepresence (to replace travel for meetings) or, in the consumer world, staycations or family road trips (instead of a regular family vacation).

If there's anything that's inevitable, it's the swinging of the pendulum as it returns to rest and equilibrium. Yet for some reason, the scenario of doom and gloom is typically met with desperation, despair, and defeatism, whereas the converse—when times are too good to be true—is often characterized by arrogance, hubris, and unrealistic expectations of sustainability.

The point is that history is on our side.

People will no doubt continue to buy stuff. And sell stuff. And do both on eBay. It's just that they sometimes go on hiatus when they're distracted. And if you're in the business of business, chances are that the extremely bad times will be canceled out by the extremely good times, and you'll settle somewhere nicely in, on, or around the middle.

During these uncertain times, it's important to keep the fires burning. It's also vital to avoid extinguishing a flame that is always much harder to reignite than it is to keep alight. This analogy is most relevant and applicable for our customers from a retention standpoint (more on that later).

BOLDNESS (RISK TAKING)

I'm a big fan of taking risks, and yet the rest of the world seems to disagree with me.

At the end of the day, we're in two separate yet related businesses. One is about managing change, and the other is about managing (or mitigating) risk. If you think about it, today's chief marketing officers got to where they are not by managing risk but by mitigating it.

Does this sound like a strategy worth banking?

Risk is the ability to do things that have never been done before, to boldly go where no brand has gone before. In marketing speak, to differentiate; in business speak, to lead. At least, that's my definition of risk. According to the dictionary however, it would appear that risk is in fact associated with *negative* consequences, not positive ones. Wikipedia defines risk as a "concept that denotes a potential negative impact to some characteristic of value that may arise from a future event." These events or conditions—especially ones characterized by uncertainty—are thought to have harmful or negative effects. In everyday usage, risk is often used synonymously with the probability of a known loss—an ironic certainty, indeed.

At the end of the day, only you can decide on which side of the fence you sit. While you're thinking, consider this:

- Risk is relative. What is risky to one person is not to another.
- Risk can be calculated, or measured. Managing it can be both a science and an art.
- As the saying goes, "If I had known then what I know now, I would never have done it." Sometimes just doing it trumps analysis paralysis and fear of the unknown.
- The risk associated with doing nothing and sticking to the status quo may ultimately outweigh the downside of doing something differently and erring in the process. Case in point: spending millions of dollars on campaigns that nobody notices (unless you're counting hits on YouTube as your barometer of success).

Boldness is not about taking chances; it is about being confident, decisive, and laser-focused when making the right decisions for the right reasons at the right time. It's also why—if you're the only one pro-actively marketing during a time when no one else is—standing out from the crowd quite literally becomes inevitable.

An Association of National Advertisers (ANA) study from February 2009 measured sentiment within the marketing community and compared it to six months prior (August 2008). Pretty much every indicator was negative to downright depressing. When asked about cutting costs (which wasn't an "if" but a "how" type of question), here's where marketers were slashing their budgets:

- Department travel and entertainment restrictions (87 percent versus 63 percent in the previous survey)

- Reducing advertising campaign media budgets (*77 percent versus 69 percent previously*)
- Reducing advertising campaign production budgets (*72 percent versus 63 percent in the previous six months*)
- Challenging agencies to reduce internal expenses and/or identify cost reductions, aka layoffs (*68 percent versus 63 percent*)
- Eliminating or delaying new projects (*58 percent versus 61 percent*)

I'm less concerned about the decreases pertaining to advertising, because, quite frankly, this relates to an inevitability that has been decades in the making. I *was* interested in the "eliminating or delaying new projects" category, which, incidentally, was the only category that actually did not increase in terms of cuts. Although it wasn't clear to what extent this covered investment in technology, innovation, or experimentation (as opposed to a new photo shoot, over-the-top Super Bowl campaign, or glossy rebranding effort), budget cuts were hopefully more of the latter and less of the former.

Either way, this number is still too high. During constricted times like these, an obsessive focus on thinking smartly, creatively, shrewdly—even laterally—is required. This kind of thinking does not and cannot happen in the absence of risk. When Hyundai launched their simple promise along the lines of "Lose Your Job, Return the Car," they took a risk that they'd be sitting on a heap of returned cars—especially considering that January 2009's job losses (598,000[1]) were the worst in 34 years (and that a whopping 1.8 million jobs were lost in the United States in the three-month period of November 2008 through January 2009). But when last I checked, this hasn't happened. In fact, Hyundai's sales were up 14.3 percent[2] in January 2009. That's what happens when you trust your customers like you would want them to trust you in return.

CONTINUITY

In media terms, we'd call this the antidote for going dark on our customers, in other words, maintaining a consistent dialogue with one's consumer base. As mentioned in *Join the Conversation*, this is the

---

[1] http://money.cnn.com/2009/02/06/news/economy/jobs_january/index.htm?postversion= 2009020610.

[2] www.forbes.com/2009/02/04/hyundai-mazda-mitsubishi-markets-equity-0204_auto04.html.

ability to create a systematic process and contact management system that ensures and encourages frequent and meaningful dialogue with your consumer—on *their* terms.

At the very core of the definition of "branding" is the word "continuity" or "consistency"; in this context, they are one and the same. It is absolutely imperative that we remember that business does not occur in staccato. For some reason, our acute inability to present a smooth, integrated solution to our customers runs starkly in the face of how they live their lives. Our mission is to ensure that there's always a trail of breadcrumbs that leads us to our customers and back again. I often refer to this as connecting the dots or establishing (and reestablishing) meaningful connections if and when they're needed.

Along the same lines as keeping the fires burning is the need for sufficiency. What's the minimum acceptable level of contact, presence, interaction, and/or commitment we need to stay in the game and maintain some kind of workable dialogue and business momentum? Clearly, every company and industry is different, but these are vital questions that must be addressed and ultimately answered—preferably long before they actually need to be.

Companies that maintain consistent rapport with their customers during tough times insulate themselves against inroads that come at the hands of undercutting and undermining competitors—as well as promote a renewed sense of loyalty. As the saying goes: *A true test of a friend is not during the good times, but during the bad times*. When the going gets tough, we reveal our true colors—and hopefully the color we display is not yellow.

Now here's the funny thing: The chapter thus far really has *nothing* to do specifically with operating in a recession. Sure, these truths are *exacerbated* by tough times, but if you think about it, poor economic and operating environments just amplify an already existing and often unmet need to serve the lifeblood of your business—your customers.

We always remind ourselves that the primary goal or role of advertising is to sell stuff, but that's really just one piece of the puzzle. Our cardinal mistake is to forget that it is these four simple truths (or metrics) that keep us in business:

1. Getting more customers to buy from us
2. . . . More often
3. To spend more with us in the process
4. . . . AND to recommend us to their friends

So why, then, do we seem to concentrate the lion's share of our dollars on point 1 ONLY?

What if we've got it all wrong? Or what if we had the right idea all along but just went about our business the wrong way? Take the marketing and sales funnels, for example (they're somewhat different). These tools from the classic marketing tool belt were designed to sift through an inordinate amount of suspects and prospects to extract the gold nuggets (customers) from the dirt (everyone else) by gently guiding (or sometimes forcing) them through a linear progression from awareness through action. But what if, instead of *ending* with the purchase action by the converted customer, we *began* with this action and, in doing so, focused on achieving three distinct goals:

1. Building solid, ongoing, and authentic bonds or relationships with our customers (customer service and experience)
2. Transforming customers into returning clients and ultimately advocates (customer relationship management)
3. Harnessing the unstoppable power of referrals, recommendations, and word of mouth for outreach to other potential customers (social networking or even a new kind of Affiliate Marketing)

What if, by following these rules, we were able to essentially flip the funnel and *reverse-engineer future growth from a platform or foundation of current growth?* What if we could use the sparks of satisfaction to generate a raging furnace of preference, precedence, and insistence?

From the few come the many: That's the mantra of the flipped funnel. As you'll see from this book, it can be applied to any business in any industry, as it can be applied to you and me, in both our personal and our professional lives.

3

Charity Begins at Home

Indulge me for a moment and break out your sales into four categories:

1. Business that comes from marketing-led acquisition or conquering (i.e., first-time customers)
2. Business that comes from repeat customers (as defined by two or more times)
3. Business that comes from successful upgrading or migrating of customers to increased or higher tiers of spending (often defined in loyalty terms based on levels of spending)
4. Referrals from existing customers (new business from old customers)

Then again—that is if you even know *how* to break out your sales into these categories in the first place. It's always surprising to me how few companies are truly on top of their customer data—or are able to classify their revenues into just four high-level buckets.

For this reason, let's make it even simpler and instead break out your sales into just two groups: acquisition-related business (category 1) and retention-based business (categories 2 through 4). Once you have these priceless percentages, I'd like you to overlay these against the total amount of money invested against each of these respective groupings. My gut tells me that there's probably a huge imbalance between the two analyses.

Why is this the case? Why do we continue to allocate our financial resources inefficiently relative to what really matters?

THE THEORY OF RELATIVITY

Listen—this is all relative at the end of the day. Budgets are fixed. Time is precious. Attention spans are in short supply and under constant threat from the barrage of noise, clutter, and irrelevance. We ourselves are hard-pressed—during bad times or good—to deliver more from less. And if all of this is true, then we need to figure out better, smarter—and, yes, cheaper—ways to teach our old dogs new tricks.

HOW WE'VE DONE IT IN THE PAST

The process of allocating budgets and making investments from them is not exactly rocket science, but perhaps it should be. This is one case where art is unwelcome at a table that really needs to be laser focused on three primary variables: inputs, outputs, and outcomes. Return on investment (ROI) remains the simplified metric that we covet in order to validate our decisions, assure us we're heading in the right direction, and extrapolate to project and predict future spending.

For many companies that have no clue how to calculate meaningful return on investment, there's a less-foolproof method of using last year's budget as a baseline or benchmark for next year—and in the interim, making sure all unallocated money is spent in a use-it-or-lose-it power play. Increasingly, however, companies are turning to marketing mix modeling (MMM), which helps them figure out how to optimize their media spending and reallocate their marketing dollars from one bucket (say, advertising) to another (say, public relations or digital marketing). It's a zero-sum approach that attempts to maximize both the efficiency and the effectiveness of paid media impressions in order to yield the best possible levels of reach, frequency, and impact.

Optimization makes all the sense in the world and will no doubt continue to do so. Tweaks, reallocations, and redistributions of available funds across the full spectrum of acquisition tools, platforms, media, and approaches are a powerful way to get more bang for your marketing bucks. Getting your message in front of the right people in the right place at the right time *using the right channels* is the right thing to do. Improving your chances and maximizing your potential for being seen by those who are of the right mind-set to consider purchasing—or, better yet, *make* the purchase—is a no-brainer.

Robbing Peter to Pay Paul

But what if the *real* optimization that needs to take place is from acquisition-led efforts (all of the preceding) to retention-led ones? What if this entire game of musical chairs and budget shifts is taking place on the deck of the Titanic? Put differently: Achieving the double-barreled goal of effectiveness and efficiency (the contraction of chairs as a metaphor for shrinking budgets, especially during tough economic times and/or more demanding levels of accountability) is meaningless if the ship goes down.

Over the past few years, we've witnessed more shipwrecks than we'd ever thought were possible. There are many reasons why a company fails, but doesn't it all just come down to an inability to sustain the business based on actual sales from actual customers? The entire acquisition process is a tenuous one at best; significant dollars are allocated without any guarantee of generating sales or the ability to sustain those sales over time. Sticking with a seafarer's theme, it's like fishing with a net full of gaping holes. As quickly as you catch the fish, you lose 'em. Or—taking the metaphor one step further—when, on rare occasions, we do hit the mother lode and rake in a boatload of fresh fish, we'll end up abandoning them by either leaving them out too long or improperly freezing them. You get the drift: We continue to focus our efforts on landing the big one but ignore, forget, or neglect what happens *after* the sale. Or we don't allocate enough resources—RELATIVELY SPEAKING—to sustain the catch of the day and turn it into catch of the year, decade, or lifetime.

When Acquisition Acts as a Retention Driver

Don't get me wrong; there *is* some merit in aiming acquisition-led efforts at existing customers. Customers experience a sense of reassurance and even pride when exposed to *their* bank or *their* auto manufacturer or *their* toothpaste. And our ability to reinforce some (ideally positive) kind of presence, equity, or association by surrounding existing customers with warm and fuzzy messages of hope, promises, and reasons to believe they all made the right choice plays a key role in keeping customers within arm's reach. And back to that zero-sum game—If it isn't our message they're exposed to, it's going to be our competitors'. And we wouldn't want that now, would we?

That may be so, but at what point should we be shifting our mindset from one that is always reaching out to that arm's-length customer to one where we bear-hug the living daylights out of our customers with meaning, passion, and complete submission instead?

The practice of executing big ideas is designed to entice consumers into considering the brand in question in the future. However, there's no discrimination between new and existing customers. If anything, the messaging almost biases *against* existing customers, with special offers, discounts, or promotions aimed at the mistress (two in the bush) versus the spouse (bird in the hand). In order to find new customers, these big ideas often take direct aim at other brands' customers, but truthfully, from a brand-loyalty, preference, and advocacy perspective, messages that are intended to enrapture are most likely going to fall on deaf ears when aimed at an already enraptured customer.

And so we come back to the same question: *Why—if our customers are the lifeblood of our business—are we not relatively investing in them accordingly?*

On any given day, about 75 percent of e-tailer Zappos's sales come from repeat customers. In 2007, first-time customers had an average order size of $123, and repeat customers had an average order size of $156.

In 2008, customers who made only one purchase *ever* accounted for 28.6 percent of Zappos's sales. Customers who made two lifetime purchases accounted for 12.6 percent of sales, and those who made three lifetime purchases accounted for 8.6 percent of sales. Customers who made *more than three lifetime purchases* accounted for 50.2 percent of 2008 sales.

Zappos is one of a handful of companies that both feeds and rewards retention with investment and commitment. They are also the exception to the rule.

Perhaps the solution in part lies in elevating the back-office role of retention marketing to a front-and-center, highly visible, and mission-critical imperative. Customer relationship marketing initiatives have never exactly been the star of the show or item #1 on the agenda in the board room.

Until now, that is.

If we've learned anything from the unpleasant recession of 2009, it's a return to fundamentals—cutting out the nice-to-haves in favor of the have-to-haves. And there's no "have" that's more important to have than loyal, returning, and crowing customers. Yet companies continue to focus on sweeping, broad-based, outside-in initiatives, without the equilibrium of inside-out efforts to provide balance and order. The result is chaos: a recipe for surefire disaster. Is it a coincidence that in the past few years, we've seen countless companies wiped from the face of the Earth?

Nothing is forever.

For sure, there were a slew of *external* variables that contributed to these companies' demise—not the least of which was the economy. For sure, they encountered a litany of *internal* factors from management (or mismanagement) to financial leverage, credit, and cash flow–related judgment calls.

Consider for a moment, the operating philosophy and corporate legacy of the average company: focused on expansion, diversification, line extension, acquisition (as in mergers)—building and growing exponentially by applying the outside-in doctrine over the inside-out alternative. How many of the companies in Figure 3.1 failed with this game plan in place? How many might have benefited instead from one that focused intently on customer experience, loyalty, and community? How many of them had fully activated affiliate and customer-referral programs in place? How many of them adequately treated customer service as the heart and soul of their organization?

I suspect we all know the answers to these questions, but here's a question to which only you will know the answer: How does *your* organization compare? Is customer experience an oxymoron or a religion within your walls?

Take Starbucks, a company that seemingly went from most con- sumers' biggest fan to also-ran by taking their eye off the ball in prioritizing and pursuing the two birds in the bush above the one already in their hands. By automating the specialized coffee process and

	Company Name	Year Shut Down	Years In Operation
Banking & Finance	Lehman Brothers	2008	158
Banking & Finance	Washington Mutual	2008	119
Retail	Circuit City	2009	60
Retail	KB Toys	2009	87
Retail	Fortunoff	2009	87
Real Estate	Thornburg Mortgages	2009	16

Figure 3.1   Snapshot of Company "Closures"

diversifying into music, movies, books, and other decidedly non–coffee-related activities, they took their foot off the gas pedal of customer experience. The message received was simple: *We don't care about you as much as we used to.*

Which would you rather pay $5 for: a grande soy no-whip no-foam, extra-shot latte that comes from the blood, sweat, and tears (hopefully not as ingredients) of your favorite barista, or one that comes from the push of a button?

The customer interpretation of that message: *You're too damned expensive.*

Starbucks' response? An ad campaign to *protest* or *insist* that, in fact, they *weren't* too expensive. Usually, when a company moves into defensive or damage-control mode with customers, it's a sign that they've lost a vital edge in the trust stakes. They become guilty until proven innocent instead of the other way around. What would have happened to Starbucks had they taken those advertising dollars and instead passed on the savings to customers in the form of cheaper coffee or other value-added services?

For purposes of speculation, I'm going to assume that the fine folks at Starbucks did not do any of the number crunching and data due diligence that would have helped them accurately break down their business into the following categories:

- New customers
- Repeat customers (frequency of transactions)
- Bigger basket size (value of order size)
- Influence and word of mouth–based

If they had been able to accurately quantify these categories, they surely would have been able to determine exactly which customers from which buckets found them to be too expensive. And with this kind of customer segmentation in place, they might have carefully constructed and deployed a unique set of strategies and commensurate tactics to deliver against the concerns, perceptions, and/or pushback accordingly.

As I type this particular part of the book *while sitting in a Starbucks,* I'm guessing the people to my immediate left, my immediate right, and my immediate self would not exactly be complaining about the cost of their joe, especially those with their Starbucks cards, free Wi-Fi (from their Starbucks cards), and 10 percent discount from their Starbucks Gold Cards. Starbucks currently has a number of fine initiatives in place to recognize and reward their most loyal customers, from free pastries via their Facebook fan page to MyStarbucksIdea, a crowdsourcing hub which invites—and even acts on—customer suggestions. They offer a number of high–value-added benefits and advantages in the process. Now *there's* something worthwhile to communicate to the world via advertising, wouldn't you say?

Here are a few other ideas or suggestions to help Starbucks counter the perception (real or otherwise) that their prices are too steep:

- Take the total cost of the advertising and invest it in $5 Starbucks cards. Hand out said cards like free samples of Caramel Macchiato, with a short, sweet, and succinct elevator pitch along the lines of "Did you know that by registering this card online, you can get free Wi-Fi, discounts, and special offers . . . plus you can refill, check your balance, and all sorts of things in the process?"
- Distribute two $50 Starbucks cards to any blogger who participates in an influencer or content-creation program: one for them, and one for their community.
- Create an automatic pricing incentive that lowers the overall cost of the coffee based on volume/dollars spent. Once again—using the Starbucks card that provides foolproof tracking and reporting—pass on savings to customers based on their business. The more you spend, the more you save.

SAYING AND DOING ARE NOT ONE AND THE SAME

The reason Starbucks didn't do any of these things is that they have historically been focused on an acquisition mind-set—regardless of whether they were talking to existing customers (baby, please don't go) or trying to woo new ones (come to my window). Acquisition mind-sets prompt us to try to talk our way out of our problems instead of just solving them and letting our actions do all the talking.

If Starbucks had flipped the funnel—and they're beginning to— might they be in a different position then—and now?

What about you? Do you agree with the central premise and hypothesis behind this book? Namely, that we've got it all wrong by doggedly pursuing an acquisition-heavy and biased approach to marketing, when in actuality the real lift and magic occurs from a shift to an inside-out approach, a refocus, reprioritization, and realignment of effort, energy, and budget to a customer-centric strategy?

And if so, I want you think about *why* it's taken us so long to do anything about this. Why do we continue to pay lip service to a simple, profound truth that has the ability to transform the way we do business and ultimately our very success and longevity?

Probably for the same reason people why morbidly-obese people continue to stuff their faces with jelly-filled doughnuts. Fear. Habit. Denial. Even hubris.

My hope with this book is that it is the strategic equivalent of an intervention, sort of like posting a photograph of your naked Michelin-Man body all over your Facebook page. Call it the *before* picture. I hope that this motivates you to work toward an *after* picture of reduced customer churn; boosted loyalty, morale, and shareability; and ultimately, increased sales via the establishment of a platform, foundation, and framework that revolves around customer experience, loyalty, dialogue, word of mouth, trust, relationship, and partnership.

WILL THE NEXT "BIGGEST WINNER" BE YOU?

It all begins with what you can control as opposed to what you cannot control. You cannot control what happens when you punt your messages into the ether that is the media market. Granted, you'll sink millions of dollars into research, planning, and production to craft the perfect 30-second elevator pitch. You'll even carefully choose *where* that message runs, based on meticulous evaluation against indexes and weighted targeting. And yet you'll still see a Ford F-150 paired up against a commercial for tampons. So much for being in control!

But it goes way further than that. Take the Olive Garden, for example. They created a television commercial advertising that their chefs are trained at an Olive Garden Culinary Institute in . . . wait for it . . . *Tuscany*. That's Tuscany, Italy, as opposed to the Tuscany Suites & Casino in Las Vegas. They even launched a promotion whereby individuals could win trips to the Institute (it's *real*, people!). According to one comment on a popular food hub called CHOW:

> McD's has a hamburger university, it doesn't make their food any good. Given that most of the stuff prepared by OG comes out of a can, box or freezer bag, what exactly do you think the curriculum is in Italy? Wouldn't

you feel bad after going to Italy and sneaking out of the dorm for a real Italian meal only to go back to the USA to serve what they serve?

In other words: you can *SAY* whatever you want, but it doesn't necessarily mean people will *BELIEVE* whatever it is you say. Perhaps in this case, Olive Garden might want to focus their attention and efforts on their customers and employees (especially those who've actually visited and graduated from the institute). Give *them* the ability to talk, crow, share, and spread. Let *them* engage, converse, and evangelize. Build credibility from the inside out, as opposed to the outside in.

This, in essence, is what flipping the funnel is all about.

4

Time to Spurn the Concept of Churn

What would happen if a business ran out of viable customers? What if the pipeline of new blood permanently dried up? Sound far-fetched? It's not as outlandish as you might think. In fact, this is precisely what happens in entrenched categories, industries, and brands that are trading in otherwise mature and/or stagnating markets.

In the early days of any new product or category, there is the shiny-object syndrome that operates in a business's favor. Everything is new and exciting, invites trial and experimentation, and rewards curiosity and intrigue. Sometimes all it takes to fill a store that has previously been vacated is just to open the doors.

For most companies, there just isn't enough pixie dust to go around and get people in the store. And so we turn to gimmicks: Take a walk down any given street in Manhattan and you'll be overwhelmed with the number of Grand Opening signs (it used to be Under New Management). Soon enough, however, you'll come to realize that the only thing *Grand* about the opening was the purchase of the actual Grand Opening sign. And once the sign is lowered and stored with the Under New Management sign, fake Christmas tree, electric menorah, pumpkin, and other window candy, it becomes a simple numbers game: prioritizing quantity (foot traffic) over and above quality (service).

This game works up to a point, but soon the magic wears off and consumers are in on the secret. No longer do bells and whistles differentiate or disguise the lack of substance and consistency. In the freakiest of cases—like that of Manhattan's famed "Soup Nazi"—complete disregard for service actually entices people to line up for more (abuse). However, for the other 99.99 percent of us, our fortune cookie will read EVERYTHING MUST GO if we aren't able to find a healthy balance between getting people in and keeping them coming back for more.

Oh, yes, and then there's advertising—often referred to as "Spray and Pray" or "Command and Control." In reality, this has become synonymous with a different act—that of Churn and Burn (with apologies to Texas Hold 'em). The continuous rotation of campaign taglines, creative messages, and clutter-busting noise helps keep a baseline level of acquisition activity. But what happens when advertising budgets dry up (as they have in recent times)? What happens when people aren't watching commercials anymore, or when they are, they're no longer convinced there's anything grand about the opening to entice them into the store and give the new management one more shot at redemption?

The entire process of managing churn is flawed at best and suicidal at worst. It is predicated on a simple formula: that people coming in need to counteract those going out. And as long as the former outweigh the latter, the cash register gives the illusion that all is well in commerce-land. To make this madness that much more scientific, there are even various levels of churn that are deemed to be acceptable.

Let me be clear: No level of churn is acceptable. *Ever.*

Call me old-fashioned, but I was always taught to treat every customer as the most important and/or last one. It's an incredibly dangerous game when people become nothing more than statistics, and a laissez-faire approach to business health and wellness is adopted in the process as long as the numbers conform to the norms.

Churn, in any form, is intolerable; it's as simple as that. Companies need to obsess on reducing churn to zero. No self-respecting cable customer should ever *have* or *need* to switch to satellite, and vice versa. No person should ever *have* or *need* to abandon Colgate toothpaste for Crest. No human should ever *have* or *need* to switch from AT&T to T-Mobile, from Dell to Lenovo, from Visa to Mastercard, from K-Mart to Wal-Mart. And yet many do. We give our customers way too many reasons to make the switch. We make it easy for them and for our competitors:

- From lack of caring or simple neglect
- By giving poor customer service (response and responsiveness)
- By losing touch with our consumers
- By failing to close the loop
- From lack of innovation

LACK OF CARING OR SIMPLE NEGLECT

In a world where perception is reality, we're awfully good at giving the impression that we just don't care. We're relatively unreachable, inaccessible, and unresponsive. Truthfully, any business that banks on acceptable or default levels of churn doesn't care nearly enough about its lifeblood. The very existence of churn requires a third pillar — containing investment, budget, and specific tactics — designed to complement acquisition (gaining new customers) and retention (keeping them). Call it attrition if you like (preventing them from defecting, leaving, or being stolen.) Although retention and attrition might seem to be the same thing, they are most decidedly not.

If acquisition's weapons of choice are advertising and promotions, and retention's arsenal consists of customer relationship management (CRM) and loyalty marketing, then attrition's tools of the trade might include customer service 2.0, commitment to conversation, and affiliate 2.0. (as I'll elaborate later). So ask yourself:

- How does your organization operate with respect to acceptable levels of churn?
- Do you have specific resources dedicated to preventing churn and/or countering attrition?
- To what extent do you court lapsed or lost customers in a concerted, intense effort to woo them back to your brand(s)?

Throughout this book, I'll be coming back to an acronym I coined in *Life after the 30-Second Spot:* C.O.S.T. (Cultural, Organizational, Strategic, Tactical). For every decision made, there is an opportunity cost; for every decision *not* made, there is an opportunity lost. To truly embrace change, companies need to hit all four of these drivers: cultural buy-in; organizational change and process; strategic architecture, foundation, vision, and planning; and finally (last and least), tactical implementation.

Although execution is critical — especially when it comprises "proof of concept" — we frequently witness tactics in search of strategy or solutions in search of nonexistent problems. Indeed, without its soul mate of strategy, all the tactics in the world become nothing more than a series of disjointed and fleeting punches, occasionally capable of winning the odd round but ultimately losing the match. Strategy is both the grounding force and the aspirational vision that empowers companies to innovate, adapt, and evolve. That said, without some kind of organizational structure and process, all the plans in the world will similarly hit a ceiling in terms of potential and impact. Without process, there is no integration, continuity, or longevity. Without the appropriate buy-in, it is extremely difficult to integrate any idea or initiative into the organization—having the effect of isolating any program, no matter how good it is and no matter how much potential it possesses.

Which brings us to the most important—and, unsurprisingly, hardest to implement—element of the formula. Without cultural buy-in, organizational process, resource allocation, system integration, and best practices are like a transplanted organ rejected by its host body: a short-lived success with a pretty grim and unpleasant ending.

In many companies, divisions and departments are separated by both literal and figurative walls, and it's not easy (or painless) to break down these walls. Incumbency and legacy trump ingenuity and originality in many businesses. Therefore, most companies do extremely poorly when it comes to adopting and adapting to change.

That's my way of saying, "I understand." But it's also my way of saying, "I don't care, and neither should you, when it comes to rethinking the way you've done business and, hopefully, the way you'll do business moving forward."

In what appeared to be a genius effort, wireless provider Sprint ended a television commercial that featured their new CEO, Dan Hesse, with an incredibly novel call-to-action. Instead of the tired and meaningless www.insertbrandurlherebutgivenoactualreasontovisitthewebsite.com URL, they provided an e-mail address—and not just any e-mail address, but Dan's: dan@sprint.com. What better way to make good on the promise of a wireless revolution—just as the ad promised, and in doing so, demonstrate commitment to customer care and experience.

Unfortunately, when a customer actually did e-mail the CEO, this is what they got back in return:

Dear Valued Customer,

Thank you for contacting Sprint. Thank you for sharing your feedback on the new commercial featuring Dan Hesse. We will pass your feedback on to the appropriate group. We really do appreciate you taking the time to show us your voice your opinion. Thank you again for contacting Sprint. We appreciate your business.

Sincerely,

Teri W. Sprint

In this case, any care being communicated was superficial and contrived at best—and blatantly false at worst.

Poor Customer Service (Response and Responsiveness)

Customer service and servicing customers are not necessarily the same. Whereas the former conjures up images of well-trained, eloquent support staff located somewhere in India, the latter is typically associated with some kind of in-store or face-to-face transaction. The former is exceptionally process-driven, with well-oiled yet stale scripts adhering to dotted i's and crossed t's; the latter is more of an art form, with loosely followed and often unpredictable results. Of course, there is crossover, for example, when the customer-service agent on the other end of the phone goes off script in the worst possible way and subsequently loses it with you and somehow takes offense at your raised voice and tonality—forgetting, for a moment, exactly what they do for a living and the reason you're calling—and consequently hangs up on you because you said something heinous like "bullshit." (The preceding story may or may not have happened to me about a thousand times.)

Value for Money Is as Much a Product of Customer Service as It Is About Product Quality

Whichever way you look at it (and I'll do that in more detail shortly), churn is directly related to our inability to overdeliver or our propensity to underdeliver, relative to our customers' expectations of how they deserve to be treated in the first place. There's no reason for a customer to leave if they feel that they're treated well, appreciated, and getting their money's worth (value). To that end, the very interpretation of value becomes so much more than just objective evaluation (product intrinsics). Rather, it is a host of personal, emotional, and subjective factors, including—but not limited to—how customers are treated and appreciated.

How many times have you lobbed the kiss-of-death threat (or bluff) at a service provider? From the "I'll take my business elsewhere" ultimatum to the less forgiving "you've just lost a customer," our ability to retain customers, loyalty, and repeat business will always be closely linked to our ability to treat them as we would expect to be treated in return. And though this may sound painfully obvious and elementary, it is somehow completely bypassed when we play the numbers game and reduce our customers to figures and data points.

So what can you do about it? For starters, when customers threaten to take their business elsewhere, don't attempt to call what you may perceive to be a bluff; instead shift gears into high defense and open up a new playbook designed to counter this threat. Ask, "What can I do to prevent you from leaving?" or "What will it to take to change your mind?" After all, what's the worst that can happen? They leave anyway, and you tried your best; nothing ventured, nothing gained. But what's the *best* that can happen? They remain in the fold: Loyalty: 1, Churn: 0. Ultimately, the answers to the questions are almost always going to be "solve my problem" or "help me." Other times, it may require an "I'm sorry" or an assurance that "it won't happen again."

Asking customers to give you another chance is as easy as asking the question. The hard part is making sure that whatever has offended them never happens again, and the only way to prevent a relapse is to make sure customer service is integrated into the organization's business processes, knowledge centers, and learning systems.

Jet Blue did just that when, following a horror incident in February 2007, when passengers were stranded on the JFK tarmac for more than 10 hours, they introduced a customer bill of rights.[1] This document covers items like departure delays, overbookings, onboard ground delays, and flight cancellations. It begins with the following words:

> *Above all else, JetBlue Airways is dedicated to bringing humanity back to air travel. We strive to make every part of your experience as simple and as pleasant as possible. Unfortunately, there are times when things do not go as planned. If you're inconvenienced as a result, we think it is important that you know exactly what you can expect from us. That's why we created our Customer Bill of Rights. These Rights will always be subject to the highest level of safety and security for our customers and crewmembers.*

The Bill of Rights was last updated in July 2008, demonstrating that customer service and adapting to customer needs is very much a live work in progress. (To view the Bill of Rights, visit www.flipthefunnelnow.com and click on "enhanced content.")

I actually wrote about this incident in my previous book, and to my knowledge, no similar incident has occurred since, further proving that brands *do* get a second chance at making a great second impression.

---

[1] /www.jetblue.com/p/about/ourcompany/promise/Bill_Of_Rights.pdf.

By Losing Touch with Our Consumers

Practically the entire business of marketing revolves around consumer insights. We plow endless amounts of money into gaining a better comprehension of what makes them tick. Our logic is simple: If we can understand them more clearly, then we can better connect with and serve them, with timely, relevant, useful, and helpful information.

But somewhere along the line, we kind of lost touch with our customers. At no time was this more prevalent than during the recession of 2009 and, in particular, during the Super Bowl, with the likes of Monster.com and Careerbuilder.com making light of "being stuck in a job you hate" while millions of Americans were busy losing their jobs and desperately trying to figure out how to keep a roof over their families' heads.

In the very same Super Bowl, one brand, Hyundai, stood out from the crowd by using the opportunity to announce their assurance program (as outlined in Chapter 2), where people who lost their jobs could return their cars. To be clear, the fact they used the Super Bowl is less significant than their incredibly smart (opportunistic?) move to stand for something valuable, especially during challenging times. Perhaps I'm wrong, but I think this was the single most significant and potentially differentiating move this otherwise commoditized brand (and aren't they all?) had done in its entire marketing life span operating in the United States.

As an aside, since Hyundai made this move, several other companies predictably jumped on the "brandwagon" and followed suit with similar programs.

By Failing to Close the Loop

Marketing is not a campaign; it's a commitment. The same is true of customer bonds or the connections between a brand and its community. In today's marketplace, our relationships with customers seem to mirror the current divorce rate (which is way north of 40 percent in the United States, and rising.) There's an acute lack of patience and staying power when it comes to forging lifelong, inseparable ties with customers. Perhaps the reason for this is an insufferable focus on short-term results and the immediate gratification that comes from making the sale. It's really emblematic of what I call "sales sickness," an epidemic of sorts, where there is a wholesale abandoning of the ship at the exact moment the cash register chalks up the transaction. Call it after-sales support on its basic level, but it's more than that. Failing to close the loop is lack of follow-through or follow-up. It's an inability to stay the course, and stay connected in the process.

An interpretation of failing to close the loop is neglecting to use the knowledge, insights, and feedback from customers to actually change or improve things. Using customer suggestions—either solicited or un-solicited—as market research is absolutely mission critical, but it's wasted and worthless if it doesn't have a direct line back to the powers that be to assess and ultimately implement. For example, pharmaceutical giant Merck changed its entire commercial model after extensive customer research revealed that their customers wanted more than just products; they wanted service.

Virtual worlds—which were all the rage circa 2006 and 2007—are making a comeback as a powerful market research tool or focus group. Companies like IBM are using online environments to learn more about their customers and are able to parlay what they've learned into improved customer service.

> How does your organization close the loop when it comes to feeding the strategic-planning side of the business with feedback from the customer interaction side of the equation? Do you have a Voice-of-the-customer program in place? To what extent are your listening strategy and customer input integrated into your core knowledge networks?

By Lack of Innovation

Closely following on the heels of market research as a means to close the loop—that is, supplying valuable information to the insights side of the business—is the idea that these nuggets are not just how we can incrementally *tweak* the model to make things better, but how we can *exponentially* improve or make things *significantly* better. Build a better mousetrap, so to speak. Put differently, how can we change the game by incorporating these insights into the very R&D process or engine that powers our company? Without the ability to greatly improve the work product, the best-case scenario is stagnation, and the worst is extinction.

It's naive—and almost negligent—to assume your competitors are sitting around, waiting for something to happen or for you to make the first move. Innovation is a high-stakes game, and more often than not, there is only one winner. Will it be you?

Innovation is inarguably the lifeblood for any company. Without it, there is the risk of becoming old news, boring, predictable, a me-too, and the list goes on. And with any one of these factors or a combination of them in play, the risk of defection increases, and the vicious circle of churn continues.

Grandfather of business management Peter Drucker once said that "the business enterprise has two—and only two—basic functions: marketing and innovation. Marketing and innovation produce results; all the rest are costs." I'd respectfully add a third to this mix: customer experience. However, this would equally be satisfied to the extent that customer service and general retention efforts also fall under the innovation banner.

BORING YOUR CUSTOMERS INTO LOOKING ELSEWHERE IS NOT A BANKABLE STRATEGY

It's time, once and for all, to spurn the churn. To do this, we typically have two variables to influence: boosting acquisition and/or lowering attrition. But there is a third pressure point: retention *itself* as a starting point rather than an ending point. By increasing our success and competence in the retention category—not only in terms of lowering net attrition and churn but also through *activating* this base and *ultimately* flipping the funnel—we have an opportunity to transform retention from a reactive or passive task to an active, actionable, and impactful strategic imperative. It also allows us to rely less on acquisition as an addiction to fuel the illusion of growth.

5

Technology and Relationships—a Love-Hate Relationship

As the previous chapter intimates, minimum acceptable levels of churn are nothing more than a fragile and temporary masking of the real challenge: keeping, cultivating, and nurturing existing customers and establishing unbreakable bonds with them.

A common theme that runs throughout this process is the rise and role of technology, which has irrevocably changed the way we do business. It has proven to be the consummate method of delivering both unprecedented levels of efficiency and effectiveness boosts to many businesses, industries, and categories.

Take the ATM (automated teller machine—did you even know what it stood for?), for example. The ability to install and distribute machines that dispensed cash, accepted deposits, spat out bank statements on demand, and performed other service-related tasks 24/7/365 had a powerful transformative effect and impact on the business:

- **Efficiency**—the ultimate saving in the form of a lower cost per transaction fee. As much as we hate to admit it, computers are less costly (over time) than human beings. There are no union complications, no lunch breaks, no sick leave, and no political games (unless you count Y2K, but I guess even that was man-made). The ATM has had a profound impact in terms of increasing the number of transactions (notwithstanding the 90-year-old granny in front of you using the machine for the first time, bless her) and lowering the cost to the bank in terms of facilitating the exchange.
- **Effectiveness**—The ability to bank and/or transact before 9 A.M. and after 4 P.M. was a game-changer. Suddenly, banks were open for business around the clock, and with this ease of access came an exponential increase in the *number* of *cheaper* transactions,

producing a one-two profitability punch. The second piece of the effectiveness puzzle came in the form of networking (the machine kind): The ability to connect all the ATMs—not only from one bank, but indeed across competitive banks—created the kind of access and scale never before imagined. And with premium fees for out-of-network transactions, even more revenue materialized where there was once none.

- **Intangibles**—I would be remiss if I didn't include the less obvious service elements as well: Decreased frustration from smaller and faster lines, less disappointment from arriving at the bank 12 seconds after closing time (and we know how many banks keep their doors open 12 seconds after closing time), and of course, more effective resolution of inquiries provides an invaluable suite of additional benefits.

Though an obviously dated example, ATMs are nonetheless prevalent and relevant in terms of illustrating the role and power of technology. Perhaps if our global banks had gone back to basics and stuck to the same steady-and-sure-wins-the-race fundamentals, we might not have landed in the mess that we are still recovering from (but that's a story for another day). The more recent proliferation and adoption of PC banking has accelerated technology's transformational drive toward changing the way we bank—and the way banks bank the profits from the new ways we bank! Perhaps that's why Intuit acquired personal finance darling, Mint.com

The problem with technology, however, is this little paradox I like to call[1] numerator versus denominator. With every compound fraction, there is a numerator (the number on top) and a denominator (the number on the bottom). In order to increase the size of the fraction (and thus the size of the pie), we have two options: increase the numerator or decrease the denominator; $\frac{1}{4}$ is smaller than $\frac{3}{4}$ (bigger numerator) and $\frac{1}{2}$ (smaller denominator). Now with apologies to those of you (I assume 99 percent) who just felt like they were back in third grade, we need only substitute "effectiveness" for the numerator and "efficiency" for the denominator in this situation. And here's where we go off the rails: Companies today don't look at technology as a numerator but rather as a denominator. Instead of embracing and investing in technology as a

---

[1] Actually, thanks goes to Len Hause, who first referenced this, and I owe its attribution to him.

profoundly transformative game-changer, they consider it a way to lower costs. Simply put, by automating processes, we negate those pesky organisms with their human errors and unpredictable emotions in favor of the kind of standardized scale that would make Morpheus[2] wet his pants.

Web sites have become dead ends to customer contact and continued conversation. Problems and concerns are rolled up into a bland and *templatized* FAQ (frequently asked questions) section. It's damned near impossible to contact an actual human being on these sites, with their seemingly endless wild-goose-chase options that are all designed to get you back to the FAQ section anyway. The only commonplace source of contact is the e-mail customer-service link, which itself is just a code name for "welcome to the black hole of despair," that is, the predictable, cold, impersonal autoresponder (see the Sprint CEO example in the previous chapter) with an unreassuring consolation promise of a 24-hour response. Seriously, what's up with that?

Customer-care lines or 800 numbers are not much better. A cacophony of howlers dominate this beleaguered space—from horrible Muzak, to the banal "Your call is important to us and will be answered in the order it was received," to the maze of "press 1 to continue in English" options that make me wish for a rotary phone (whatever that is). It's an invariable comedy of errors, the main one being our error in judgment in taking our customers for granted. The intent of the telephone from a technology standpoint is telegraphed a mile away: to make it as hard as humanly possible to actually speak to another human being. Some companies (maybe yours) force the web site URL down callers' throats to the point of gagging them (see web sites). Others give callers an approximation of wait time, only (a) to be inaccurate and (b) to drop the call just when there is a connection; still others send their prized customers on one-way Easter-egg hunts, with no path of return despite the number of times they hit the 0 button.

And with all that technology, you'd think the person on the other end of the line would know who you are, considering that you punched in your 10-digit telephone number, your account number, and all other identifying information. But you'd be wrong. What's the first thing you hear when the sound of a human voice comes on the line? "Can I have your name and account number, please?" "Your mother's maiden

---

[2] A reference to the movie *The Matrix*, as if you didn't already know.

name?" "Your first pet's name . . . yes, the one that got squelched by a bus?" "Your bra size?" The list goes on.

Perhaps that's why—as I wrote in *Join the Conversation*—Paul English started www.gethuman.com, a web site designed to share the various cheat codes to fast-track a customer care call to get an operator or technician on the line. For example, when calling Comcast, *"Press*#* at each prompt, ignoring messages. Or—don't press any button nor say anything. It will ask but then after 3 'no response's will put you through."*

And then you have companies like eBay that validate this entire section, with no human beings whatsoever on the other end of the line. As per GetHuman: *"This number is no longer available. eBay no longer has any published customer-service phone number on their site, but instead recommends that you click on Help > Contact us on the home page. From there, there is still no direct way to contact by phone."*

> Note to eBay: Perhaps you might sell a little more by introducing human beings to help other human beings become more comfortable with technology, as opposed to using technology to help people become even more unconfident and unsure of using technology. I once thought that was why you acquired Skype. But then you sold it. So much for that theory.

DELL IS DIFFERENT

Whether you're a Mac or a PC, you should be able to appreciate moments when technology *exponentially* improves the overall customer experience. Dell didn't always understand consumer care, but thanks to Dell Hell,[3] it's a completely different company today. Dell now installs software on its customers' computers that makes contacting the company incredibly easy. In addition, the first thing you'll be asked when you get on the line is *your* telephone number—just in case you get disconnected. This is a far cry from the industry norm (*"unfortunately, we're not able to dial out"*) or the probing, clarifying questions devoid of empathy, care, or concern. Dell also utilizes software that allows the technician to take over your computer, that is, to see what you see. They can remotely access your PC and, in doing so, are able to troubleshoot as

---

[3] Case study noted extensively in *Join the Conversation* or just search "Dell Hell" on Google.

if they were there in the room with you (a feat that would make Scotty[4] proud).

APPLE IS DIFFERENT

Apple really *is* different. After all, they're the ones who came up with Think Different, which would be useless if they didn't act differently to walk their talk. They are unconventional, original, and unique in almost every way. They've not only brought back the human element but have even celebrated the physical person by putting said humans at the Genius Bars in their Apple Stores. It's a decidedly unplugged version that creates the perfect contrast, given the technical nature of the conversations.

IBM IS DIFFERENT

In my first book, I introduced the notion of multiplatform engagement, which—like multichannel selling—is designed to give people more opportunities to interact with a company. When it comes to buying stuff, the hypothesis is dead simple: The more opportunities we give our customers to transact the *more likely* they'll be to transact. Brick-and-mortar stores, pop-up retail or satellite outlets, e-commerce and e-tail Web presence, catalog or direct mail, and/or a toll-free number all support the more-the-merrier adage.

In the media business, the same proposition is true. Why try in vain to connect with today's elusive, skeptical, and marketing-weary consumer through the tried and tested media of television, radio, and print (symbolized by the three primary colors of red, yellow, and blue) when there is an entire box of crayons to color with (the 96 Big Box, for example, by crayon manufacturer Crayola)? Instead of chasing our consumers on our terms with our preferred channels, why not give them a rich and diverse array of connection points or communication channels through which to engage, interact, seek, and connect? Going back to the hypothesis, we're banking on the notion that the more options we give our consumers to participate, the more likely they'll be to do just that.

---

[4] That would be Scotty from *Star Trek* and, yes, gratuitous *Star Trek* references *are* necessary.

With *customer* (versus consumer) dialogue, however the same logic and rationale apply. The more opportunities we give our customers to engage us (as opposed to *us* engaging *them*), the more likely they'll be to do just that.

IBM makes it ridiculously easy for people to get in touch with them. Who would have ever imagined that Big Blue would encourage First Contact[5] in one of the more progressive suites of options:

- E-mail contact.
- Toll-free line.
- Message boards/FAQs.
- Live chat (text).
- VoIP talk (someone will call you right back on your phone).
- Virtual world meet-up: You can actually beam in to meet a dedicated IBM person in an online environment and interact on a simulated face-to-face basis. It's a sublime way to humanize the otherwise impersonal technology space, as well as demonstrate and showcase various product offerings, configurations, customized setups, and so on. It also shows that there is life after Second Life.[6] (See Figure 5.1[7])

MICROSOFT IS NOT

Surprise, surprise. Microsoft is stuck somewhere in channel purgatory with a combination of not-made-here and pass-the-buck mentalities that put the onus on their customers—instead of the corporation—to solve their problems. For example, if you purchase an HP laptop from Best Buy that's preloaded with Vista (hopefully not for much longer with the introduction of Windows 7), do you call HP, Best Buy, or Microsoft when you get the Blue Screen of Death? Good question. Damned if I know the answer, although it rests somewhere in "depends if it's a hardware, software, services, or support issue." Even if you corner "software," you'll still be flirting with the direct versus reseller branded

---

[5] That would be *Star Trek* reference #2.

[6] The virtual world and economy from Linden Labs, which was first hyped and then abandoned by both mainstream media and the corporate world. It still lives, by the way, at www.secondlife.com.

[7] Reprint Courtesy of International Business Machines Corporation, copyright 2009 © International Business Machines Corporation.

Figure 5.1   IBM Multi-Channel Customer Service

Source: Reprint Courtesy of International Business Machines Corporation, copyright 2009 © International Business Machines Corporation.

or customized version of the software, aka, the Not-Made-Here Syndrome. And should you ever make it to the leprechaun guarding the pot at the end of the rainbow, he'll probably tell you that you're not a premium customer and therefore he can't help unless you add to *his* pot of gold. Put succinctly, it's a mess.

Microsoft's online support is not exactly much better, with its endless stream of "Was this helpful to you?" messages which, if you think about it, is kind of like hitting a dead end in a dark alley, with a sign that reads, Dead End: Turn Around, Dummy.

Technology was meant to liberate us, not shackle us and inhibit us further. Our goal should be to use it as a game-changer—a numerator, as opposed to a cost-cutting or cost-saving denominator. When it comes to establishing and nurturing relationships, it's no longer good enough to play dumb and pretend we don't know everything about our customers. Now is our chance to prove that all the data collection has been worth it and, in doing so, solve problems, engage our customers, and build relationships like never before.

THE DEATH OF THE HUMAN BEING

Everything begins with what happens in your stores, dealerships, banks, and web sites. This is the essence of flipping the funnel: focusing or refocusing all efforts on the magic (or lack thereof) that is ultimately responsible for making a sale or not. Of course, every business is different. Many industries, sectors, and verticals do not have physical stores and, therefore, best practices like greeters, information kiosks, accessible managers, and any other human guide designed to answer questions, solve problems, and eradicate confusion.

A little piece of us dies when we turn to marketing and customer automation; I call this the death of the human being. Every day we read about how technology advances obliterate the precedents set the previous day, week, or month. By 2013, a supercomputer will be built that exceeds the computational capabilities of the human brain, and by 2049, a \$1,000 computer will exceed the computational capabilities of the entire human species.[8] That's awesome . . . now how do I find a @#$%$ @$# human capable of solving my problem?

CONGRATULATIONS, DREAMHOST, YOU JUST MADE MY BOOK

I *used* to have a web site for my second book, *Join the Conversation*. It was a beautiful web site (www.jointheconversation.us) that featured a public/open blog for which any reader of the book could register to become a contributing guest writer. It contained multimedia, various contact information, and a range of other related or useful information associated with the book. Then, one day—it was gone. I was left with nothing but an unceremonious message that eloquently read: *error id: "bad_httpd_-conf."* After a long and laborious search, I found out that this was associated with a company called Dreamhost, the apparent hosting company for my site. I wouldn't know, as I wasn't the person who originally set up this service. After a few unsuccessful attempts to contact technical support (I didn't have log-in credentials, as I didn't know I was even a customer), I managed to find an obscure e-mail address associated with "sales." Long story short: It turns out that the credit card used to procure this service had since expired, and an invoice for \$190 had not been paid.

---

[8] www.youtube.com/watch?v=cL9Wu2kWwSY.

Here's the incredible part: Dreamhost callously suspends the account and then deletes the entire web site. Let me repeat that: they deleted the *entire web site*. Every single file. Every single blog entry. All. Gone. *Forever.* This is a company that trades in data and, for some unexplained reason, does not have backup or the capacity to archive or store files for extended periods of time (and apparently for less than $200). They had evidently sent some really badly constructed and poorly disclosed e-mails, which did not even indicate the domain in question. They essentially read like SPAM to this human AND ended up in my SPAM filter to boot (so apparently the machine shared the human's sentiment).

The moral of this story was that this relationship is severed beyond any point of reconciliation and repair. For now, I'm forwarding the site to my blog (http://www.jaffejuice.com/join-the-conversation-2007-wiley.html), which works for me, as most of the new thought leadership that pertains to the book is on the blog anyway. I'm also telling the story to anyone who will hear it with the point that if data is mission-critical to you, you probably don't want to trust a company like Dreamhost. I e-mailed Dreamhost politely (okay, maybe not politely) and explained to them that they were doing such a great job at customer service that they were going to be included in my new book's Hall of Shame. Mission accomplished.

If Dreamhost had taken 60 seconds of their time to actually visit the site, they would have realized that it was indeed legit and belonged to a relatively newly released book. They would have easily been able to contact the webmaster or, in this case, the actual author (me!) and point out the outstanding amount owed them. But they didn't . . . because human beings are costly, and machines are not. Contrast this with GoDaddy, a web site hosting company that begins each call by raising the bar and expectations, calling their service "world class," and they don't disappoint. It didn't take me long at all to talk to a human who helped me redirect my URL to my blog. I suspect GoDaddy will be in business for a long time to come, and Dreamhost (a man can dream!) will not.

In your industry, you have the exact same situations that present themselves to you on a daily basis—whether you know it or not. A great example is the banking business. The difference between flat-out rejection in the form of a bounced check for an overdrawn account versus a courtesy call, text message, judgment call, and/or provision to keep a customer's account and dignity intact is the difference between attrition and loyalty. Thank goodness my bank is not run by the folks at Dreamhost; if it were, they'd probably close down my account, delete all my funds, destroy my credit history, and repossess my house (all for an overdraft of less than $200).

What you can do about it? Following are 10 tips to turn technology from a denominator to a numerator:

1. Technology should bring out the humanity in your company, not mask it. Like being able to call someone by their name, for example.
2. If your customer-care operators at your call center are not allowed or able to call out, change that immediately.
3. Adopt a multiplatform or multichannel approach to building relationships. The easier you make it for your customers to connect with you, the more likely they'll be to engage with you.
4. Like the ATM example, think about ways you can change the game by transforming your business and customer relationships.
5. Efficiency and effectiveness are not necessarily mutually exclusive. Attempt to achieve a balance between cost and benefit.
6. Don't take the intangibles for granted or discount their importance. Indirect benefits like service, goodwill, and perception of being an innovative company are as important as hard metrics like number of transactions and cost per transaction.
7. Consider tiered systems for different segments of customers. Like airlines, your business can also segment and reward customers with accelerated and upgraded service relative to their loyalty and/ or business.
8. Automation is not always the answer. Balance technology with a good old-fashioned analog or manual solution, namely, human beings.
9. Personalization is the gift of technology; intimacy is the gift of humanity.
10. Scale is often the enemy of service. When things get too big, they usually begin to suck. Figure out ways to keep things small and manageable. This doesn't mean sacrificing bigger-picture thinking, but rather rolling up and implementing what you've learned on a global scale.

Section II

A New Way Forward

6

Time to Flip the Funnel

In Chapter 1, I described how the traditional marketing funnel is anything from outdated to flat-out broken, and I introduced several key themes and terms that traditionally have been absent from strategic planning and agenda-setting in the board room: retention, attrition, churn, and technology as a numerator.

ONE SOLUTION: EXTEND THE FUNNEL

In this day and age of the Long Tail, we'd almost expect a rather long trickle of a tail to stem from the end of the funnel. But even if this were the case, it wouldn't substantially address any of the shortcomings mentioned in Chapter 1, at least not in the kind of way that could have the potential theoretical impact of halving your budget, while simultaneously doubling your revenue. With this theory, the funnel would just get narrower and narrower and represent one or both of two extremely undesirable scenarios: less investment against fewer and fewer customers, with no guarantee of positive (versus negative) outcome. Granted, there's value in acknowledging that something should happen after the moment of truth—that is, the purchase—but what? Is it customer relationship management (CRM). Loyalty marketing? One-to-one marketing? All three? Or something completely different?

The goal is not simply to extend the goodness; it's to enhance the value, impact, meaning, and purposes associated with customer loyalty and experience. As the doodle in Figure 6.1 illustrates, perpetuating a purchase without necessarily improving on it is just as likely to lead to a negative result as to a positive one.

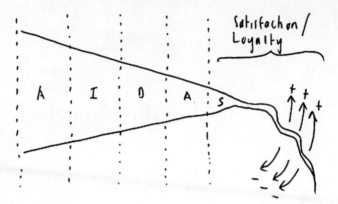

Figure 6.1   The Long Tail of A.I.D.A.

Source: © Joseph Jaffe.

ANOTHER SOLUTION: TURNING IT ON ITS SIDE

In Seth Godin's e-book *Flipping the Funnel,* the author makes the great point that your customers are essentially underused "assets." Given that practically every company has more customers than salespeople, isn't it logical that customers should have an amplifier or a megaphone (hence the funnel flipped on its side in Figure 6.2)?

Godin astutely notes that former customers or those with grievances already use certain channels—predominantly the Web—as an amplifier. It's thus incumbent on us to make sure our fans or friends have the same opportunity. Let's call it equal opportunity for customers.

I'm certainly not criticizing the idea of turning the funnel on its side—except for the fact it's really comparing apples with carrots insofar as it's a smart, lateral, and even literal interpretation of a theoretical concept. It also represents a part of the solution to the multitude of problems associated with the traditional funnel (*namely, an unhealthy obsession on an acquisition-led process that is neither efficient nor effective*).

ANOTHER SOLUTION: FLIPPING IT COMPLETELY

Why not turn the funnel on its head? Instead of ending with your customers, why not begin with your lifeblood, the single biggest—if not the only—reason you're in business today?

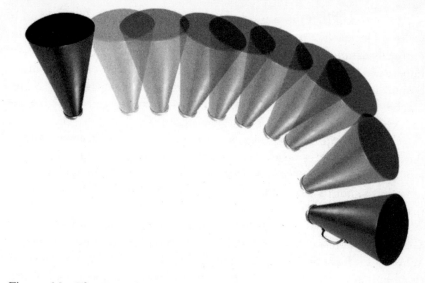

Figure 6.2   The Funnel Becomes the Megaphone
Source: Seth Godin. Reprinted by permission.

We need not abandon the customer acquisition process or minimize the role that awareness and/or action play in terms of moving
prospective customers from unawareness to paying customers. The
same could be said for my championing of new media over old, or
conversation over communication—one does not necessarily *replace* its
predecessor or counterpart. However, it does bring with it new and
differentiating thinking. From the standpoint of investing in both
human and financial resources, it also reprioritizes strategic thinking
and mind-share *from* an otherwise saturated space *to* one that essentially represents virgin territory in terms of upside, potential, and
impact. It's also an acknowledgment that the proposed space in
question is significantly evolved:

- The sharp and clinical scalpel of digital trumps the blunt hatchet of
  advertising.
- The fluid and pervasive conversation washes away the uni-
  directional current of communication.
- The meaningful and long-lasting commitment of retention deeply
  resonates over the superficial and materialistic attraction of
  acquisition.

I *am* saying that there is a better way. There just has to be. And if we're able to elevate retention (customer service, dialogue, and customer outreach or affiliate 2.0) to the point at which it becomes a strategic imperative at the expense of the traditional acquisition efforts from an optimization and budget allocation standpoint . . . then maybe, just maybe, we'll be able to change the way we do business for the better. Forever.

On one hand, this represents starting with your customers, and if there's time, effort, energy, and budget remaining, hop on over to the pool of uninitiated prospects. On the other, it speaks to repairing the holes in the net to assure that you'll enjoy more fruitful results the next time you go fishing.

There should always be room for *both* acquisition and retention. Why can't the respective potentials of both be achieved simultaneously? Why does it have be a zero-sum game? Or what about the really radical thought that we might never *NEED* to invest in acquisition again if we're able to deliver effectively on retention?

When I was Down Under in Australia—the perfect place to be flipping anything on its head—I proposed this thought to one of the nation's largest banks when they told me that they "didn't really need" any new customers (they had enough). *What if you announced that you would not be taking new customer accounts or applications (at least for a period of time)? What message would that send to your* existing *customer base -- and to those who weren't yet part of your family in terms of aspiration, motivation, and desire? Would it make them want you more or less?*

Radical thinking aside, any changes you make to your existing methodology and process—however small—will have major organizational implications when it comes to budget allocation, prioritization of objectives, time, and initiatives. That doesn't mean it's not worth doing—on the contrary. But your decision will ultimately depend on the company's tolerance for risk (usually low) and its fervent belief in the power of its customer base—in terms of both staying and buying power. Regardless of whether you flip the funnel on its head in one decisive motion or experiment with tilting it just a few degrees, I hope you'll acknowledge that the hypothesis on offer is a shift of the very foundation of marketing management as it relates to consumer behavior. At the very least, it's an enhancement on *existing* theory and best practices; at the most, a complete and utter rethink.

Ultimately, where it fits and how far you take it is up to you, but I hope you'll give this serious thought in terms of making permanent changes that permeate your organization. Of course, I believe that this could be the x factor for which you've been searching so hard. It certainly is not going to come from a new advertising campaign or manifest itself in an obtuse new web site, either.

The Death of Loyalty

Before we get into the flipped-funnel methodology, it's important to tackle—and possibly debunk—one of the most misused and even abused words in the marketing lexicon: *loyalty*. It's a word that is liberally thrown around to refer to customers. It's wholly interchangeable with a random impersonal e-mail that doesn't even mention the customer by name, an indulgent and overpriced *techmology* (hat tip to Ali G) and database solution, or a frequent-purchase program that penalizes returning customers at every turn, such that they are helpless to use their miles or points with any reasonable ease. All of this drives them to the point at which they end up expiring, along with the customer's tenure and so-called loyalty. Talk about a vicious circle!

It's time for renewed thinking on loyalty. It's best to begin with a clean slate—one without any sacred cows, predisposed thinking, or incumbent assumptions.

Consulting firm McKinsey & Company offers thinking on the customer journey, and seems to have blended the acquisition and retention processes together as fluid and circular. McKinsey segments loyalty into active and passive, as in "I'll never purchase any product other than yours" versus "I'm open to purchasing yours in the future, and I'm equally open to purchasing other, similar products as well," respectively.

The diagram of McKinsey's consumer-decision-journey theory in Figure 6.3 sheds some light on four current market truisms when it comes to loyalty:

1. Loyalty today is predominantly passive rather than active.
2. Companies mistake or confuse passive loyalty with active loyalty.
3. Companies need to segment loyalty in to several more meaningful categories.
4. Companies generally approach loyalty (programs such as CRM and the like) as equally or commensurately passive, that is, noncommittal, indecisive or lacking a clear and firm position.

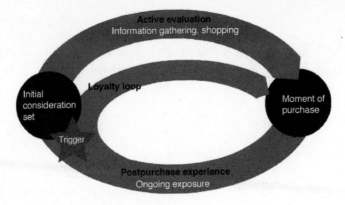

Figure 6.3   The Consumer Decision Journey

Source: Exhibit 2 from "The consumer decision journey," June 2009, The McKinsey Quarterly, www.mckinseyquarterly.com. Copyright © 2009 McKinsey & Company. All rights reserved. Reprinted by permission.

Case in point: According to research from Forrester (see Figure 6.4),[1] loyalty programs have virtually *zero*—and in some cases, *negative*—correlation with loyalty in the banking, mobile phone, CPG (consumer packaged goods), and durable goods sectors. By contrast, prior experience, trust, and reliable service—in other words, consistency—had the closest correlation with loyalty.

It's time to address the elephant in the room when it comes to loyalty.

That Elephant in the Room Is Your Customer

Although they may not segment loyalty per se, most businesses today (sadly) do divide their customers into three very distinct categories, all of which exist within the animal kingdom: Lemmings (the hapless victims to mass-media hype and pop-culture indoctrination), Dogs (playful and loyal to a fault), and Goldfish (inherently forgetful). In reality, customers today are more like Chameleons (adaptive, unpredictable, ever changing, and contextually original), Dolphins (highly intelligent), and Elephants (terrific memory!). Besides their reputation for possessing incredible memory, elephants are also known as highly

[1] Q3 2007 North American Technographics Customer Experience, Marketing and Consumer Technology Survey.

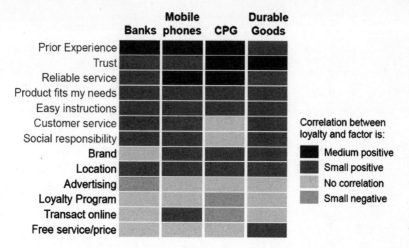

Figure 6.4 Loyalty Programs and Loyalty Are Not One and the Same

Source: Forrester Research Inc.

social animals who engage in greeting ceremonies, complex communication, courtship, teaching, and communal care.[2] They're also an endangered species—hunted and targeted as they simultaneously fight to adapt to shifting terrains and landscapes. Sounds kind of like how we treat and what we do with our customers, right?

If we want to show our customers that their purchase is just the beginning of a long and mutually beneficial exchange, then we need to think of them more as dynamic chameleons, engaged dolphins and mighty elephants. Look up to them. Acknowledge their presence. Stroke their egos. Feed them. Nourish them. Cool them off. And for heaven's sake, get out of the way if they go on a rampage.

Enthusiasts versus Influencers

And as long as we're rethinking the notion of loyalty, it's probably also a good idea to do the same with the word "customer" itself. Who exactly is a—or specifically, *our*—customer? Is it someone who pays money or attention; consumes our products or services; or simply one who uses our intellectual property or brand equity?

[2] Smithsonian National Zoological Park.

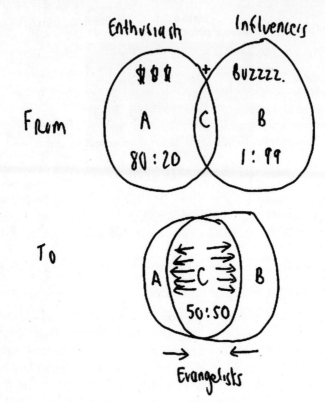

Figure 6.5   Three Types of Premium "Customers"
Source: © Joseph Jaffe.

We do a fairly satisfactory job of segmenting our prospects in the marketplace; but how do or should we segment our customers—both direct (compensation) and indirect (attention)?

Figure 6.5 above offers a breakdown of three types of premium customers:

1. The 80:20 rule: The prototypical 20 percent of customers responsible for 80 percent of revenue
2. The 99:1 rule: The 1 percent of influences, iReporters,[3] or content creators responsible for 99 percent of our buzz
3. The sweet spot: customers who both talk about *and* purchase from the brand

---

[3] Using CNN's descriptor.

Using this segmentation, several key implications emerge:

1. Companies should utilize and deploy three distinct approaches when it comes to engaging walkers, talkers, and a hybrid of the two.
2. Companies should distinguish and differentiate between enthusiast and influencer behavior.
3. There's no black and white, but rather 256 shades of gray. Although there are generalizations, customers exhibit both enthusiast and influencer behaviors. Companies should therefore treat their customers as influencers (the *I* in the flipped funnel) . . .
4. . . . and at the same time, it is worth considering pure influencers as customers (having some bearing, however indirect, on future sales).

As we think about flipping the funnel for our customers, keep in mind that we're establishing long-term, meaningful, credible, and valuable relationships with them in the process—far beyond any level of dedication we've demonstrated in the past. As we hope to realize their lifetime value, we are slowly but surely committing to *them* for life. We expect them to trust us, and so we need to trust them in return. We must also acknowledge the value of both business *and* buzz by constantly engaging in conversations with enthusiasts *and* influencers, offering incentives for different types of customers, and activating these respective social networks—both internal and external—to great effect.

Picking Up Where We Left Off: The Tip of the Traditional Funnel

Congratulations! You've arrived at the *A* of Action. Now what? You just secured a purchase of a Big Mac, 2-ply roll of Charmin toilet paper, Honda Pilot, or iPhone from AT&T. Think your work is done? On the contrary, it hasn't even begun.

It's time to flip the funnel and when you do, you'll notice that your previous journey's pinnacle is now the tip of the iceberg of your next one.

Introducing the new flipped funnel, A.D.I.A.:

- Acknowledgment
- Dialogue
- Incentivization
- Activation

ACKNOWLEDGMENT

When did you last thank your spouse for the hot cup of coffee waiting for you in the morning, or the extra hour you got to sleep in over the weekend? When did you last tell your coworkers how much you appreciate them and what a great job they're doing (or at least how hard they're trying)? When did you last thank your customers for their business, loyalty, return patronage, and/or referrals?

Acknowledgment bridges the chasm between everything that happens when we convince someone to buy something from us and what happens next. It's a sad and universal truth that the very second the sale is complete, all genuine empathy and service seem to go out the window. That overeager and attentive salesperson turns his or her back on you and refers you to some peon in technical support or customer service — or worse, lobs an 800 number or web site address in your general direction. If you're feeling just a little guilty right about now, fret not; you're certainly not alone.

Acknowledging our customers affirms their importance to us and places both tangible (the purchase itself) and intangible (future business) value on them. It is the first step in a new continuum that anticipates future interactions between company and customer, both monetary and otherwise (insights).

On the flip side, our customers enter a phase where they're craving acknowledgment, from us, others, and themselves. They want to know they're important, that they made the right decision, and that their purchase counts. On one end of the spectrum, they want to justify to themselves that they chose the right brand. On the other end, they're voting with their wallets or purse strings, thereby extending a vote of confidence to the companies they patronize. And not just the first time; every time, and increasingly so. Think one person can make a difference? In isolation, perhaps not. But add 'em all up, and devastation can occur when customers are underappreciated or taken for granted.

TYPES OF ACKNOWLEDGMENT

Acknowledgment can take a few different forms, and thanks to the explosion of contact points available to companies today, via a variety of ways.

Thank You

This is the simplest form of acknowledgment and the two most powerful
words in any playbook. A company that recognizes a customer's
patronage conveys a sentiment that can touch even the coldest heart.
The problem today is that people have become jaded. Trust in companies
has declined, and customers' default reaction is typically a guarded one;
they are waiting for the catch, the trap, the fine print, or to be sold to.

Prove them wrong, already.

Additionally, thank-you gestures can often come up short by falling
on deaf ears. So standardized and predictable, they risk becoming white
noise, especially in the form of an automated, *templatized* e-mail with zero
degrees of personalization. Don't throw in the towel, though; this is a
battle worth fighting, and typically a thank-you works best when it isn't
expected. A note on a customer's birthday is a great way to take the
opportunity to thank someone for their loyalty.

The band Coldplay expressed the ultimate thank you when it gave
away an entire album to its customers without any strings attached
(Figure 6.6). They weren't asking their customers to use the honor

Figure 6.6   Left, Right, Left, Right, Left Coldplay Album Giveaway
Source: 3D Management.

system to ante up whatever they thought the album was worth into a tip jar (like Radiohead did). Instead, they just said thank you. Short. Sweet. Powerful.

Good intentions aside, Chris Martin and company aren't dummies. They captured e-mail addresses as part of the value exchange, which itself is part of the process of flipping the funnel, namely, extending dialogue. And as altruistic as this might sound, there's no question that Coldplay expects to make up on the roundabouts (future sales, loyalty, buzz) what they lost on the swings (free music). However, none of that should take away from the band's overt demonstration of trust in their customers and authentic commitment in the relationship, which—if it were so obvious and commonplace—everyone else would be doing. And they don't.

Progress Report

A restaurant environment is a great example of a place where tacit acknowledgment works best. It can simply be a manager popping by a table to introduce himself and making friendly banter with the patrons. He is also checking subtly on the waitstaff to ensure quality control and making himself available to answer any questions, address any concerns, and/or follow up on any requests. It's also a way of saying, "we haven't forgotten about you."

In a digital environment, in-progress acknowledgment could include any of the following examples in the form of an e-mail:

- Your order has shipped.
- Since you placed your order, the price has dropped, and the difference will be applied to your account (something Amazon. com does very well, I might add).
- We've received your inquiry, and someone will get back to you in the next 24 hours or *less*.

The 24-hour *autoresponder* is perhaps the single biggest missed opportunity to meaningfully connect with a customer, insofar as it is generally devoid of any personalization and standardized to a fault. Why not provide additional information to customers that they might find relevant, or helpful? For instance – if a customer has just sent in a query ticket to GoDaddy due to problems with a domain, why not provide a list of freelance web developers and webmasters whom the organization has preselected to help with similar queries? Why shouldn't GoDaddy be in the same business as Craigslist (customer service as a value-added resource and revenue generator) and, without necessarily needing to do a direct sell, give their customers another option to make their lives easier? (And by "their" in this particular case, I mean both the customer—with an expedited, direct process—and the company, by a decreased burden on the customer-service function via providing other outlets of service.)

COURTESY CHECK-IN

You've selected that beautiful new Audi Q7 and signed the three-year lease. Now imagine your surprise when you get a call from the dealership three months later to ask you how you're enjoying the ride. I happen to drive an Audi myself, and I receive a call like this every year on the lease's anniversary. To be honest, I always feel a little guarded when I get this call—waiting to be sold to—which has never happened.

Courtesy check-ins may seem innocuous, but in reality, they're anything but. They should never be about selling, at least not from any immediate standpoint. Instead, they reaffirm a connection and keep the brand in the game—perhaps not top *of* mind, but rather *in* mind.

FOLLOW-UP

The follow-up contact is affirmation that any promises or intentions were genuine and earnest. This is not only acknowledgment in and of itself but also clearly demonstrates commitment toward a customer— which is precisely why it is likely to yield disproportionately positive results down the road. In a rapidly changing marketplace—one that's becoming more conducive to a two-way conversation versus one-way communication—many *listening strategies* fail because there is inadequate follow-up, response, or responsiveness. Customers today demand our presence long after the sale is complete, or they'll likely fade into obscurity (and fall into the clutches of our competitors). Regardless of whether we're dealing with a new purchase or a query on an existing one, it is critical that we execute an indiscriminately robust and comprehensive follow-through that would make Tiger Woods proud.

The corollary has even higher stakes and more severe repercussions: *A halfhearted attempt is probably worse than no attempt at all.* If we start something, we need to see it through to completion. Anything less telegraphs a lack of commitment and a lack of care.

I recently received a call from the head of the Audi service center following a service appointment in which my car's battery had to be restarted. They just wanted to make sure everything had gone according to schedule and that I was back up and running again.

Can you see the pattern? Do you believe I'll be back to renew my lease? Do you think I might tell someone else (or tens of thousands) about this experience? Well—I just did.

REMINDER

Truth be told, reminders aren't really essential. Customers are more than capable of remembering service appointments, or that a new product is arriving at a store.

Or are they?

It might seem a bit insulting to underestimate our consumers' ability to remember us, but it's probably still better to err on the side of caution and proactively manage a client's schedule when transacting with our brand. We also do ourselves a disservice when we overestimate our own self-worth by assuming that we're constantly at the top of our customers' minds.

That said, there is a happy medium that recognizes our customers' extremely busy, often preoccupied, and almost always overloaded lives. For that reason, anything we can do to help them out—perhaps by giving a friendly nudge—can leave a lasting impact.

"APPOINTMENT LOYALTY"

There's appointment viewing, so why not appointment loyalty? The simple ability to make an appointment with a customer-service representative in the Genius Bar in the Apple Store goes a long way toward validating the customer's importance. It also gives the brand an opportunity to *formalize* a two-way commitment and become part of a consumer's schedule.

Expect to see a significant rise in and democratization of concierge services no longer exclusive to the Rich and Famous (such as American Express's Platinum Card or Visa's Black Card), offering an expanded suite of concierge services to help schedule appointments with customers, manage conflicts, and remind them when key milestones or announcements are drawing near. Personal shoppers are nothing new, but what about personal experience or service consultants?

THE ROLE FOR MARKETING

With the traditional funnel (A.I.D.A.), every stage of the process that corresponding to a distinct consumer behavior has an accompanying and defined role for marketing. For examples:

- ESTABLISHING awareness—typically via communication or messaging (advertising and the like)
- AROUSING interest—likewise via advertising, using emotion; using the ability to inform, educate, and provide necessary information and details
- CREATING desire—using trial, sampling, or more importantly, some kind of incentive in the form or promotions or special offers
- FACILITATING action—anything that helps bridge the gap between intent and commitment: in-store and online signage, offers—from 25 percent extra to free shipping

By the same token, A.D.I.A. has its own series of corresponding roles for marketing to play in terms of achieving the necessary stage of *enlightened or evolved customer behavior.*

Marketing's goal in the case of acknowledgment is to CONFIRM it. Typically, confirmation has to take place EXPLICITLY between BOTH parties; it is decidedly mutual. The purpose at this critical stage of the flipped funnel is to show customers that they're part of a process, that their business and patronage is important, and that the company in question is committed to nurturing a long-term relationship that will hopefully enjoy the fruits of repeat business. Without establishing the clear link between the *A* of action and *A* of acknowledgment, a vital connection to the rest of the flipped funnel is likely to be broken.

Ten Ways of Confirming Acknowledgment

1. A thank-you from an actual manager and salesperson.
2. A personal, handwritten note.
3. A gift. Why not? The bigger the purchase, the bigger the gift; this is just common sense.
4. Enrollment in a club or community with some kind of status involved.
5. A subtle mention at the *next* point of purchase. *Aaah, Mr Jaffe, good to have you back at the Four Seasons. I see it's been three weeks since your last stay at our resort.*
6. Gratitude without benefits: pulling the heartstrings with no strings attached.
7. Gratitude with benefits: A reward at the next point of purchase. Technology has an even better memory than human beings (at least those who work for corporations).
8. A tacit yet effective reminder of tenure. American Express's "Member since" on their credit cards reminds both customers and merchants how long they've been aboard. Many companies, including several primary credit card competitors, have since followed this lead.
9. Integrating appointments into personal Outlook or Entourage calendars using simple Web-based functionality.
10. Extending these ideas to the social web using widgets, feeds, and other applications.

DIALOGUE

You've established a connection between customer and company. No longer are you a faceless corporation, or they a transactional data point. Now it's time to start delivering on the promise of commitment and continuity by setting ground rules for future, ongoing conversation. Establishing parameters or guidelines for future dialogue makes it a lot easier for customers to reach out to companies, and vice versa.

GUILTY UNTIL PROVEN INNOCENT

We're jaded. We're skeptical. We're damaged goods. We've become wary of corporations' intentions when it comes to trusting companies

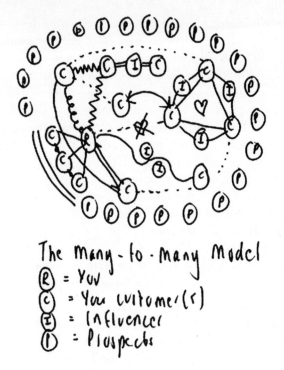

Figure 6.7   The Many-to-Many Model
Source: © Joseph Jaffe.

today. And leading the charge or rationale behind this accusation is advertising itself. A 2009 Harris poll stated that 66 percent of consumers felt that advertising agencies bore at least some responsibility for the recession, because they "caused people to buy things they couldn't afford." Is it therefore any wonder that our defenses are up when we interact with a company? It took a while for me to get used to Audi's periodic check-in calls, which—after almost eight years of sticking with the brand—still arouse some suspicion on my part.

We need to change this perception with our customers. Perhaps the adage to draw on is "if at first you don't succeed, try, try, try, try again." And then again.

As depicted in Figure 6.7, we live in what I call the *many-to-many era,*[4] characterized by a seemingly endless series of conversations

---

[4] As introduced in *Join the Conversation.*

between a multitude of constituencies (R=Brand; C=Customers; I=Influencers; P=Prospects). In a perfect environment, companies talk early, often, and honestly to their employees; customers talk to the company and its employees (and vice versa); and finally, customers talk to one another. These dialogues may occasionally skew negative in the form of complaints, concerns, and challenges. On other occasions, they'll consist of glowing praise or congratulations; and sometimes they'll just be about making conversation. But one thing remains constant: companies and brands need to be ready ALL THE TIME to continue the dialogue with customers—on *their* terms.

As the funnel widens, the nature of conversations expands as well, not only in terms of quantity and quality but also in terms of sentiment, intensity, authority, and influence.

Sentiment—A tendency to skew positive or negative that increases as people's experience's with the brand deepen.

Intensity—The words "love" (versus like) and "hate" (versus dislike) tend to be used a lot more by our customers than does the word "satisfactory" (as in customer satisfaction). (Do a search for your brand plus "love or hate" on Google or Twitter,[5] and you might feel a little woozy.)

Authority—The degree to which one or more parties are considered to be credible, unbiased, and/or independent voices on any given issue.

Influence—The tendency for sentiment, intensity, and authority to sway another person's perspective toward a brand. This can be based on the size of one's community or just the ability to break into a more manageable inner circle of like-minded *influentials* (you are the company you keep). There's no scientific formula here, save the recognition that this becomes an exponentially expansive set of contact points:

Sentiment × Intensity × Authority × Influence = WOW!

Pretty much the only way to deal with this dynamic framework is to engage in constant dialogue. Keep your ear to the ground, and stay close to your customer. This is when a conversation's strength can make or break a company.

[5] http://search.twitter.com/search?q=love+OR+hate.

Take the now-extinct Circuit City, for example, and contrast them with B&H Photo,[6] an institution that opened its doors at the back of Manhattan's Madison Square Garden in 1973. Think of B&H as a kosher Willa Wonka chocolate factory for cameras and other electronic paraphernalia. Owned by Orthodox Chassidic Jews, the store shuts down on Friday afternoons and reopens on a Sunday because of the Jewish Sabbath. On the multitude of Jewish holidays, the store (and astoundingly, its web site, which accounts for 70 percent of its sales) is closed for business. Yet B&H is perpetually bustling with activity and sales. B&H actually stands for Be'ezrat Hashem (Hebrew for "with the help of G-d"), and perhaps it is divine intervention that keeps this company afloat. Or maybe it's just a customer experience that's second to none—from traditional haggling or negotiation through the buzz that follows customers into their homes and beyond.

This is the stage of the funnel where customers exercise their natural tendency to share opinions with others (which I call "shareability")—whether they want to hear about it or not! There is another phenomenon that is unearthed at this stage of the flipped funnel—a customer behavior that shows how the purchase and consumption of products, services, and accompanying experiences is *inherently social.*

DIALOGUE IS NOT A ONE-OFF

The *A* at the end of the traditional funnel might as well stand for Alone (or even Asynchronous). Without Acknowledgment, there is really nothing more than a one-off transactional exchange. To make it through this next stage of the funnel, companies need to understand that dialogue is not a superficial chat that ends when a consumer pays the cashier or ends a phone call with a service center. Instead, customer conversations need to be as fluid as the water in the ocean and as pervasive as the air we breathe. There is no alpha (beginning) and there is no omega (end). There only is.

Conversations don't necessarily depend on high- versus low-involvement purchases nor are they a function of purchase price or frequency. Your home mortgage, for example, might be something that spans a 30-year time frame between purchases, but that doesn't mean you won't refinance at some point or that you won't purchase another

---

[6] www.wendistry.com/branding/it-isnt-the-economy-stupid/.

complimentary product or service offered by the same company (and the larger the company, the more the ability to one-stop shop.) And finally, there's that magical thing called the word-of-mouth recommendation that has the ability to influence family, friends, colleagues, and even complete strangers through advice and recommendations.

Once the flipped funnel widens, people increase the number of contact points between themselves, the company, and like-minded people. For instance, spotting another person on the same flight with a Kindle or nook instantly sparks exchanges about pricing, quality, experience, and hacks, which can quickly segue into related dialogue about travel, family, and even opportunities for collaboration. If this happens naturally, can you imagine the power and potential that could be harnessed if we could leverage this energy in intentionally?

This complex and ever-expanding social web of possibility is best represented by a visual constructed by Brian Solis, coauthor[7] of *Putting the Public Back in Public Relations: How Social Media Is Reinventing the Aging Business of PR.* (See Figure 6.8.)

With its coat of many colors and endless possibilities, the Conversation Prism[8] may scare living daylights out of you—or mesmerize you. Either way, it's a far cry from the conventional communication wheel used by so many agencies to spam their wary targets with marketing messages. Whereas the communication wheel is typically one-way—emanating *from* brands *to* consumers—the conversation prism is decidedly two-way, emanating *from* consumers *to* other consumers and, occasionally, *to* brands as well—perhaps even yours. So the question is: Are you paying attention?

Customer service itself has traditionally been a one-way street, and is often associated with solving problems that involve heightened and usually unpleasant emotions. It's a reactive process that requires a customer to contact the company to begin a problem-solving exercise. That's a pretty narrow and incomplete view of reality. In reality, people talk—a lot. And though they talk even more when they have something to complain about, that's not always the case. In fact, it could be just as true to say that people talk a lot when they've got something to talk about. (Now that's a Yogi-ism[9] if I've ever heard one.)

---

[7] Deirdre Breakenridge also co-authored *Putting the Public Back in Public Relations.*

[8] Source: Brian Solis and Jess3. More here: www.theconversationprism.com

[9] A reference to Yogi Berra, legendary Yankees' captain and catcher and keeper of a plethora of esoteric and pithy quotations.

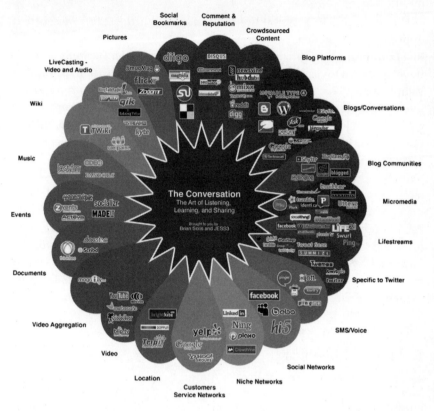

Figure 6.8   The Conversation Prism

Source: Brian Solis and Jess3.

When people have something to say, they're going to share their thoughts, feelings, opinions, and recommendations to friends, family members, colleagues—anyone that will hear what they have to say. Anyone whom I encounter through any form of media is going hear what's on my mind. You don't even have to ask, and you'll probably regret it if you do.

To that end—and all too often—companies focus only on the opposite ends or extreme scenarios. The most positive ones are usually taken for granted and stapled to the conference room corkboard, whereas the most negative are elevated to crisis status. It's the vast stretch in the middle, however, that holds the most potential for companies. Like the retail manager who approaches customers with questions about everything from how their day is going to how their shopping experience is shaping up. The possibilities that ensue from this otherwise benign approach are sublime.

In this rapidly digitizing world, however, there's an alarming scenario developing: an invariable ghost town, with nothing more than the random sample survey cascading across your screen—carefully evading your futile attempts at hitting the X button—to break up the monotony of the chirping crickets (or clicking mice). There's no dialogue here; at least not within a corporate framework. In consumerland however, it's a completely different picture. There's a raging party going on in the nether regions of the online world (once called Web 1.0, but now with a 2 or even a 3 preceding the period). It's not on the bloated home pages of the once-mighty but now whimpering defeated portals like MSN, AOL, and Yahoo!. Rather, it is on a combination of social networking hubs and start-up or upstart consumer-generated presences. This world— governed by blogs, podcasts, social networking, and messaging—represents an orgy of activity and sentiment, with endless possibilities for dialogue, initiated by ourselves, our fans, or our critics. Good times indeed.

Isn't it time we stepped up and joined the party?

ROLE FOR MARKETING

Simply put, we need to *encourage* and *engage in* dialogue by providing our customers with multiple ways to contact us at will, whether they have a purpose or not. We need to get them talking about the little things, the big things, and everything else in between. We also need to come to terms with the fact that they'll talk, whether we want them to or not; and the only thing worse than our customers talking negatively is not talking at all. The choice is therefore twofold:

1. Do we want them to talk about us to our faces or behind our backs?
2. Do we want to be masters of our own fate or victims of it?

The answers to both are pretty obvious.

Here are five things companies can do to activate dialogue *with*—as well as *among*—its customers:

1. Establish customer *clubs, forums, communities, groups, or hubs* (more on this later) where people can connect with each other, ask questions, provide answers, and socialize.

2. Make the first move: *Outreach proactively* to your customers. It's a tough sell, but one that can build over time through a combination of permission-based invitations, rewards, and most important, demonstration that there is genuine intent to act.
3. Implement a robust *listening strategy* to get a real-time handle on customer conversations where and as they happen.
4. Design a comprehensive and intense *response strategy* to provide timely and relevant information to ongoing conversations.
5. Find an optimal mix between *technology* and *human resources* designed to maximize your ability to participate effectively and efficiently with customers and their communities.

INCENTIVIZATION

Our customers are feeling the love, satisfied that their purchase counts and that they're not just another statistic. Their problems are being met proactively and comprehensively. They're also sharing their experiences with personal contacts — and even *selling* product for you. At this point of the funnel, customers are essentially recognized and rewarded both for their repeat purchase(s) and for their ability to influence *other consumers'* purchases — typically via positive sentiment, word-of-mouth, and specifically recommendations and referrals.

REPEAT PURCHASE BEGETS REPEAT PURCHASE

Surprising fact: Just 12 percent of shoppers[10] are responsible for 80 percent of Coke sales, 6.5 percent of shoppers account for 80 percent of Diet Coke sales, and less than 3 percent cover 80 percent of Coke Zero sales. Who do you think these sales are coming from: new or returning customers?

Do you know what percentage of *your* total number of purchases come from the same — in other words, returning — customers? If it's higher than two-thirds of your total sales — and more often than not, it will be — ask yourself: "What am I doing to address the people who come back to buy again and again and again?" On the flipside when we take repeat customers for granted, at some point, they're going to ask, "What

[10] Source: *Beverage Spectrum Magazine.*

have you done for me lately?" They're going to feel unappreciated, taken advantage of, and essentially abused. And we hasten this process by heaping endless discounts and perks on new customers, thereby basically slapping our existing loyal customers in the face.

At some point, these loyal customers are going to turn their backs on us — for good. At least, they *might*, and just the threat or possibility of that happening should have us all scuttling like crazy to our battle stations to make sure this never occurs.

One obvious way to avoid this is to reward our customers. Loyalty programs have long been the expression of this kind of best practice. Frequent-flier programs are the perfect way to segment repeat customers into tiers based on their patronage and frequency of purchase. American Airline's Executive Platinum program is unmatched, and does pretty much everything except preventing flight delays. The leap from Platinum to Executive Platinum is like the giant leap Neil Armstrong once took when setting foot on the moon. (I exaggerate a tad, but as an Executive Platinum member myself, I can attest to this level of service).

American created a program that rewards customers both functionally and emotionally. The peace of mind and the satisfaction that come with a first-class check-in in a foreign country is invaluable. The ability to save time and energy and enjoy a little bit of luxury in the process when traveling constantly on business makes a huge difference.

But what happens when a frequent flier misses the milestone? What happens if he or she has encountered a situation where travel isn't as frequent as it once was? This is where this and other types of programs tend to fall short. There isn't enough consultative selling or proactive outreach to help customers figure out how to maintain their status and avoid being downgraded. In American's case, however, there is *"the challenge."* And I realize that I'm sharing one of the best-kept secrets in the business, spread only via selective word-of-mouth, but then again, it's just you and me right now, and you won't tell anyone else, right? The challenge is a three-month second chance where American Airlines gives you the ability to hold on to your status if you prove to them, via repeat business, that you can maintain a prorated number of qualification miles. Ask for it next time by name and tell 'em Jaffe sent you! That's an incentive in and of itself, but it's still just the tip of the iceberg. I'd like to see the airline do more, perhaps even something as extreme as *lowering* the number of qualification miles based on the number of years the customer has been an Executive Platinum member! One technique used by fliers who are short of their milestones by 10,000–15,000 miles is literally to fly coast to coast (and, if necessary, back and forth once again) to make the grade. But why make a customer have to eat all that airline food in order to prove themselves worthy of maintaining their status? Shouldn't the brand demonstrate *its* loyalty to its best customers, in addition to the other way around? Why not let them purchase the miles without having to make the trip? In a host of other ways, American could not only preserve the loyalty of their most loyal customers but actually boost it—and all the while, increasing revenue and repeat purchases. Delta, for example, sent me a letter informing me that they had deposited 10,000 complimentary Medallion Qualification Miles into my account to help me requalify for Medallion status in 2010. They "understand your ability to travel is more restricted this year, due to the economy and other factors." They've also instituted rollover miles where one excess year can subsidize the next. (Right ideas; however, as you'll read later in this book, I wasn't flying less, just flying THEM less.)

Taking our customer for granted translates into an acute lack of recognition and reward for repeat purchases and considered referrals. In an acquisition-heavy world, we pull out all the stops to woo a stranger to sample our wares, yet we ignore the very people who essentially fund our acquisition efforts in the first place. It is tantamount to feeding yourself by holding a steak knife the wrong way. Not only will you go hungry but also you'll end up in the emergency room.

INCENTIVIZING WORD-OF-MOUTH

How many times have you said to yourself, "*I've sold so many units of Company X's product, they should pay me! In fact, I might as well work for the company.*" At a time with such abundant choice and difficulty getting the attention of consumers, I believe there's going to be an awakening among consumer nation for a quid-pro-quo partnership; a mutual back-scratching effort where failure to reciprocate will be short-lived. As a blogger, I can tell you that I am wholeheartedly aware of the power I possess when I hit the publish button. When I say something about any company, it's going to find its way all the way up the totem pole—often to the CEO or chairman of the company. When I recorded an episode of my video show on how much I loved Charmin toilet paper, I promptly received free toilet paper in the mail. *Them's the perks, my friends*. I subsequently created follow-up shows for my new favorites: Tiffany, Lamborghini, and Rolex. (I'm kidding, of course—about Tiffany.)

Right now, the majority of blogger-related conversations are spontaneous, informal, and generally snarky when it comes to brands. Things are changing quickly, however. The explosive rise of Mommy Bloggers (or Mothers that Blog, which is now apparently the politically correct or acceptable term), Blogging Networks, and Sponsored Conversations are giving us a glimpse into the propensity, intensity, and potential of word-of-mouse.

Don't get me wrong: Having customers who *naturally* feel the urge to spread the love and take on the role of honorary VP of sales with zero compensation on behalf of your company is spectacular. But it's also about as likely as hitting the jackpot. Unless, of course, you're Apple—a company that has enlisted an army of zealots who feel a sense of calling to spread the gospel of Job(s), who surely will be martyred as possessing a once-in-a-lifetime gift of activating the collective passion of the spirit of raw, undiluted, and pure creativity. Halleluyah.

For everyone else, you're SOL, so to speak. You'll need to figure out ways to formalize structure and ultimately incent people who are inclined to talk about you. And why wouldn't you? You're already indirectly paying a network, publisher (magazine or web), or radio station money to persuade people to purchase your product. So why not cut out the middleman and pay them directly?

The hypotheses here (there are several) are as follows:

- Rewarding customers who recommend you to others will increase the probability of the *number* of recommendations.
- Rewarding recommendations will counter any potential backlash or dissonance associated with being taken for granted.
- Compensating formalized referrals will increase the loyalty associated with the referrers, which in turn will lead to their increased purchases.

Call it Affiliate 2.0 if you like: a win-win-win situation. The referrer wins, the refer-ee wins, and you (the brand) win. Who would argue with a methodology that compensates every party at the table while maintaining integrity, authenticity, and transparency in the process?

THE ROLE FOR MARKETING

Our role, in essence, is to ante up, and make it easy to spread the word. Increase opportunities to refer a friend and, at the same time, recognize and reward the referral.

To be sure, it's going to happen without you. But how much bigger could it be? The entire premise of the Net Promoter methodology is centered on people's propensity to *naturally* recommend a product or service to a friend. That said, does that mean we are powerless to join in—catalyze or accelerate—this process? Does this mean we need to stay detached or disconnected from our customers—especially our most active or proactive?

Figuring out ways to recognize and reward our customers is about making sure we don't look a gift horse in the mouth; but rather giving that gift horse a big, fat smooch on the lips. In a world where we chase elusive, marketing-weary consumers with outdated, blunt, and ineffective instruments of mass deflation, shouldn't we create economies of scale based on the explosive and exponential power of word-of-mouth—both directly (through referrals) and indirectly (by rewarding frequent purchases and thus the goodwill that leads to increased talkability)?

ACTIVATION

The final part of the flipped funnel is about flipping the switch of community or social networking. Up until now, our efforts have been focused on individuals or one-to-one interaction. Now it's time to connect the dots and activate the collective potential of the wise crowds.[11] This explodes the number of potential connections and subsequent transactions, based on formalizing some kind of structure around which all customers—including current employees—are connected.

Whereas the first three stages of the funnel are more commonplace, this final phase is decidedly *not*. In fact, as the flipped funnel widens, we notice an inverse relationship in terms of adoption, incidence and usage. That's not a coincidence, given the fact that every step away from the *A* of Action is one more step removed from the norm or status quo.

That's not to say it's not going to change—it is . . . and soon. Eventually, everyone reading this book will likely investigate some kind of customer activation program that goes way beyond loyalty to a point at which customers become an inextricable part of the brand's evolution and life-force. So consider this *your* opportunity to activate the final phase of the flipped funnel, hopefully before your competitors do.

[11] A reference to *The Wisdom of the Crowds* by James Surowiecki.

Activation is the final piece of the puzzle where returning and referring customers become explicitly part of something bigger—arguably, part of the marketing ecosystem itself, at an authentic and communal partnership level.

Take Nike, for example. They sell millions upon millions of pairs of running shoes to individual customers around the world. But what connects these customers together? What unites two shoppers both reaching for Dawn, Wisk, or Tide down the aisles of the supermarket? And while I'm waiting to check in at the airport Hilton, do I have more or less in common with an Honors Blue versus Silver, Gold, or Diamond VIP based on my own membership tier? Depending on our shared interests—and, specifically, our frequency of purchase activity—what can we learn from each other? What role could the brand play in terms of unifying or enabling us in terms of our loyalty, patronage, and purchase behavior?

Nike's Run London, Human Race, and Nike+ initiatives demonstrate the power of activation. Nike flipped the funnel by creating a sense of belonging to their customers by acknowledging them through membership (or subscription); dialogue via content creation, curation, and conversation; incentivization via recognition and achievement; and finally, activation via getting out on the road and running as part of a global community. Good job!

What about those who purchase an HD camcorder but for the most part only know how to hit the record and play buttons? Or those who have a fancy 50-billion-megapixel camera but no clue how to get rid of red eye, compress a photo, crop or convert to sepia tone, or upload to Flickr? That's where consumer electronics company Panasonic stepped up to meet the challenge.

In late 2008, Panasonic began to reach out to various families across the United States who had submitted an audition to a promotional program called Living in High Definition (LiHD). Once selected, these families were surrounded with a suite of high-definition products—from HD TV to Lumix Camera to IP Camera to Camcorder—and became charter members of a fledging community. My company, crayon, began to work with Panasonic to build out this community far beyond the initial promotional element. Today, the LiHD community (www.livinginhd.com) is open to anyone and, more important, has become a haven for any Panasonic customer (or even their competitors' customers). It's available to educate, inform, empower, and inspire others with tips, tools, tricks, tutorials, stories, ideas, reasons to believe, and reasons to behave. It's an unprecedented activation that both humanizes the brand and counters the threat of commoditization, which occurs all too often in the technology space.

After a while, all the technical mumbo jumbo just seems like meaningless gibberish to the average consumer. This is why the iPod succeeded: It was so dumbed down it didn't even need a manual.

Panasonic's LiHD community (Figure 6.9) recognizes that the product itself and its gift-wrapped brand promise need a final ingredient: the delivery against that promise, in this case, the context and experience of activation.

Ten years ago, I might have been telling you that there would soon come a day where every self-respecting brand in the word would have a web site. I might also have gone as far as to predict that this digital presence would be on a par—if not superior—to their brick-and-mortar

Figure 6.9   Panasonic's Living in High Definition Community

presence. You, on the other hand, might have laughed me out the room
(or even had me forcibly removed). Turns out I would have been 100
percent on the money. Now, I'm going to give you another prophecy and
this time, I think it's likely to come true within a much more compressed
timeframe than 10 years.

> Within the next 5 years (or less), every self-respecting brand will have some
> kind of digital or virtual community in place.

Time starts . . . . NOW!

THE ROLE FOR MARKETING

The role for marketing here is to almost literally IGNITE Activation. Unlike
that unused gym membership, which is equivalent to flushing money
down the toilet, Nike gave its customers five of the new marketing six Cs:
context, community, content, customization, and conversation in a complete flipped-funnel package. (The final C—that of "Commerce"—will be
Nike's reward.)

> Activation represents a new marketing system where organizational process
> supports a new customer-centric ecosystem—one that is powered by loyalty,
> word-of-mouth, and most important, sales. It's a self-sustaining environment
> with its own currency of both intangible intellectual property and tangible
> exchange of goods and services.

OH, AND ONE MORE THING . . .

Just like A.I.D.A. had a suggested *S* on the end representing Satisfaction, I'll suggest another *S* to support A.D.I.A.: the *S* of Sustainability.
As one might assume that Action and Satisfaction need to fit together,
the same logic would equally apply to the notion of a fully functioning,
self-sustaining ecosystem.

There's also a more profound interpretation of Sustainability here,
beyond the notion of merely closing the loop. Rather, it's the ability
to create a smarter, more efficient, and more environmentally and
socially friendly system of marketing, promotion, communication,

and distribution. Imagine a world where customers are literally hard-wired into the DNA and infrastructure of the company itself. Imagine the power and potential of a feedback loop that is inextricably inter-woven into the very nerve center of the organization.

It's not unrealistic or inconceivable to improve marketing efficiency by more effectively managing customer relationships and ultimately empowering customers to manage themselves and/or others (in the form of bringing in new business). After all, we talk about media efficiency—that is, getting more from less—which normally takes the form of cost savings and efficiencies realized from scale (the denominator). Why, then, would we not look at innovative ways of improving this in the form of higher returns, sales, and, ultimately, payback on investment?

The ability to create initiatives that sustain themselves—that is, grow over time, and gain momentum and value in the process—offers corporations a powerful point of differentiation and competitive edge. Not only does it give customers reasons to both believe and behave but it also provides them with a reason to keep returning and avoid going elsewhere.

LADIES AND GENTLEMEN . . .

. . . I give you your flipped funnel as depicted in Figure 6.10 on the next page. The diagram in question depicts a funnel that widens instead of narrowing, and in so doing, expands the number of customer connec-tions, conversations, and potential conversions (via repeat purchase and referrals).

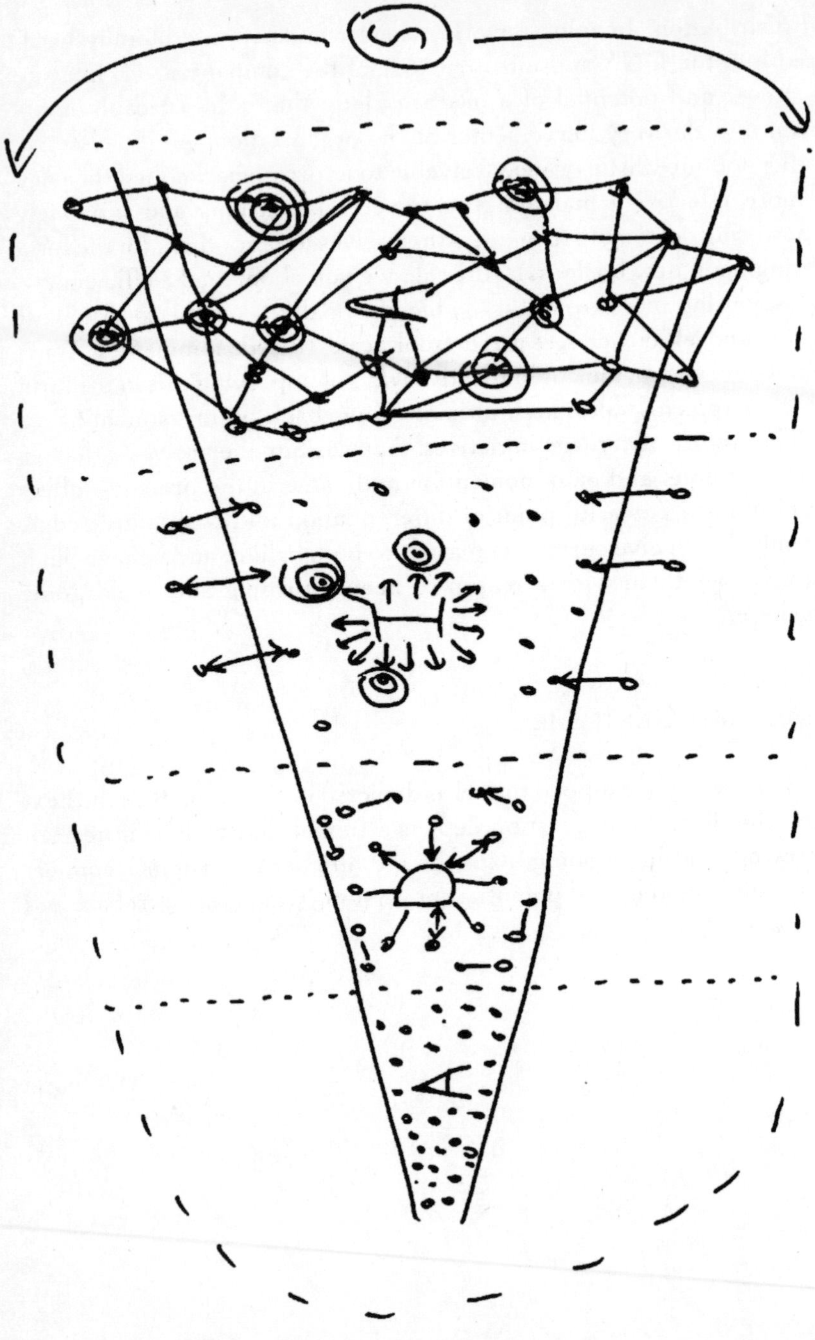

Figure 6.10 A.D.I.A.—The Flipped Funnel

7

Politics, Shoes, and Insurance: Three Examples of Flipping the Funnel

You just got a taste of a new conceptual framework, drizzled with several real-world examples to bring this thinking to life. Now I'd like to expand the focus and shine the spotlight on three very specific and diverse examples that really illustrate the theory in practice.

BARACK OBAMA FLIPPED THE FUNNEL

Barack Obama (that's Mr. President to you) was not the first presidential candidate to develop a new-media grassroots strategy to mobilize voters; Howard Dean did it in 2004. What Obama did differently, however, was the following three things:

1. Utilized *new media* as a strategic driver and imperative (have-to-have), versus an optional add-on (nice-to-have). Obama recognized that new media was the platform of choice for both younger and/or disenfranchised or disengaged voters, so a program that involved and empowered potential voters was critical to the eventual success and outcome of the campaign.
2. Deployed both new media and social media in unique and differentiated ways that fulfilled and maximized their roles and potential. This was less about reach and frequency and more about the power of *two-way interactivity and involvement.*
3. Flipped the funnel by focusing on his core, converted, and most *loyal customers.* Here's how.

Acknowledgment

On one level, Obama's and his team's outreach was as diverse as the very people he was trying to access. Their campaign efforts mirrored the overall U.S. trend toward digitalization and mobilization. For example, the Obama iPhone application demonstrated the Democratic candidate's awareness of his audience (and, by inference, how to better serve them) with a mix of always-on and up-to-date news, information, and multimedia content, combined with examples of unprecedented innovation.

My personal favorite was the call-friends feature, which literally rearranged and sorted a user's entire rolodex by state, prioritized by battleground states. Theoretically, I was just a click away from calling Pete Blackshaw in Ohio to encourage him to vote for Senator Obama in the general election. Once this call was complete, the call stats would have acknowledged my call and crossed him off the list. The application also made full use of the locator-GPS functionality to match up the user with local meetings, regional news, and other participation and partnership-based activities. And finally, there was a little green button that contrasted nicely with the deep sea blue background, allowing the user to donate to the campaign. (See Figure 7.1.)

The Obama iPhone application was the epitome of the flipped funnel. It was probably a guarantee that anyone who installed this app was most likely voting for this particular candidate. Yet Team Obama was able to extend and maximize value far beyond a single vote by using the ability of that one vote to influence additional votes, participate in the campaign, and contribute monetarily.

Obama's micropayment strategy was, in fact, especially in genius. By flipping traditional campaign fund-raising theory on its head—that is, counting on fewer numbers of larger contributors—Obama was able to amass unprecedented levels of financing from a spectacular breadth of average people *just like me* (the same group that trusts someone *just like me*). Most of the money Obama received came from small donations of less than $300. And every single contributor was acknowledged in some way, shape, or form. In fact, early in the campaign, donors not only were rewarded by invitations to fund-raising events (which they ordinarily would never have had a chance of attending) but also, even more remarkably, were guaranteed to meet the presidential candidate. In fact, Obama would come over to *their* table to exchange a few pleasantries. This kind of access was unheard of before the 2008 election.

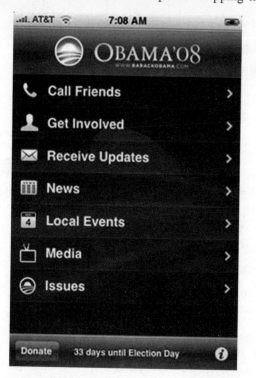

Figure 7.1   Obama iPhone App

Photo credit: CNET News.

Dialogue

Obama developed an online following that reached far beyond www .barackobama.com. Not only did he establish a presence on at least 15 major social networks—including Facebook, MySpace, AsianAve, MiGente, and BlackPlanet—but he also created a social network of his own called MyBO, which served as a central hub for both online and off-line activities (Figure 7.2). The platform became the nerve center for all online grassroots initiatives.

By developing a healthy roster of digital content in the form of a thought leadership blog, podcasts, e-mails, text messages, contests, Web videos, games, and widgets, Obama engaged his community in a series of ongoing, two-way dialogue and conversations. In addition, through various blogger outreach initiatives (including conference calls with the campaign team), Obama established online credibility with very vocal and influential audiences.

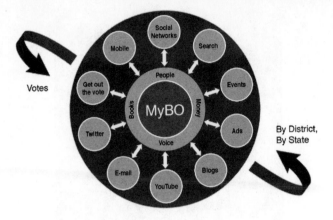

Figure 7.2   MyBO Social Network Overview

Source: Edelman.

Incentivization

Something that cannot be attributed to Obama's social media utilization is the core reason that people were driven to actively participate in arguably the most historic campaign in this nation's history. The significance and emotion associated with being a part of something revolutionary was an incentive in and of itself that campaign strategists carefully developed and leveraged throughout the campaign. People commonly referred to this as the Hope Factor. Hope and Change were the central themes of his campaign, and *Yes We Can* became the primary tagline and major incentive to participate. Quotes like "I'm asking you to believe. Not just in my ability to bring about real change in Washington . . . I'm asking you to believe in yours" rallied people around an idea this was more than an election; it was a movement.

Following his election, voters were taken by surprise when some received an actual *invitation* to the inauguration (sent to contributors by the campaign committee). It's unclear how they were selected or how many were included, but a million invitations were allegedly sent out. Although anyone could attend the inauguration and the invitation didn't gain the recipient special privileges, it showed how the campaign went the extra mile to make the community feel appreciated. One blogger-contributor, who received the invitation (Figure 7.3), as well as a Christmas card, had this to say: "*I feel so special, honored, due to the fact a nobody like myself can honestly receive this special invitation from the Obama committee. I had tears roll on my face.*"

The Presidential Inaugural Committee
requests the honor of your presence
to attend and participate
in the
Inauguration of

Barack H. Obama

as President of the United States of America

and

Joseph R. Biden, Jr.

as Vice President of the United States of America
on Tuesday, the twentieth of January
two thousand and nine
in the City of Washington

Figure 7.3   Obama Inauguration Invitation

Activation

This brings us to the matter of how Obama activated this movement—arguably the most important phase of the flipped funnel for Obama. He empowered his friends, followers, and fans (converted and safe voters) with a variety of tools and offered countless ways for people to assist, based on their level of commitment. These tiers were broken into three categories: Personal, Social, and Advocate.

A Personal supporter could start by making Obama a friend on a social network and signing up for text messages and e-mail to stay informed. After Republican vice presidential candidate Sarah Palin's attack on Obama's community credibility, it was the lowly e-mail blast to the community of customers that activated a fever pitch of response—which led to the single biggest fund-raising day in U.S. political history.

Once further invested as a Social supporter, people were able to evangelize (through referrals and recommendations) to contacts in person or via social networks. From existing and more formalized networks like MyBO to personal groups on Facebook, the more the merrier was the order of the day when it came to customer-based outreach.

Finally, Advocates became content creators by writing blog posts, posting photos, and uploading support videos to YouTube. This approach to content was what micropayments are to fund-raising. You didn't need to be Will.I.Am to leave a mark and make an impression. Advocates were literally and prolifically creating free (and credible) media impressions by the score as they become part of the elaborate tapestry of preference and precedence that spread over the entire country with infectious waves of passion and loyalty.

The results were evident on MyBO, which provided people with videos, speeches, photos, and other raw materials to remix and create their own original pro-Obama content. Supporters ended up creating more than 400,000 videos and posting them to YouTube. They also wrote more than 400,000 blog posts on the site. Advocates were also able to host offline events, where they would ask fellow supporters to donate money, register to vote, canvass, or phone-bank.

These three tiers of support gave everyone—regardless of how small or large a commitment they made—a chance to make a difference.

The Power of the Product

Whether you're a Democrat, Republican, Independent, unaffiliated, interested foreign observer, or comprehensively uninterested, there was no denying the uniqueness of the offering: an African American, with a middle name of Hussein, looking to make history in a country that only 150 years prior did not even recognize the right of a black man or woman to be free.

Many critics were quick to discount the new or social media influence and activation as nothing more than hype or misdirection associated with a more fundamental truth: the product must be differentiated and superior in order to stand a snowball's chance of being embraced, internalized, passed around, and talked about.

They may very well have been correct. There's no question that the product was unquestionably different, but so, too, was the marketing and in particular, the customer experience associated with it.

The Funnel Lives on . . .

The Obama campaign turned every single converted voter into an evangelist. By making them special and *not* taking them for granted, the campaign was able to achieve the ultimate in political strategy: activating the median voter theory by making every single voter feel significant. Only in this case, it wasn't about showing up and voting Democratic but rather about spreading the word and essentially growing the business from the inside out.

From the few come the many (Figure 7.4 summarizes the key numbers).

The genius of the Obama strategy was that it began with and focused on the converted, the *A* of Action in the traditional A.I.D.A. model. By flipping the funnel, Obama was able to use existing customers to gain new ones. By giving supporters the power to create their own commentary and conversation, ordinarily what might have been perceived as a marketing message from a controlled source (yes, even Obama created those horrible political ads) became the equivalent of a credible, unbiased, and independent customer review.

But it didn't stop there.

During the second week of December, thousands of Obama for America volunteers held house parties to celebrate the victory, as well as to discuss the next steps on how to help push legislation through Washington. And then there's 2012 and reelection and, as history will ultimately prove or refute, the ultimate endorsement and/or validation of customer experience, retention, and loyalty marketing.

As a sidenote, within his first year in office, President Obama ran into several hurdles associated with the economic stimulus recovery

Format	Results
E-mail	13 million people on the e-mail list who received 7,000 variations of more than 1 billion e-mails
Donors	3 million online donors who contributed 6.5 million times
Social Networks	5 million "friends" on more than 15 social networking sites 3 million friends on Facebook alone
Web site	8.5 million monthly visitors to MyBarackObama.com (at peak) 2 million profiles with 400,000 blog posts 35,000 volunteer groups that held 200,000 offline events 70,000 fundraising hubs that raised $30 million
Video	Nearly 2,000 official YouTube videos watched more than 80 million times, with 135,000 subscribers 442,000 user-generated videos on YouTube
Mobile	3 million people signed up for the text messaging program. Each received 5 to 20 messages per month
Phone Calls	3 million personal phone calls placed in the last four days of the campaign

Figure 7.4   Obama Campaign By The Numbers

Source: Edelman.

program and specifically health care reform. Some might argue that he *failed* to harness, *activate* or even *sustain* his newly-built community in order to help him with his mission. Put differently, "campaign" prevailed over "commitment."

ZAPPOS FLIPPED THE FUNNEL

"We're not a shoe company that happens to give great customer service; we're a service company that happens to sell shoes."

Those are the words of Zappos CEO Tony Hsieh. Ordinarily, claims like that are nothing more than lip service, the kind of spin not worth the paper it's printed on. But Zappos is no ordinary company; and it walks its talk in the most extraordinary of ways.

How? By flipping the funnel.

What began as a challenge to overcome a hurdle in the traditional funnel—getting consumers to purchase—became one of the industry's guiding lights and a competitive differentiator second to none in the flipped: a legendary customer experience.

It's also the central reason why little David was acquired by the mighty Goliath (Amazon.com) in July 2009.

Hsieh and Zappos founder Nick Swinmurn believed that consumers would purchase just about anything on the Web as long as it was easy to reverse the transaction. In fact, Zappos's return policy alone went a significant way toward easing consumer apprehension about buying shoes. The company's tagline, Powered by Service, exemplifies a commitment that makes buying from the company painless, risk-free, and pleasurable. It is such a simple process that Zappos hasn't merely separated itself from its competitive set of shoe e-tailers but has also become a beacon of exceptional customer service among brick-and-mortar retailers. Whereas most companies are almost impossible to contact, Zappos provides a 24/7 800 number on every page; whereas most companies make it difficult to return items, Zappos allows free return shipping and an unprecedented 365-day return policy.

Getting people to make an initial purchase is one thing; getting them to return again and again is an entirely different nut to crack. At some point, Zappos made the successful leap from superior to sustainable customer service and, in doing so, flipped the funnel from a transaction-based brand to an experience-based brand.

A prime example is the "I Heart Zappos" story (Figure 7.5) in which blogger and Zappos shopper Zaz Lamarr bought seven pairs of shoes for her terminally ill mother. When only two of the pairs fit because her mother had lost so much weight, Zaz was forced to return the rest. However, she was unable to make the shoe return a priority, given her circumstances. When Zappos e-mailed her, asking about the returns, she told them the story—and in an unprecedented gesture, Zappos took the initiative to send a UPS truck to pick up the shoes. But that's not all they sent; they also surprised Zaz with a bouquet of flowers from a florist.

Figure 7.5   I Heart Zappos

Source: © 2009 Zappos.com, Inc.

Growth—and rapid growth in particular—can often kill a company's spirit, dexterity, responsiveness, and intimacy. Not so with Zappos, where it appears that scale has actually *helped* the company formalize and solidify both its core beliefs and its ability to deliver on them. To support this expansion, the company developed 10 core values and, as only Zappos can, transparently communicates them to the outside world.

1. Deliver WOW through Service
2. Embrace and Drive Change
3. Create Fun and a Little Weirdness
4. Be Adventurous, Creative, and Open-Minded
5. Pursue Growth and Learning
6. Build Open and Honest Relationships with Communication
7. Build a Positive Team and Family Spirit
8. Do More with Less
9. Be Passionate and Determined
10. Be Humble

Delivering WOW service is the bedrock of these values and a key part of how Zappos flips the funnel at every opportunity with its loyal customers. Tactics like surprise upgrades to overnight shipping—and even direction to competitor web sites when items are out of stock—consistently demonstrate a commitment that goes above and beyond what would be considered to be any industry norm.

None of this would be possible if there wasn't an unprecedented and deep-seated Cultural and Organizational commitment to customer experience (ranked against the C.O.S.T. methodology, they overindex against C and O at record-breaking levels). Zappos inventories all of their products, which means no drop-shipping, and runs their Kentucky warehouse 24/7. This flies in the face of e-tailing giant, stalwart, and now parent, Amazon.com. Like USAA (as you'll see shortly), they do not log call times for call center reps.

Zappos strongly believes that their employees are the key to providing the best customer-service experience, which is why they are so adamant about hiring the right people. They put all Las Vegas staff through five weeks of extensive culture, core values, customer service, and warehouse training. They even offer employees a $2,000 incentive to quit after the first week of initiation if they don't feel they're a good fit for the company. They publish a culture book and put at least

50 percent weight in both interviews and performance against core values and culture fit.

Perhaps that is why *Fortune* magazine ranked Zappos as No. 23 on its "100 Best Companies to Work For" list.

Proof That Flipping the Funnel Drives Business Growth

Delivering an experience that is centered on customer service translates into tangible results for Zappos. On any given day, about 75 percent of purchases are from returning customers, and those repeat customers order at least 2.5 more times in the next 12 months. Zappos's repeat customers have higher average order sizes. First-time customers in Q4 of 2006 racked an average order of $111.98, and returning customers during the same quarter spent an average of $143.22 per order.

As the chart in Figure 7.6 (direct from Zappos) illustrates, the company embodies a flipped-funnel methodology to growth their business via repeat customers and word of mouth (using existing customers to gain new ones).

Figure 7.7 shows repeat customer data.

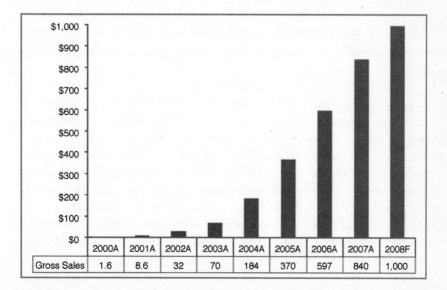

	2000A	2001A	2002A	2003A	2004A	2005A	2006A	2007A	2008F
Gross Sales	1.6	8.6	32	70	184	370	597	840	1,000

Figure 7.6   Power of Repeat Customers and Word of Mouth

Source: © 2009 Zappos.com, Inc.

	% customers who buy again within next 12 months (repeat customers)	avg # purchases by repeat customers over next 12 months	% repeat customers multiplied by avg # purchases
March 2001	20.4%	1.50	0.31
March 2002	27.0%	1.74	0.47
March 2003	33.5%	1.96	0.66
March 2004	44.6%	2.36	1.05
March 2005	51.0%	2.53	1.29
March 2006	51.3%	2.66	0.47
March 2007	54.9%	2.68	1.47

Figure 7.7   Repeat Customer Data for Zappos.com

Source: © 2009 Zappos.com, Inc.

Zappos scores highly and consistently throughout the A.D.I.A. process, but it is perhaps through its constant dialogue with its customer base and community that it registers the most engagement and resonance. In fact, Zappos follows one of my central messages to marketers: *Forget social media and instead focus on putting the social back into media, the social back into marketing, the social back into commerce.* They've put the social back into e-commerce and buying stuff; they've made an otherwise inanimate and cold transaction into a human, engaging, and fun activity.

And they do this in a highly transparent manner. In fact, Transparency is one of the four elements that Hsieh believes is pivotal to building a brand that matters (along with Vision, Repeat Customers, and Culture). Zappos maintains an open and ongoing relationship with its employees, partners, customers, and even business community via a variety of techniques and platforms, including blogs (blogs.zappos. com), a web video brand (www.Zappos.tv), a presence on several social networks and networking platforms, and a foundational approach to employee–customer conversations via microblogging and a presence platform, Twitter (twitter.zappos.com). Hsieh even uses his own account to share details about his personal and professional life, gives followers an inside look of what it's like to work at Zappos, and every now and then, launches contests in which he gives away free shoes. The company conducts experience tours at their head office and has developed new revenue streams by advising and consulting for other companies on how to achieve similar levels of commitment to customers through premium subscription portals and events such as their Insights Live Bootcamp.

In hindsight, it's probably inaccurate to say that Zappos flipped the funnel, because they never operated their business using the traditional method. The flipped funnel has always been the norm for Zappos, and that is why they are the darling of a very conventional business world desperately searching for change.

USAA FLIPPED THE FUNNEL

You might not have heard of USAA before, but I guarantee that after reading this case study, you'll never forget them. USAA is a Fortune 500 financial services company that offers banking, investing, and insurance to people and families that serve, or served, in the U.S. military. Because its customers are both active and retired members of military, its 13,000 customer-service employees (60 percent of the company, 15 percent of which are military themselves) are trained to understand the struggles and challenges of families pressured by war, deployment, and in some cases, death.

Perhaps it's this empathy that naturally lends to a philosophy and culture that is closely aligned with a flipped-funnel methodology. It's also why USAA is one of the most highly regarded companies in terms of positive customer experience, with top two rankings on *BusinessWeek*'s listing of Customer Service Champions. They've also enjoyed stellar showings on Forrester's 2008 Customer Experience Index (CxPi) for both its credit card division (#2) and insurance provider division (#16). Here's how:

- *The service they provide is on their customers' terms.*

   Too often, companies migrate (force) their customers into channels that require them to essentially serve themselves. USAA offers free financial advice led by more than 175 advisors who help members over the phone or by e-mail, not because it's necessarily cheaper, but because it's an efficient method for military personnel overseas who have easier access to the Internet than to a phone.

- *Personalized scale.*

   Unlike most companies, USAA does not sacrifice or trade off empathy for scale. With employees responding to more than 55 million phone calls per year (no, that's not a typo), this company refuses to succumb to the denominator pressures at the expense of numerator outcomes. Case in point: One employee, Angela Castillo— a USAA member for 10 years and an employee for 1—attributes a big part of her job to simply listening. She was once on the phone for an hour with a recently widowed member who was crying during her call about her homeowner's policy. Castillo walked her through money-saving changes to the policy and finished the call with "Thank you for your trust in USAA."

• *Time is relative.*

Much like Zappos, employees at USAA don't follow scripts, and calls are not timed. They're given the power to make executive decisions about a member's plan if they believe that it is in the best interest of the customer, even if that means not selling them any- thing. We have "a dedication to keeping the decision-making at the lowest level of the company," said David Travers, a senior vice president in USAA's property and casualty insurance business, about USAA's approach to answering customer calls.

Retirement specialist Jayson Sacco said that he worked with one member for four months to help her out of $100,000 in credit card and auto loan debt—and didn't sell her a thing. "I call her every few weeks. She's a real nice member," Sacco said. "When that happens, the best you can do is just listen." The financial advice unit is shorthanded, and calls for advice take a lot of listening. Sacco worked 600 hours of overtime in 2006 and was promoted for his hard work in March 2007.

• *Good goes around—both tangible and intangible.*

Employees receive hefty perks for their work. In 2006, all employees—from execs to reps—saw bonuses approximating to 22 percent over and above their pay, on top of 401(k) matches and a company-funded pension. Employees receive full tuition reimbursement, free financial advice, and extras such as on-site child care and massages.

Travers claims the biggest of all the perks is something he calls "psychic income," which is being treated like a professional in a position that is traditionally considered the lowest rung in corporate America. "At the end of the day, we're all kind of wired the same way," Travers said. "We like to go home knowing that we did something worthy, that we contributed in some way that was measurable and meaningful. It's just a little more visible when you work at USAA."

- *Walking a mile in a customer's flak vest.*

The company goes to great lengths to educate its employees on *who* their customers are, the lives they live, and how much it should mean to them to have USAA at their side. During Stevie Salinas's new-hire orientation in 2007, she donned a military helmet, a 65-pound backpack, and a flak vest and ate the same MREs (meal ready to eat) that soldiers eat in the field. She even got letters to read from troops in Iraq. The letters she received were from a soldier who later died in the war and were addressed to his mother.

Policy service manager and Air Force reservist Chin Cox once gave her 17 agents—who had to work on a Saturday—MREs as a reminder that, while the cafeteria was open, soldiers in the field didn't have the same luxuries. "The reason we have choices is because they're out there giving up theirs," Cox says.

- *You can't fake authenticity.*

Getting employees to truly care about their members and the sacrifices they're making is the company's key criterion for hiring. USAA Executive Vice President for People Services Elizabeth D. Conklyn, claims that it takes 10 applications to find each person who fits the company's expectations. "If they don't get goose bumps when they see the training video, they're probably not going to work here," Conklyn said.

- *Flipping the funnel.*

USAA doesn't need more customers; keeping the members of the U.S. military safe both home and abroad kind of takes care of that part of the funnel. Instead, USAA focuses on the lifetime value of the customer—with a particular emphasis on the word LIFE, as opposed to TIME. The company's commitment to retention is not a business strategy; it's a cultural imperative and a calling. It's beyond good business sense or even common sense; it's just the right thing to do.

Expanding on the A.D.I.A. methodology:

Acknowledge: USAA takes this to new and powerful levels of emotion and connection by paying tribute and respect to their customers' sacrifice for their country. This is purpose-based context with a big-picture vision that almost seems unreal.

Dialogue: Empathy can't be faked, and USAA takes as much time as is needed to see a policy or claim through to completion.

Incentivization: USAA fulfills against both its internal and external customers with a powerful mix of tangible and intangible benefits on multiple levels.

Activation: A community of veterans provides an ever-present ecosystem that USAA does not take for granted. By uniting both employees and customers—and nurturing the very fabric of this base—the company helps to perpetuate and strengthen the very reasons that the U.S. military remains a volunteer-based organization, propped up by a select group of patriots who are prepared to make the ultimate sacrifice in the name of civic duty and responsibility.

8

The Key Is Customer Experience

You've just been introduced to three organizations that successfully flipped the funnel. You observed a 180-degree change in what would otherwise be considered normal business process: from the standard top-down or outside-in approach to a bottom-up or inside-out methodology.

This chapter is going to introduce a phrase (perhaps you've heard of it already?) that—mark my words—you'll be hearing a lot more of going forward. Feel free to start the idea virus yourselves within your own organization, and time-stamp or date-stamp the moment you did for posterity and bragging rights. The phrase is "customer experience," and in many respects, it cuts across the entire flipped funnel. I'll even give you a definition: *Customer experience is the sum total of all contact points, interactions, transactions, and encounters between a customer and a company, its brands, and its various product and service offerings over a determined period of time.*

CUSTOMER EXPERIENCE IS *NOT* CUSTOMER SERVICE

Customer-service is just one component—albeit a very important one—of the customer wheel. In keeping with the metaphor, it's the grease or oil that keeps the wheel turning smoothly. As the mantra goes, "The squeaky wheel gets the oil," and this couldn't be more appropriate or accurate when it comes to customer service. That said, there's so much more involved in tapping into and leveraging existing customers in order to gain new ones, increase sales, and ultimately grow your business. In the musty world of advertising, there's an absolutely correct saying that everything communicates. The logic can be applied to the entire customer–retention process and the ability to create a holistic customer experience that either exceeds or falls short of customer expectations.

In order to truly understand customer experience, it helps to focus on the "experience" part of the phrase. As per www.dictionary.com:

–noun

1. A particular instance of personally encountering or undergoing something: *My encounter with the bear in the woods was a frightening experience.*
2. The process or fact of personally observing, encountering, or undergoing something: *business experience.*
3. The observing, encountering, or undergoing of things generally as they occur in the course of time: *to learn from experience; the range of human experience.*
4. Knowledge or practical wisdom gained from what one has observed, encountered, or undergone: *a man of experience.*
5. *Philosophy.* the totality of the cognitions given by perception; all that is perceived, understood, and remembered.

Our takeaway from definition 1 is that experience is personal and thus internalized and contextualized on an individual level. That doesn't mean that there are no shared or community experiences; there most certainly are. In fact, a big part of the Flip the Funnel theory banks on this. However—and it's a big however—the point of origin is at a personal and individual level. The other takeaway is to avoid our brand being perceived as "a bear in the woods" or a frightening experience. You'd be surprised how true this is when it comes to dealing with companies and their supposedly satisfactory customer service on the flipside, how frightened companies are to step out from behind the velvet curtain and face up to their customers.

Definitions 2 and 3 reinforce one another and validate the "everything communicates" mantra. In other words, while an experience can be a one-off and/or absolute evaluation or determination, it is also the sum total of these individual encounters, observations, or personal contacts *over time*. This is, after all, a process, which implies or alludes to the ability to create and deploy some kind of formalized evaluation methodology. That's both good news and bad news for your organization, depending on whether you're able to address or execute accordingly. The other takeaway is the *whole versus sum of its parts* thinking, which one might presume would present a foundation on which to build over time. Ordinarily, that would be true, except that we need to allow for the very real and frightening (like encountering a bear in the woods frightening) reality that *at any stage in this process,* our entire body of hard work can be literally undone in one misaligned, misdirected, and misguided *speedwobble*.

Take Domino's Pizza, for example. In 2009, they encountered the kind of nightmare that puts the "crisis" in crisis communication and earned the franchise a place in marketing and PR textbooks for generations to come. Two allegedly disgruntled—or just plain bored—employees filmed a series of distasteful and disgusting videos displaying some of their kitchen antics and uploaded them to YouTube. Although the two EX-employees *claimed* it was all a hoax and that none of the food prepped with, shall we say, items that belong in noses and not in subs – actually went out the door, the damage was well and truly done.

Literally within hours, the blogosphere erupted with commentary, disbelief, and postmortem backseat criticism (constructive or otherwise). However, Domino's remained silent, *hoping* that the fervor would subside before hitting the mainstream media.

It did not. The company took a position that they would *not* issue a press release (an attempt to control or channel the speculation); rather, they would respond to anyone (including bloggers) who reached out to *them*. Although it was admirable that they were prepared to move beyond a *no comment* iron veil of silence, they weren't addressing the hundreds upon hundreds of blog posts or articles that—like a moth to a flame—were attracting Google juice by the truckload. In fact, just type "Domino's Pizza" into Google, and you'll probably find several references to this debacle on the homepage no less!

Ultimately, Patrick Doyle—president of the North American operation of Domino's Pizza—appeared on YouTube in what can only be described as a cross between deer-in-headlights and teleprompter 101. His apology was stiff and uncomfortable, and he seemed uneasy and reluctant to have to step up to the proverbial podium. It also appeared to be too little, too late. Sadly, the Conover Domino's Pizza store closed its doors several months after this incident due to pretty much a 50% reduction in business[1]

Quite frankly, it's grossely unfair for Domino's to have to pay so dearly for the unforgivable actions of two rogue employees. Regardless, it still doesn't mask the reality that, when it comes to customer experience, you're just as strong as your last and weakest interaction, which

---

[1] http://www2.hickoryrecord.com/content/2009/sep/28/lost-business-gross-out-clips-forces-dominos-close/news/

is part of an ongoing process that is apparently pretty vulnerable and fragile at the best of times.

This brings us to definition 4 of "experience": the ability to learn from the past in order to be wiser and more competent in the future. In the case of Domino's, the blogosphere was not short of suggestions and recommendations for the fast-food franchise operation. I even offered my own suggestion: to install IP (Web) cameras in as many Domino's stores as the individual franchisees would allow and then randomly scroll from one to another in order to demonstrate commitment to cleanliness and vigilance to the highest standards of employee compliance. It's an international trend, after all, to show restaurant kitchens in a more transparent light, and in this case, I believe it would have worked wonders to restore customer confidence in Domino's.

Here's a more official indication of lessons learned: I reached out to Tim McIntyre, vice president of communications as Domino's, with a few follow-up questions. As the saying goes, there are three sides to every story: yours, mine, and the truth. In pursuit of the third, it made sense to go straight to the source. To read Tim's response to the following questions and other related material pertaining to this example, please visit www.flipthefunnelnow.com and click on "enhanced content":

- *Question 1: Is the store that this happened to, still in business? (we now know the answer is "no")*
- *Question 2: What do you think was new/innovative/effective in Domino's response to the backlash/criticism/rumor/speculation?*
- *Question 3: What have you learned from this whole incident?*
- *Question 4: What steps have you taken to keep this from ever happening again?*

This brings us to the fifth, final, and arguably most important explanation associated with the idea of experience—one that aligns experience with philosophy or culture and ironically (or not) sounds a LOT like the definition or interpretation of what brands are and represent:

A brand is a collection of experiences and associations connected with a service, a person or any other entity.

This particular explanation continues to elucidate that brand experience is the sum of all points of contact with the brand. Another interpretation as to why brands are so powerful is the consistency of expectations associated with said experience. Visit a McDonald's (unlike a Domino's) in Tel Aviv or Timbuktu and you'll get, for the most part, the same Big Mac (minus the cheese, in Israel) that you'd get in Tallahassee or Topeka. Any deviation from the expectations—perceived or otherwise—is likely to be met with anything from disappointment to anger. And while it could be argued that customer experience is a subset of brand experience—after all, it is one of the points of contact with the brand—I would argue that it is on a par with—if not more important than—the amorphous gobbledygook associated with brand mystification and justification. Customer experience, after all, is about:

- Being appreciated (or acknowledged)
- Being made to feel special or important (through ongoing dialogue)
- Being rewarded or, conversely, not being taken advantage of when it leads to increased sales for the business via recommendations or referrals (incentivization)
- Developing a sense of belonging; being part of something bigger than oneself (activation)

Customer experience is 100 percent a cultural imperative, and the difference between companies that put this front and center from the boardroom all the way through to the checkout counter and those that don't is marked. It's substantial enough to clearly differentiate—and may even prove to be *the* difference—between survival and extinction. And in keeping with the Darwinian analogy, it will require companies to evolve to avoid becoming part of the Corporate Ice Age—a period that will go down in business history as the era when companies froze out their customers and, in return, froze to death themselves.

Loyalty as a Bridge Toward Economic Value

A February 2009 Forrester Research report takes this one step further: It demonstrated a direct link between customer experience and loyalty—and not just amorphous loyalty, but specifically a high correlation between loyalty and:

- Willingness to repurchase
- Reluctance to switch
- Likelihood to recommend

Overlay this against the flipped-funnel methodology, and you should clearly see three distinct ways to grow the business (acquisition) via the process of engaging and harnessing the power of existing customers (retention).

Willingness to Repurchase

You can get everyone in the world to buy your product once. The operative word here is "once," and when I say "you," I am referring to marketing in general. All things being equal, acquisition marketing should generally be able to entice anyone — over enough time and with enough repetition — to consider, if not commit to, a purchase. But if the experience does not live up to the oft-hyped promise, it's often a very abrupt end of the line.

That thinking is actually kind of outdated. In the days of yore, the *end of the line* was typically characterized by a silent vote of no confidence. Until recently, we had no way of knowing if we failed to live up to our customers' expectations. And in an environment of constant churn, the flow of newly purchased customers often masked the gaping holes in a company's ability to hold on to its customers.

Today, of course, we have the exact opposite situation, — namely, an explosion of ways for our customers to share their sentiments and future intent with us. Only it's much more volatile, unstable, and unpredictable in that they'll tell us — and anyone else who will listen — what they think of us . . . regardless of whether we ask for it or like it.

Although it might seem like common sense that if we treat our customers well, they'll come back for more — how elementary is it really? Do our track records reflect or repel this approach? As an old mentor of mine used to say, "Marketing is common sense, but how many of us have common sense?" True dat!

Today's reality is steeped in the same cause and effect; it's just that everything else in between has become a compendium of complexity, nuance, and/or subjectivity. So much can go wrong or set our customers off. So many steps that once were taken for granted are now critical for survival, let alone success. This — intertwined with a different use of the funnel (as a megaphone) — makes things ridiculously more sensitive and therefore critical for companies and brands to nail . . . or be nailed.

Take Dustin Curtis, for example. He's not exactly a *loyalless*[2] consumer, but one company I know he's not loyal to is American

---

[2] A term I created in *Life after the 30-Second Spot* to describe today's "changed" consumer.

Airlines. It all began with a blog post titled "Dear American Airlines
. . . " in which Dustin said the following:

> Dear AmericanAirlines,
>
> I redesigned your website's front page, and I'd like to get your opinion.
>
> I'm a user interface designer. I travel sometimes. Recently, I had the
> horrific displeasure of booking a flight on your website, www.aa.com. The
> experience was so bad that I vowed never to fly your airline again.
>
> If I was running a company with the distinction and history of American
> Airlines, I would be embarrassed—no, *ashamed*—to have a website with a
> customer experience as terrible as the one you have now . . . .
>
> Very truly yours,
>
> Dustin Curtis

To read the full story, including American's response (or lack thereof,
as is indicated in Figure 8.1), as well as an anonymous e-mail Dustin
receives from a user experience architect within the company who was
subsequently fired, please visit www.flipthefunnelnow.com and click on
"enhanced content."

At this point, I suspect you've already figured out why I reprinted
this little account in great detail. It is partially to make the point that
customer experience correlates highly with loyalty, which in turn

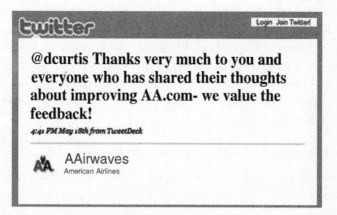

Figure 8.1   American Airlines' Anemic Response

influences willingness to repurchase. But perhaps a little more fascinatingly, I was blown away with Dustin's insight and internalization that a badly designed web site (in his opinion) is tantamount to a slap in the face from a rude flight attendant (my words); indeed, he even uses the exact phrase "customer experience." Not only does Curtis beautifully validate the very definition of experience (the sum total of EVERY interaction with a customer) but also he shows how service itself is not linked to just human-to-human contact, but also technology/automation-to-human interaction.

I don't know about you, but the way I look at web sites (through a customer experience lens of customer respect and homage) is forever changed because of one Dustin Curtis.

Reluctance to Switch

The idea here is pretty straightforward: Treat your customers consistently well, and they'll be more loyal. Over time, this will translate into an increased barrier to exit (or, conversely, an increased barrier to entry for your competitors to make significant inroads into your existing base).

You didn't really *need* me to make that last point, but let me throw a curveball to bring a new thought to the table. What about *degrees* of loyalty? For example, active versus passive loyalty in Chapter 6.

Conventional thinking holds that the more loyal customers are, the less likely they'll be to throw in the towel and defect to one of your competitors. One might also assume that the longer a consumer is a customer, the more loyalty there is likely to be. If only life were conventional.

There's another variable that needs to be considered in contemplating the relationship between customer experience and loyalty—namely, the sands of time as they relate to freshness or its opposite, staleness and atrophy. In many respects, time is the enemy of blind and/or unconditional loyalty. *"What have you done for me lately?"* has replaced *"until death do we part,"* especially when complacency, greed, and laziness creep into the equation:

Complacency = Taking our customers for granted

Greed = Focusing on acquiring new customers instead of retaining existing ones

Laziness = Self-explanatory: not putting in the necessary effort to make a difference

Companies need to have an intensive, omnipresent approach to dealing with their customers. I'd almost advocate a slightly paranoid stance: Err on the side that assumes we're only as strong as our last service transaction, *especially* when we're dealing with long-standing and/or high-value customers.

Consumers today have more choice than ever before; the world is both their oyster and their marketplace, and it's open for business around the clock. We, on the other hand, are not. For these reasons, we have to add value at every twist and turn of the customer journey, utilizing a mixture of service (doing business better using existing techniques) and innovation (finding new ways to do better business) in the process.

We've always believed that we can create impregnable fortresses to protect our investments (customers) against marauders (competitors), inclement weather (unforeseen circumstances), and the like. That may be so, and while we've probably done enough to protect ourselves from the outside-in, sometimes the enemy does lie within. By not taking care of our customers, employees, and even our culture, we run the risk of defections, mutiny, and even sabotage (Domino's). And all those high castle towers, deep moats, and taut drawbridges simply cannot withstand the rot from within.

Case in point: all of those massively complex and far-reaching frequent-purchase programs with the oodles of miles, points, and credits. Thanks to our laborious and counterintuitive terms and conditions—with blackouts, limitations, exceptions, and small print—we create what appears to be a fortress of competitive superiority that turns out to be nothing more than a house of cards.

Here's a simple piece of advice moving forward: NO MORE BLACKOUTS.

For starters, you run the risk of allowing your competitors to upstage you. In fact, every single caveat, exception, or condition is an opportunity served up on a silver platter for your competitors. Seriously, do you really want to make life that much easier for other companies looking for a reason to advertise something that actually makes sense to your customers? I think not. From a self-referential standpoint, a no-blackout policy is a clean and effective way of giving something back to your customers. Starwood Hotels (my preferred hotel group/chain) is pretty progressive in terms of making it easy for its members to cash in their hard-earned miles for free stays. In fact, they took this to a new level in May 2009,[3] when they

---

[3] https://www.spgflights.com/images_w/plg01/nav/starwoodLoyalty/TERMS.html.

announced that they would extend this no-blackout policy to airline deals (a natural complement to hotel stays) through their newly introduced SPG flights service. If you read between the lines, they're teeing up the ability to use Starwood miles in exchange for airfare and, in doing so, opening up their members' ability to pay cash for hotel rooms (read: revenue generation). Swings and roundabouts.

Blackout policies are really nothing more than blatant expressions of greed, manipulation, and opportunism. Companies telegraph their disdain for their customers by denying their ability to exchange their genuinely hard-earned points or miles for perks during what would be called peak or high season (translation: school or public holidays). In other words, all those sacrifices the road warriors made during the year really mean nothing when they can't be shared with their families. (Can you tell how unemotional I am about the subject?)

Likelihood to Recommend

The final loyalty generator comes in the form of word-of-mouth referrals. It's the Net Promoter strategy, mixed in with good old-fashioned peer-to-peer dynamics. The formula here is pretty simple: Treat your customers well enough and they'll pay it forward by sharing the love with others. We humans have some redeeming qualities, one of which is the very biblical treatment of our neighbors as we would want to be treated ourselves. Or in this case, tweaked to recommend products, services, and/or brand experiences to others, based on how we're treated and how we'd expect them to be treated in return.

Everything we do with and to our customers has an impact on customer experience; in turn, our customers flip that experience to their personal and social networks. This magnifies the number of people exposed to the message and at times even embellishes the experience (rarely with good and almost always with bad encounters). Using the wireless-telecommunications industry as an example, consulting firm McKinsey showed how even something seemingly as innocuous as how long it takes to answer the phone can translate all the way through to a company's bottom line (in the form of positive or negative personal, social, or even viral recommendations).

STORY BEHIND THE STORY

The relationships we establish and cultivate (or annihilate) between ourselves and our customers are almost the story behind the story. In many of these cases, we're not talking about the product itself at all. Yummy-tasting ice cream from Carvel, the new electric car from Tesla, or online tax preparation software from Intuit takes a back seat to the cashier who gave a free scoop after Little Johnny dropped his cone on the floor, the dealership that drove 20 miles to help with a stalled engine and brought along a loaner car, or the social networking-community tool that helps members solve the tax problems of other members.

Take CustomInk for example. Who? Exactly. But after my experience with them, it's more like "Who else?" It all began when I wanted to print some T-shirts advertising my video show, "JaffeJuiceTV (www.jaffejuice.tv)" My first port of call was the recognized name in consumer-generated merchandise, Café Press. However, for some reason that I can't recall now, I decided to look elsewhere. Upon finding CustomInk via a search engine query, I put together a design and ordered six (dearly priced, I might add) T-shirts.

My first e-mail from CustomInk was on Friday, April 24. It contained an image and link to my design, including the functionality and ability to edit it, print it, share it with friends, get a quote, review sizing information, place the order (of course), and finally, post it to my blog.

I decided to order the T-shirts and then received a second e-mail, a standard confirmation e-mail (acknowledgment) with a *guaranteed* delivery date of May 8 and instructions on approving a final proof (as I used my own artwork). To be honest, I didn't even realize I'd have the opportunity to approve my design. I was pleasantly surprised and reassured.

Then, on Monday, April 27, I got this e-mail, titled "Question on your Order":

> *Please note that we have a few questions for you that need to be addressed before we can proceed with your order. Please give us a call at your earliest convenience so we can discuss these issues. Our phone number is 866-779-3570; and please reference your order tracking number when you call.*

It turned out that I suck at designing, which was not a total surprise to me. What *was* a surprise, however, was that the folks over at CustomInk had actually taken the time and the care to recognize that I had not optimally designed my T-shirt. I had chosen a font color that would not have shown up well (or "popped") against the colored background of the T-shirt. Even more surprising was that there was a telephone number to call, and a human being waiting to help me on the other end. When I spoke with the CustomInk representative, I was offered suggestions that I ultimately took.

The next day (April 28), I received a final proof that I subsequently approved.

On May 5, I received a note informing me that my T-shirt had been printed, packed, and shipped ahead of schedule and, later that day, another e-mail confirming delivery and a follow-up to make sure that I was completely satisfied. The word "experience" is appropriately used in terms of my evaluation of the process.

On Friday, May 8, I received an e-mail from CustomInk President Marc Katz. The reply-to e-mail address is service@customink.com, although Marc's e-mail address is clearly indicated as the sender's description: marc@customink.com (why not send him an e-mail and tell him that you read about his great company in *Flip the Funnel*? I bet he responds!). Marc asked me to evaluate CustomInk's service, which I duly did.

On May 19, I received another e-mail, welcoming me to the CustomInk *community*. I have the opportunity to do the following:

You can win $100! Post a shot of everyone with their t-shirts for the chance to win $100 in our weekly photo contest.

The skinny. Get the inside scoop on new products and special offers — become our fan on Facebook.

Tips, tips, tips! Learn how to design like a pro, save money, be the best-looking group, etc.

Speedy reorders. Need to order more? Contact us for quick and easy reorders 7 days a week.

Did you notice the flipped funnel in action? Acknowledgment. Dialogue. Incentivization. Activation. And a little bit of Sufficiency thrown in for good measure and continuity!

Suffice it to say, I'm a customer for life. Or at least until CustomInk lets me down and/or one of their competitors one-ups them. Hey, no one said this was going to be easy!

9

How Employees Help Flip the Funnel

Without customers, you have no business. That's a central premise of this book. It might sound so elementary, yet it's profound; especially when contrasted against the fact that we blindly continue to chase strangers with an unhealthy emphasis on acquisition. Here's another no-brainer for you: Take employees out the equation, and there is no equation. If you want to be in the customer-experience game, it helps to have talented, empowered, and engaging employees to represent the brand—and serve as the face, heart, and soul of the company behind the brand.

As guilty as we are of taking our customers for granted, so, too, are we guilty of taking (advantage of) our employees for granted. The churn that plagues our businesses from the outside-in poses an equally massive challenge from the inside out. And although most companies struggle to come to grips with this connection point—namely, the bridge between internal and external customers—there are those exceptions to the norm: companies who do treat their employees like gold. And more often than not, this translates into a superior customer experience and is evident in bottom-line performance and results.

Take a company like Costco, where a customer once described[1] shopping as a "religious experience." It's an appropriate term, given the cultural obsession the company has with taking care of one another. It's no coincidence that Costco has the lowest employee turnover rate in retailing—five times lower than its primary competitor, Wal-Mart. They pay higher wages and offer pretty much blanket health care coverage to more than 90 percent of the workforce.

Costco is a classic example of having flipped the funnel from the inside out. They *acknowledge* their employees every day with accolades in the form of awards of recognition and service, and they continuously maintain an open and accessible stream of communication (*dialogue*)

[1] http://abcnews.go.com/2020/business/story?id=1362779.

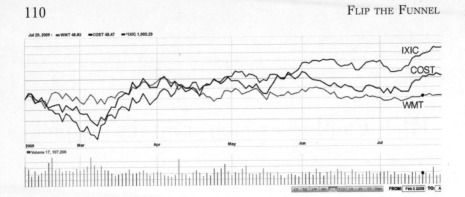

Figure 9.1   Costco's Stock Performance (COST) versus Wal-mart (WMT)

within the company. But perhaps the most significant aspect of the Costco flipped employee funnel is how they fuse *incentivization* and *activation*. Costco doesn't have a PR department, and they don't advertise; they recognize that their more than 120,000 salespeople spread the gospel both inside and outside the huge churches of discount retail on a daily basis. Last but not least, Costco *sustains* the entire process with a policy of almost exclusively promoting from within, and everyone within the company buys into this long-term commitment.

In the spirit of transparency (in this case, the bridge between the inside and outside worlds), Costco shares its benefit plans openly with the general public: www.costcobenefits.com/ and www.costco.com/Service/FeaturePageLeftNav.aspx?ProductNo=10045087. Contrast this with their chief rival, Wal-Mart, which continues to be under the gun and criticized for its lack of commitment to its employees, in terms of both hourly wages and benefits. As Figure 9.1 suggests, decisions like these are well rewarded.

Staying in the retail space, another company pulling away from its competitors—partly because its competitors are going out of business by the day—is Best Buy, through (among other initiatives) providing superior customer experience that begins with its attitude, empathy, and commitment to its employees. Best Buy employees are known as *Blueshirts* by virtue of their easily identifiable blue shirts. That wasn't always a good thing, with largely negative associations pertaining to everything from customer service to knowledge to intelligence. Even the NBC show *Chuck*—set in a fictitious Buy-More store (gee, I wonder who that's meant to be?)—depicts its employees as a cross between nerds-gone-wild and aging rampant zombies.

The truth, however, is anything but. For starters, I have it on good authority that there are very few walking undead among active blue-shirts. Second, there is a world of difference between a nerd ("nerd herd," per *Chuck*) and a geek (as in the Geek Squad, founded by visionary Robert Stephens). Third, Best Buy employees are young. In fact, across the enterprise, the average age of a Best Buy employee is 26; in the stores, it's as low as 19.[2]

WHEN IN ROME . . .

This millennial generation has grown up with technology as pervasive as the air they breathe. In particular, social computing, social networking and peer-to-peer sharing all come naturally to this networked segment. In hindsight, it seems like a no-brainer that an internal social network would be met with rapid adoption by a younger base. After all, Facebook was initially created as a novel way to keep in touch with college buddies.

Enter Blue Shirt Nation, an internal social network within Best Buy that has literally transformed Blue Shirts from a liability to an un-matched strategic asset *from the inside out.*

Blue Shirt Nation (BSN) was founded by two members of Best Buy's internal advertising department — Copywriter/Creative Director Gary Koelling and Account Supervisor Steve Bendt — who were work-ing on an upcoming campaign but weren't satisfied with the quality of consumer insights they'd been given. So they decided to go into their stores to do some of their own research with employees; however, they needed more responses than they were getting to make their research fairly representative. In order to expand the sample set, they decided to create — innocently enough — an online forum for all employees to access and use as a tool to collect insights and feedback.

What they found, however, was that this feedback platform was bigger than advertising. It became more than a place for Best Buy employees to share ideas about the work they do for their customers; it bridged the gaps among the employees themselves and even connected them to corporate, thereby filling a massive void that had previously existed.

Employees weren't told what to talk about. They were free to say whatever they felt, even if it was critical. In fact, there were a lot of

[2] Per Blueshirt Nation founder, Steve Bendt.

people who initially thought the platform sucked. However, there were also many who decided to stick around and share ideas on how it could be better.

According to Koelling and Bendt, a lot of BSN's success had to do with being in the right place at the right time. The timing was perfect from a cultural standpoint, as the spirit of cocreation had become a driving force in the business. Blue Shirt Nation went live for the first time in June 2006 but wasn't rolled out to all employees until February 2007.

After the launch, Bendt and Koelling created a 15-slide manifesto titled "An Open, Social Approach"[3] that outlined their beliefs. The document was uploaded to Koelling's blog for viewing and commenting. The manifesto's three main points were "Be believable," "Bring people together," and "Try things."

The last goal was particularly important, because the two BSN founders felt that it was critical for employees to think innovatively and not be afraid to fail. Without the confidence to openly share ideas, employee participation and collaboration across departments, stores, and the retail-corporate line would not have been possible.

DECONSTRUCTING BSN

BSN is broken into four aspects: the Water Cooler, the Wiki, the Loop Marketplace, and Tag Trade.

The Water Cooler is a fairly standard message board for employees that allows them to post, add to, and build on their own content and experiences. The Loop Marketplace lets staff members bounce innovation ideas for new services off one another, with the best ones qualifying for funding and testing from corporate. What makes this even more sublime is that if an idea doesn't get picked up, it can still be adopted by other stores and, if proven successful, the idea's success essentially overrides the corporate decision-making process. Finally, Tag Trade is Best Buy's prediction market, a Web-enabled stock-market game where employees trade stock or votes on how they think a particular idea will do. It's like an internal version of the popular consumer voting engine, Digg. Through Tag Trade, corporate predictions are reconciled with rock-face sentiment that has proven to deliver precision accuracy for the company.

[3] www.slideshare.net/garykoelling/thebigslideshow1-presentation.

The implications for inventory management, service support, and logistics planning are sublime.

BSN has become a central resource for testing and implementing several key initiatives against some of the company's core objectives. It collects real-time feedback for stress-testing and even implementing ideas in significantly shorter lead times. One particular internal challenge was encouraging younger employees to sign up for Best Buy's 401(k) program, as long-term planning is not exactly second nature to millennials. So the company ran a video contest through BSN to increase enrollment. The video that won, titled "Croft and 401K,"[4] boosted enrollment from 18 percent to 47 percent—which equated to 40,000 sign-ups.

One of the best examples of camaraderie and collaboration came from 24-year-old employee of 8 years (they start 'em young in BSN) Nick Pfeifer, who had an idea to improve videogame sales. He drafted a 108-page document, which he took with him on nine trips to his head office to discuss. However, leading up to his meetings, he was simultaneously sharing his ideas on BSN, and together—with the help of his internal social network—they were adding, subtracting, and refining sections of his plan.

Another example involved the construction of a better Employee Toolkit (the terminal used to get information within the stores). Instead of outsourcing to an external company at an estimated cost of $6.5 million and an 8- to 12-month proof-of-concept window across a test market of 10 stores, the company was able achieve its proof of concept within an unbelievable 6-week window—and a $250,000 cost.

Best Buy is now utilizing BSN to roll out mobile functionality, which is designed to access relevant information in both real time and real space, as well as personalized employee-branded online stores with their own recommended gear (if there's a Waco store, why not a Wendy or a Warren store?).

By the time you read this book, both ideas will no doubt be reality.

NEED MORE PROOF?

For the first time in the history of the company, the turnover rate is below 50 percent, down from 130 percent two and a half years previously. And when staff turnover is lower, customer service and experience are likely to be higher.

[4] www.youtube.com/watch?v=VqpKgTmkHIk.

FUSING THE FUNNEL

Whereas BSN emerged as a fairly self-contained internal initiative, the real upside lies in connecting employees with customers. Once you successfully activate an internal flipped funnel, it doesn't take too much of a leap of faith to connect with one's customers. BSN has an outside-in web interface called Best Buy Connect that allows customers to follow blog postings, tweets, and employee discussions that otherwise would have remained inside the company. Barry Judge, Best Buy's openly tweeting Chief Marketing Officer, stresses this need to be transparent in order to build trust. BSN has helped achieve this from the inside out.

The company has since launched Twelpforce, a Twitter-based service that essentially links Best Buy customers to potentially every single blueshirt via a singular Twitter profile, http://twitter.com/twelpforce, an account that essentially aggregates the individual accounts of the various blueshirts (Figure 9.2). Pretty cool.

Switching gears, Smokey Bones, a 68-unit bar-and-grill franchise concentrated in Florida and the Eastern Seaboard, did something similar in an effort to rebrand itself for a younger audience. Using a combination of local marketing, Web development, personalization, and social media, the chain recruited one staff member per location to become a Web host. Each went through social media training to

Figure 9.2   Best Buy's Twelpforce

complement their already Web-savvy aptitude. These employees essentially became the voice of each particular location and were tasked with regularly speaking with that location's Smokey Bones family members, in other words, the customer community. Each restaurant web site was duplicated on primary social networks Facebook and MySpace. Some quickly built up impressive communities of between 5,000 and 10,000 followers.

The brand struck a healthy balance between creating an authentic and intimate experience and insulating the business against inevitable turnover (commonplace in the restaurant space) by using the equivalent of a branded avatar that would remain their property. The role of a host who leaves is taken over by a new host. And it didn't hurt that hosts were paid an incremental amount beyond their normal salaries, thereby extending the longevity of these tenures—and the waiting list of replacements.

GARBAGE IN, GARBAGE OUT

It's a universal rule that what you put into life, you get out. That applies to effort, energy, investment, and commitment. And it equally applies to talent—especially when recruiting and compensating geniuses.

According to www.glassdoor.com—a less-than-scientific collection of submissions from people who claim to be employed by the respective companies—Apple's geniuses are well paid, even relative to the folk over at Best Buy. The reported average hourly salary for a Genius Bar tech was $18.30, while the reported average hourly salary for a Geek Squad Agent was $11.58. It's a Mac versus PC commercial in the making but also a reminder that talk is cheap when it comes to employee expectations regarding customer experience.

On a much larger and more pronounced level is the visible disconnect between those who prop up the economy and those who almost brought it down. It's hard to even begin comparing corporate fat cats at the likes of AIG—who earned millions of dollars a year in undeserved salary, bonuses, and spa treatments—with the average salary[5] for entry-level customer-service representatives of $28,500 in the South (which makes up the highest percentage of customer-service representatives at 27.40 percent), equating to an hourly wage of around $15. Perhaps we'll

[5] Source: www.Salary.com.

start to see this gap bridged over time, especially within companies that are experiencing firsthand the value that comes from flipping the employee funnel.

Banking on Employees

Umpqua Holdings Corp. is a bank that also considers itself a lifestyle retailer; President Bill Fike refers to the bank as "a marketing company that plays in the financial services arena." Umpqua is similar to shoe e-tailer Zappos in a lot of ways; for starters, Umpqua calls itself a customer-service company first and a retailer second. And like Zappos, the bank considers its culture to be its key differentiator.

Umpqua's branches, or stores, are furnished with large, comfy couches and offer Umpqua-branded coffee, free Internet access, mix CDs, and a chocolate coin served on a silver platter after every transaction. They also provide an experiential space for community events like movie nights, yoga classes, and concerts for local bands. The bank even has its own Discover Local Music Program, which highlights up-and-coming artists in the bank's region.

This dramatic shift in operations for the bank—founded in 1953—happened in 1994, when it conceived a profoundly unique (or is that *umpnique?*) core service and differentiation strategy, that of *delivering outstanding customer service*. The minute this shift was approved, the company began to aggressively expand its vision and horizons from banking to the hospitality business.

Customer Experience and Word of Mouth Are Referential

In 2003, Umpqua CEO Ray Davis selected seven bank associates to stay at the San Francisco Ritz-Carlton to observe and ultimately implement what they learned during their time at the hotel. Two of the many service elements they immediately incorporated at the flagship store in Portland were creating an emotional bond with customers by frequently using their names and understanding that regardless of how junior or senior a staff member is, *everyone* is responsible for providing clients with an exceptional experience.

Davis and the rest of the executive management team were so pleased with the initial training that they tapped Ritz-Carlton to maintain the bank's customer-service training for its 1,800 associates.

Several times each year, instructors from Ritz-Carlton's Leadership Center hold half-day classes at Umpqua Bank training locations. When space allows, specially selected bank customers are invited to attend as well, furthering the notion of it being the community's bank.

Customer Experience Is a Horizontal and Shared Capability

All of Umpqua's stores have managers, but the company trains employees to be Universal Associates — empowered to handle all of a customer's banking needs. This method of training eliminates the concern that customers will go from banking pillar to banking post because they went to the wrong department. And it seems to be working, having yielded several key metrics and measurements that consistently exceed industry averages, including low employee turnover, high customer loyalty, and double the average number of products per household. From 1994 to June 2008, the bank gained more than $6.8 billion in assets.

Happy Employee, Happy Customer

Umpqua's unusual training methods and commitment to customer lifestyle have generated tremendous buzz for a company you probably never heard about until just now. It's no fluke that the bank earned 13th place on the 2008 *Fortune* 100 Best Companies to Work For.

CUSTOMER-CENTRIC VERSUS CUSTOMER CESSION

This chapter makes a strong argument for balance and equilibrium between investing and committing *equally* to customers and employees. In fact, some might argue that employees are even *more* important than customers, which isn't necessarily far from the truth. Using the same logic that customers should be prioritized over prospects (remember: without customers, there is no business), so, too, could it be argued that employees should be prioritized over customers (without employees, there is no way to *do* business).

Happy Hour Is 9 to 5 author Alexander Kjerulf wrote a great blog post[6] called "Top 5 Reasons Why 'the Customer Is Always Right' Is

---

[6] http://positivesharing.com/2008/03/top-5-reasons-why-the-customer-is-always-right-is-wrong/.

Wrong." In it, he challenges the notion that "the customer is always right"—originally coined in 1909 by Selfridge's department store founder Harry Gordon Selfridge—with the following five reasons:

1. **It makes employees unhappy:** Blindly ceding to customers at the expense of employees is a dangerous proposition. In fact, when it comes to customer versus employee, it's perhaps best to give employees the benefit of the doubt (or, at the very minimum, let them be innocent until proven guilty).

2. **It gives abrasive customers an unfair advantage:** Why should abusive customers be treated better than respectful ones? Just because they make a bigger noise or create a bigger scene head-to-head with an employee in front of other customers? And what if they're in on the notion of blind acceptance (see point 1) and attempt to game the system? Whilst I'd still adopt a "customer is always right" mentality when employee conflict is *not* in play (assuming that most people are good and act accordingly), when it becomes a "them" versus "us", the result can often be a lose-lose situation.

3. **Some customers are bad for business:** When employee morale suffers because of constant conflict with difficult customers, it may be time to fire a customer, rather than perpetuate a vicious cycle of disgruntled employees taking out their frustration on each other, their families, and future customers.

4. **It results in *worse* customer service:** The corollary of the previous point is if you put employees second, they'll treat their customers likewise. Put employees first, and they'll put customers first.

5. **Some customers are just plain wrong:** The "always right" generalization takes a critical human element out of the equation: Customers don't necessarily *mind* a little spirited debate or conversation about an issue. It's actually somewhat insulting to assume they're *not* open-minded or reasonable. Certainly there will be times when companies or customer-service agents need to pick their battles; however, when there is a blatantly black-or-white impasse, putting a stake in the ground is probably a good idea.

If you think about it, we've never had a problem firing employees (just look at 2009). So why do we struggle so mightily at the idea of firing customers? In fact, preemptive and proactive action can have long-lasting positive benefits. And in the case of flipping the funnel, a bad apple can also potentially affect the entire customer community.

Double Bubble

Simultaneously overlaying a flipped funnel for employees on top of one for customers creates a symbiotic relationship that can only be described as win-win. If one does not necessarily work without the other, then it stands to reason that the two working harmoniously side by side can be an exponentially powerful one-two punch.

Perhaps it's time to make the following revisions (wordy but worthy) to the timeless adage:

Original:

Rule 1: The customer is always right.

Rule 2: If the customer is wrong, see rule number 1.

Revised:

Rule 1 v2.0: The customer is *mostly* right

Rule 2 v2.0: If the customer is wrong, don't be afraid to tell them so, and if necessary, put a stake in the ground. At the same time, pick your battles. *Black or white: pick a fight; shade of gray, (live to) fight another day.*

NEW Rule 3: Whether right or wrong, if a customer is up against an employee, do not automatically take the customer's side.

As parting thoughts, here are 10 tips to consider when flipping the funnel for your employees:

1. Perhaps the problem with business today is that companies fundamentally don't trust their employees. Change that. Without trust, our entire organizations are essentially houses of cards waiting for the wind to pick up. (See: Domino's.)
2. Empower your employees to act. Give them the freedom and confidence to go beyond the manual or playbook.
3. Allow them to make mistakes, and instead of punishing them when they do, reward their initiative for taking a chance in the first place.

4. Making the same mistake twice, though, is not cool. Integrate learning and key takeaways from all customer encounters into the organization's processes, operations, and practices moving forward.
5. Train. Train. Train.
6. Be transparent with key performance indicators that are essentially shared by the employees of the company.
7. Compensation is key—especially when tied to performance.
8. When it comes to performance-based bonuses, there are two pathways: group (shared) and individual compensation. There's no reason you shouldn't implement both at the same time.
9. There's an old saying: Not everyone can be your customer. Blindly taking a customer's word over your employee's denigrates the very integrity and respect of your own people. It's not an example worth setting, and it can be devastating on morale.
10. There's a reason why they call employees internal customers. They're just as likely to purchase from you, and more important, they're just as likely to spread both positive and negative recommendations and referrals. Don't ever forget that.

10

Customer Service as a Strategic Driver

Customer service is just one component of a much broader customer experience imperative. Yet it is arguably the most tangible, impactful, and actionable item in your portfolio of services that you can activate in a truly transformative manner. This chapter introduces the NEW RULES OF CUSTOMER SERVICE, a fresh approach comprised of openness and authenticity in customer relationships. It also puts forth a framework that will fuse word of mouth, customer recommendations, and incentivization—with a potent three-pillared formula that's redefining the very nature of customer experience. All three drivers are like layers of a cake that essentially run perpendicularly through the flipped funnel (Figure 10.1). In other words, they can be drawn on at any point in the process.

THIS *IS* YOUR GRANDFATHER'S CUSTOMER SERVICE

Well, kind of. Back in the days predating the faceless monolithic global corporations, one common thread bound these concerns together: service. Personalized and empathetic customer service was fairly commonplace. Without it, there wasn't much chance of survival. One didn't need fancy technology, computer systems, or databases to remember the names and preferences of one's most loyal and valuable customers. Today, however, it would appear that the tides have turned irrevocably and that great service has become an endangered species.

At the beginning of the twentieth century, the piano industry was one of the most popular and fastest growing in the United States; there were *literally hundreds* of piano manufacturers worldwide. Today there are but a handful, one of which is the very recognizable and popular Steinway company. Here's a little blurb from their web site[1]:

[1] www.steinway.com/protect-your-investment/.

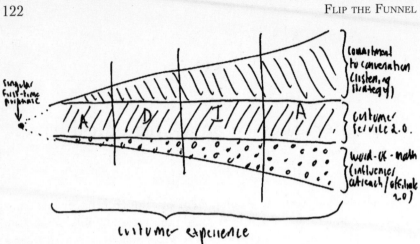

Figure 10.1   Dissecting Customer Experience across the Flipped Funnel

Source: © Joseph Jaffe.

The purchase of a Steinway-designed piano is an investment in music and an artistic musical instrument that requires general care and maintenance to ensure that it will perform to its designed specifications. To protect this valuable instrument it is important to ensure that you and your sales representative have completed, during the purchasing process, the owner's registration card that is attached to the piano. Be sure to have your piano serial number available. The serial number can be found on the cast iron plate when you open the front top of the lid on a grand piano or the lid top on a vertical piano [Figure 10.2].

> You'll find the rest of the Steinway registration process and instructions under the "enhanced content" tab on www.flipthefunnelnow.com.

Do you think it's a coincidence that Steinway is still in business today? This commitment to service is an obvious badge of pride; it shows both strength and conviction in a superior product. It's also the kind of infectious passion that is hard to contain. Idealism aside, here are some *practical* questions that you probably can guess the answers to:

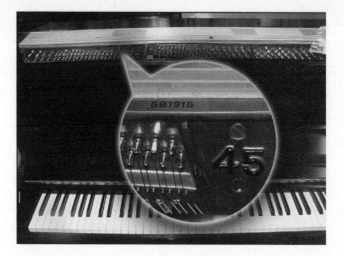

Figure 10.2 Steinway's Commitment to Customer Experience

- How many pianos do you think the average customer purchases in a lifetime?
- If and when a second piano is purchased for the home, what are the odds that both are Steinways?
- How loyal do you believe Steinway customers are?
- How many purchases from Steinway come through recommendations or referrals from existing customers?
- Is this kind of care, attention to detail, and earnest commitment solely a function of purchase price or perhaps something that runs much deeper?

Loyalty is not luck, nor is it a coincidence. Loyalty is the result of careful planning, long-term commitment, complete follow-through, and genuine empathy. And that should be music to your ears!

THIS IS *NOT* YOUR GRANDFATHER'S CUSTOMER SERVICE

It seems that the very nature of customer service has been wholly transformed with technology at the core. While being able to call a personal Steinway customer-service agent is terrific, wouldn't it be better if an iPhone application helped you self-tune your piano?

Nationwide Insurance does just that with an app that leads consumers who need to document an accident through an interactive walk-through and step-by-step guide. Although any consumer can complete the process—which allows input of accident and driver details, uses the gadget's ability to locate itself via GPS, and takes photos of the accident (Figure 10.3)—Nationwide customers can hit a button and submit the claim THERE and THEN. Now THAT'S progressive!

Off the bat, there are several key differences—or new ideas—that distance themselves from older versions of customer service, to form an entirely new paradigm:

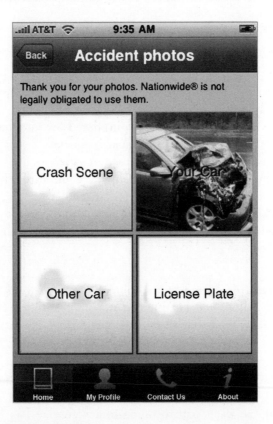

Figure 10.3   Nationwide's iPhone App

Source: © Nationwide Insurance. All rights reserved.

CUSTOMER SERVICE IS EVERYTHING (THAT INFLUENCES CUSTOMER EXPERIENCE)

Any interaction that influences customers' experience with the company, brand, product, or service is part of an elaborate tapestry that builds or breaks the bonds between all involved.

Following from this assertion, three key questions and/or marketing implications emerge:

1. To what extent should customer service *remain* part of the marketing department's area of responsibility (if at all)?
2. To what extent could customer service end up reviving, reinvigorating, or downright SAVING an otherwise tired and depleted marketing function and capability?
3. . . . and in doing so, create the kind of effectiveness, differentiation, and growth driver capable of achieving sustainable competitive advantage?

The answers to the questions above are really open-ended hypotheses that you'll need to explore through first-hand, tangible implementation, proof of concept activation, and structural or process redesign. However the text that follows should provide fairly clear illumination of which path to pursue and how to pursue it.

CUSTOMER SERVICE DOESN'T HAVE TO INVOLVE CUSTOMERS

This is an incredibly important point that makes no sense and makes total sense at the same time. Let's start with the obvious: Your customer today may become your ex-customer tomorrow; conversely, a non-customer (prospect, unaffiliated, out of market, etc.) today may become your customer tomorrow. For brands that span broader, even mass-market coverage—and for any who have ever dared to utter the foolish words "everyone's our customer"—this is *especially* for you.

Companies that have any semblance of scale *have* to think big in terms of broadening their horizons and how they grow. Step 1 is a shift from acquisition to retention; and Step 2 is a lateral broadening of what and who is considered to be a customer.

Does someone have to have paid to count as a customer? Does sending free product to what I call the "new creative class"—aka content creators, bloggers or "influencers", and the like—count? What about people who consume the brand but not necessarily the *product*? As mentioned in Chapter 6, both enthusiasts and influencers associated with the brand need to be serviced.

This is a lesson from which General Motors could have benefited, when on Monday, June 1, 2009, at around 8.30 A.M., they made a very poorly kept secret official: the company was filing for bankruptcy protection. Tens of thousands of employees, dealers, channel partners, and creditors now had their worst fears confirmed. Nervous customers in the possession of Iraqi-ready Hummers were suddenly contemplating how much a routine maintenance service would cost, adjusted for internal freight, Afghani-ready life insurance, and other military-grade small print. And then on June 2—not even 24 hours later—biG Mess (per *The Daily Show*) releases a cookie-cutter, 30-second spot conveying pearls like:

- We're not witnessing the end of the American car; we're witnessing the rebirth of the American car.
- This is not about going out of business; this is about getting down to business.
- . . . because the only chapter we're focused on is Chapter 1.

As the saying goes, who are the ad wizards who thought up *this* one? If only this call to action had come 10 years ago.

I reacted to what a complete crock I found this to be through various forms of media. Although I don't drive a GM vehicle, am I not a GM customer in the sense that I was consuming bandwidth, information, and IP associated with the corporation's future decisions and ultimate success? Could my own influence possibly *not* impact in some way the equity, sentiment, and/or perception about the brand? Did I not deserve to be serviced? And last but certainly not least, would I not be considered a customer of the future? Again, unlikely, but never say never.

Towards the end of 2009, GM emerged from bankruptcy protection with a money-back guarantee on all car purchases or leases, but—at least based on a commercial showing their government-appointed chairman Ed Whitacre—it seems unlikely that this particular old dog (the company, not the man) has learned any new tricks.

The "customer" part might be debatable; but the "service" component is carved in stone. The actions we take today will impact how we are perceived tomorrow, and for this reason, customer service can never afford to let down its guard.

MOVING CUSTOMER SERVICE TO THE FRONT OFFICE

If there's any doubt as to where customer service fits in your organization, let me state emphatically: **Customer service is a front-office strategic imperative that belongs at the same table as strategic planning, marketing communications, branding, and advertising.** It is a critical driver vital to providing brands with unique points of differentiation and businesses with a sustainable competitive advantage. I'd even go so far as to say that customer service (as a foundation-setting capability and pivotal pillar of a customer experience imperative) may very well prove to be THE single biggest and most-defined strategic and competitive differentiator.

Bar none.

However, in order to realize this, customer service has first got to move from being considered a cost to one hell of a sound investment. Second, the breadth and depth of customer service must be expanded significantly to cover a much broader spectrum of touch points and categories, with a commensurate deeper level of follow-through and interaction (à la the conversation prism or wheel). Third, this overhaul requires another kind of flip—one that's associated with recruiting, training, empowering, and compensating those responsible for customer service.

Why on earth would you outsource a crucial function as a decentralized, offshore cost center? It makes no sense to essentially pawn off (at least in terms of proximity to the center of the organization's decision-making and agenda-setting core) the one capability that we *know with certainty* represents a direct connection between customer and company. Why would you delegate this to interns or junior employees by the same token? Or conversely, why *wouldn't* you charge your most senior and talented executives with this mission-critical function?

What is thus required is a major rethink, arguably a borderline overhaul of the current level of strategic importance, organizational relevance, and cultural resonance associated with how we service our customers, *way beyond the sale.*

THE 10 NEW RULES OF CUSTOMER SERVICE

To help you on your way, I've come up with 10 new rules of customer service that I hope will challenge, inspire, guide, and channel your efforts from this moment on. I do hope you'll add to these, in terms of expansion of thought and color through the addition and association of best practices and real-life examples. You can join this particular conversation at www.flipthefunnelnow.com/newrules.

Let me introduce the new rules, and then I'll discuss them in more detail.

1. Customer service doesn't stop at 5 P.M. on Friday.
2. From "everything communicates" to "everyone communicates." The paradox of customer service: The lower down the totem pole you go, the more impactful and important customer service becomes.
3. All customers are equal; but some are more equal than others. Pay particular attention to WHO is doing the complaining. ("Do you *know* who I am?").
4. Customer service is not only about solving problems.
5. Customer service lives in the now. Real-time response is not a nice-to-have but a have-to-have.
6. Customer service can be a revenue generator (and even an acquisition tool).
7. Customer service lives in the public domain.
8. Customer service is an ongoing commitment, not a one-off happenstance (customer service needs a memory; integration is innovation. Who owns the customer?).
9. Customer service can be proactive and anticipatory.
10. Customer service is alive. Feedback loops need to be active, direct, and effective at improving and evolving the business.

CUSTOMER SERVICE DOESN'T STOP AT 5 P.M. ON A FRIDAY

Isn't it amazing how most problems in your home happen late at night or on the weekends? The toilet overflows, the heating stops working on a grim winter's day, the fridge goes on the fritz, and the cable is scrambled, on the only two days that you don't have work. Is it part of a massive cover-up or an elaborate ruse to get us to pay those premium overtime rates?

Turns out Murphy's Law doesn't discriminate between customers and marketers nowadays . . .

Figure 10.4　Motrin's 30-Second Spot About "Babywearing"

Source: Johnson & Johnson.

In early 2009, Kathy Widmer clocked out on a Friday afternoon after an undoubtedly satisfying week in the office. Kathy was a content marketing executive. She had a brand-spanking-new campaign on television, print, and no doubt radio—the big three, no less. She had gone through all the due diligence, dotted her i's, and crossed her t's. In her particular neck of the woods, no campaign could ever be vetted—or even conceived—without extensive research, all of which was specifically crafted to deliver cutting-edge, proprietary consumer insights, trends and, truths. These would (hopefully) in turn become the backbone of a messaging thrust for Motrin.

In this fortunate case, Kathy was banking on the cool trend of babywearing: the practice of wearing or carrying a baby or child in a sling or other form of carrier (Figure 10.4). And viola! This 30-second baby was born.

The copy for your reading pleasure:

Wearing your baby seems to be in fashion.

I mean, in theory it's a great idea.

There's the front baby carrier, sling, schwing, wrap, pouch.

And who knows what else they've come up with. Wear your baby on your side, your front, go hands free.

Supposedly, it's a real bonding experience.

They say that babies carried close to the body tend to cry less than others.

But what about me? Do moms that wear their babies cry more than those who don't?

I sure do!

These things put a ton of strain on your back, your neck, your shoulders. Did I mention your back?!

I mean, I'll put up with the pain because it's a good kind of pain; it's for my kid.

Plus, it totally makes me look like an official mom.

And so if I look tired and crazy, people will understand why.

And with that, the Twitterverse and blogosphere erupted into spontaneous combustion, ignited by very vocal and pointed criticism from the all-knowing and all-powerful Mommy Blogger community—a group that has become a force to be reckoned with. The result was a proverbial firestorm of negative commentary and very heated conversation, all aimed at Motrin and its parent, Johnson & Johnson.

Did I mention that this all happened over the weekend and, as a result, went almost completely unattended and essentially ignored? Can you imagine if the Fire Department responded to a brush fire with *"Terribly sorry, but we don't work weekends!"*

In this particular case, the lack of feedback and/or responsiveness had a disproportionately negative impact on the brand. As the mob reached a fever pitch, Motrin reacted by pulling their advertising and in doing so, yielded to the angry gaggle of Mommy Bloggers. I personally disagree with the decision to capitulate to the few over the many—unless, of course, this reaction was truly representative of the total populous. Regardless, the brand's commitment to its influencer (and no doubt, part enthusiast) base was nevertheless commendable.

Kathy Widmer no doubt took solace in and benefited from her own product to help her through this fiasco. Here was her response to me on Jaffe Juice:

Yours is among the most thoughtful assessments I've read on our Motrin situation—and I've read plenty. This mom—as you rightly suggested in your post—was, in fact, in the kitchen last Sunday . . . on my laptop (my husband was cooking—though not barefoot). What I saw on Twitter was both scary and fascinating. I did what came instinctively. Maybe it was right . . . maybe wrong. I suspect this is all about building new instincts. The learning continues. Have a Happy Thanksgiving.

J&J is not alone. I conducted an unscientific exercise at around 1:35 A.M. on a Sunday morning to test the responsiveness of some other well-known companies. First, I timed how long it took to find an actual number to call via the brands' respective web sites, and then I determined how long it took to actually reach a human being (or not, if no one was available). The unscientific results are shown in Figure 10.5

	Round 1	Round 2	Human
Wal-Mart	1:33	No Number	No
Exxon Mobil	1:08	No Number	No
Toyota	:18	Closed	No
ING Direct	:56	Closed - :44	No
General Motors	2:10	Closed	No
General Electric	:39	Closed - :33	No
Ford Motors	:29	Closed	No
AXA	1:41	Closed	No
Citibank	:34	2:50	Yes
Bank of America	:42	Closed	No
AT&T	:35	4:02	Yes
AIG	:27	Closed - :26	No
Samsung Electronics	:39	Closed	No
Hewlett Packard	:34	1:44	Yes
IBM	:25	Closed - :30	Yes

Figure 10.5   Company Response Time Experiment

Source: © Joseph Jaffe.

Implications: Customer service should be operational 24/7/365. Restricting customers' problems, concerns, queries, or questions to office hours is flawed, selfish, and shortsighted—not to mention detrimental to the company and the brand's equity, goodwill, and trust.

Although outsourcing elements of customer service offshore is not always the best solution, it can help to keep the lights on after hours.

(*continued*)

(continued)

The important point here is to make sure customers can reach you when they need to and that you can contact them when you need to—and you do indeed *need to* when they're having a problem, venting frustration, or simply calling out for help.

FROM "EVERYTHING COMMUNICATES" TO "EVERYONE COMMUNICATES." THE PARADOX OF CUSTOMER SERVICE

The world always warms to the unlikely hero, especially if it's someone just like you and me. Reality TV is somewhat based on this premise: ordinary today, extraordinary tomorrow. All it takes is a little magnification or spotlight.

Our customers are now providing that spotlight or platform. And more often than not, it's a hapless and disempowered customer-service rep, cashier, sales clerk, or other junior employee in the trenches who is the cause or catalyst—and subsequent (disa)star of the show!

Every single employee in an organization represents the company as a window into the business, and as far as your customers are concerned, they are the only window they look through. Best to make sure that what lies beyond the window is suitable viewing, don't you think? Customers don't care that you have 10,000 employees in 200 offices out of 80 countries; they just want their problems solved by as few people as possible. They also don't care if the person they're speaking with has an Indian or American accent as long as—you guessed it—the person solves their problems.

When it comes to serving customers, creating a flat organization of democratized access, care, and responsiveness makes a huge difference. As outlined in Chapter 7, Zappos puts an enormous emphasis on its frontline workers. All of its employees—431 total, pre–Amazon.com acquisition—are Twittering without the filter of a public relations department. The notion of opening the door for all employees to speak freely is exactly what "everyone communicates" is all about.

I offer a tip for the other 99 percent of you to help you fulfill this new rule: Whether customer service is decentralized and/or outsourced offshore—or literally fragmented across hundreds or even thousands of stores in one or multiple countries—you must make sure the entire crew of employees, agents, and partners are with you for the ride. In other words, companywide commitment to world-class service must be clearly communicated to everyone who is responsible for its delivery, buy-in must be comprehensive and universal, and finally, performance incentives should be inextricably and directly tied to the achievement of world-class service.

Companies that are "with the program" usually telegraph this commitment a mile away. Employees at Internet domain registration provider GoDaddy answer the phone saying something to effect of "How can we help you today *with our world-class service?*" Talk about setting themselves up to fail . . . or in fact, succeed, which (the latter) is typically what they do. Imagine that, a technology company that actually *invests* in human beings to solve the problems of other human beings. It's a beautiful thing!

The corollary of this rule is that customer service is the responsibility of everyone in the company, from CEO to secretary. Ironically (yet not surprisingly) enough, the people that suck the most at service are the ones at the top of the corporate pyramid. They're the most aloof and detached of the bunch, and they struggle to break out of all the bureaucracy and red tape to reveal their human side. It always amazes me how poorly the C-suite performs at any customer-facing activity. Case in point: Domino's deer-in-headlights President of the Americas Patrick Doyle. Your average minimum-wage cashier, on the other hand, has no choice but just to be herself. It's completely up to her to utilize whatever skill sets and/or empowered faith you place in her to leave your brand's permanent imprint on your customers' soul in the brief 4 minutes and 12 seconds that it takes to check them out.

Implications: Customers form their impressions of the brand based on the sum total of experiences, transactions, and interactions with the people behind the brand. Every single contact point is a moment of truth that has the potential to end a relationship for life and even adversely affect the brand. But the flip side equally applies, so when the going gets tough, don't take it personally, and train your customer-service people not to take it personally. Sometimes you gotta suck it up, take it in the gut, and deal with an unhappy customer who needs to vent. A bit of profanity is okay if it's part of a cathartic healing process. Customer-service is all about empathy, and it takes a degree of thick-skinned resilience to prevail.

(continued)

(continued)

   Ironically, the people to whom these angry customers are exposed most often are usually those whom we pay the least (both in terms of compensation and attention). Under these conditions, it takes major cultural mojo to inspire and/or motivate them to deliver brand magic at every twist or turn. The trick is to empower your employees to deliver world-class customer service, no matter where they stack up in the "who's who in your zoo" pecking order.

   Up top of the totem pole, revisit the old MBWA (Management by Walk About) dictum and get back in the trenches, whether that means sitting in on customer-service calls or—better yet—taking them yourself. If you have a retail outlet, get in the aisles and make a difference. Besides keeping you fresh and close to the business, you'll gain firsthand insights that no research or focus group could ever reveal.

ALL CUSTOMERS ARE EQUAL, BUT SOME ARE MORE EQUAL THAN OTHERS

Every single customer deserves to be treated well, respected, and given the appropriate attention and effort. In other words, the minimum level of your bar needs to be higher than the minimum level of your competitors' expectation bars, as well as higher than your industry and competitor averages. That said, different tiers of customers deserve different levels of treatment. Conventional marketing theory holds that more loyal and valuable customers should be treated with elevated levels of service. That absolutely still holds; however, I'd like to inject a new variable into this mix: influence.

We've all witnessed that awkward moment or major meltdown where a celebrity shouts at the top of their lungs to some poor schmuck working as a valet to make a few extra bucks, "Do you *know* who I am?" This is obviously meant to instill fear in said schmuck, to essentially accommodate the self-entitled prima donna.

Well, guess what? Yesterday's celebrity is today's Web-celebrity. With sites like FlyerTalk or blogs such as "The Consumerist" waiting to pounce on big dumb companies' missteps—not to mention the ability to amplify a conversation, interaction, or heated debate—it becomes critical to *do your homework* when engaging in conversation with your customers. And more often than not, they'll gladly volunteer this information to you on a silver platter. I know I do. In fact, I politely explain that I am a fairly well-known (at least in my immediate family circle) blogger who happens to take a particular interest in all things service-related. I continue by stressing that this disclosure is not a threat, per se (even though it probably is), just additional information served up as a courtesy that might provide them with a little more context and clarity regarding the scope of the encounter. Granted, most don't know what the hell I'm talking about. What kind of Juice is Jaffe and what exactly is a pawdcawst?[2] But accent aside, there is still a major disconnect today in linking customer service with word of mouth.

The reality is that most agents just don't care about these kinds of blogger disclosures and either don't know and/or haven't been trained on how to deal with this growing "concern." I've yet to encounter the person at the other end of the e-mail or line who gushes, "OMG, you're *THE* Joseph Jaffe???!!!"

Here's a personal example of one company that perhaps should have reacted this way. I call it *"Delta Skelter,"* and what follows is an excerpt from my blog on June 4, 2008 (the full version in all its unedited glory is available on www.flipthefunnelnow.com under "enhanced content"), after Delta unceremoniously bumped me from a paid business-class seat to a coach seat on a more than nine-hour flight to São Paulo, Brazil.

I'm writing this post from a cramped 16E on Delta's 10 hour Flight 21 from JFK to Sao Paulo. The tray table is so small it doesn't even support my laptop, so I'm literally using my PC as its name suggests: on top of my lap.

I guess I'll write for as long as I can until the battery runs out (because there is no power in these seats either).

To my left and right are scenes from a horror movie—people curled in embryonic positions; . . . sleeping on the floor; others doing things with their bodies I didn't think were even possible.

I want to just state here and now before moving on to the real essence of this post that I think coach class is borderline unacceptable. Airlines need to seriously think about taking out rows of seats and give their customers something that doesn't threaten to break human rights violations. I completely understand the trade-offs that might come with a vacation (especially during these trying times)—price is a major consideration and I guess, with discounted prices comes an inevitable trade-off.

---

[2] My South African accent's butchery of the word, "podcast."

Business travel is different. And it is what happened to me on Delta that has prompted me to take a stand and dig in my heels to let this airline know that I WILL NOT GO AWAY QUIETLY. Not this time.

I didn't want to be the "Jeff Jarvis," the "Doubletree Hotel" duo i.e. coming good on the "I have an influential blog" veiled threat, but here's the thing:

1. I am a *Platinum* Skymiles customer. Platinum is Delta's *highest* frequent traveler tier.
2. I booked (paid for) a Business class seat (in the region of $5,000 USD).
3. I have an American Express Delta Skymiles affinity credit card.
4. I am a customer.

You would think that any one of these criteria would give Delta cause to treat me special, look after me, and help solve my problem. Delta barely met the minimum; in fact, they failed miserably treating me as a customer, let alone of their most frequent (and loyal?) ones.

In a twist on a normal customer-service dispute, I decided to experiment by taking the initiative to actually tell (via the blog post) Delta what I wanted from them in return. I did this because I had little faith they'd react, respond and resolve my problem, and as it turns out, that lack of faith was completely justified.

Here's what happened after I posted this blog:

- Within 24 hours, I received a voice mail from Delta's customer-service department. I was not shocked as it seemed pretty obvious and inevitable that *someone* (who read my blog) would know *someone* who knew *someone* in corporate customer service.
- That's probably the high point of the brand's response, as it all went downhill from there.
- When I called back, the person in question had left for the day. It happened to be on a Friday, and so the entire weekend went by without a resolution.
- When I did speak with customer service, the best offer I received was a $300 voucher and two upgrade certificates *on upgradable fares* (i.e., not cheap). Typically, a passenger who volunteers to get bumped from a flight in coach would receive the same offer. Hell, they might even get an upgrade on their next flight.
- I indicated that I would think about it, but most likely would respectfully decline this offer, and that was pretty much the end. I never heard from Delta again. They never called. They never

wrote. They never commented. You could almost sense the exact moment I became *persona non grata* to them; I simply wasn't worth pursuing anymore.

After that, there was no follow-up or follow-through, no commitment to resolving the problem, no haggling, no negotiation. *Nothing*.

To be honest, I'm not sure I ever expected Delta to yield to my demands, namely give me two first-class round-trip tickets anywhere in the world. I would gladly have accepted *one*, or even a lifetime Platinum Medallion status (okay, 10 years) (okay, 5 years) (okay, 3 years—but that's my final offer). Or perhaps a page in their in-flight magazine to promote one of my *other* books (as opposed to this one that documents their horrible customer service).

Instead, they stood their ground, and for what it's worth, I stood mine as well:

- In the 12 months since Delta Skelter, I've flown just over 10,000 miles in total on Delta. In 100 percent of these cases, the decision was because Delta was the only airline that met a specific schedule requirement or restriction and/or flew direct.
- As a yardstick, I've flown well over 200,000 miles on other airlines.
- My Platinum Medallion status has lapsed. I'm now Gold Medallion, and soon I'll be whatever comes underneath that.
- I've closed down and cut up my Delta "affinity" credit card.
- To this day, people from around the world approach or e-mail me with their Delta horror stories.

And none of this stopped Delta from sending me a supposedly exclusive invitation to their Reserve credit card (Figure 10.6), because I'm one of their "very best customers." I. Think. Not.

Delta may have forgotten me, but I haven't forgotten them.

And apparently, neither has Google (Figure 10.7).

Implications: Playing the ignorance card is no excuse for not doing your homework on your customers. Train your customer-service people to anticipate and respond to customers who have a word-of-mouth distribution platform such as a web site, blog, podcast, or in an analogue world, community pulpit. If necessary, be a little more proactive with collecting information from customers, either through registration forms, profiles, or

(continued)

Figure 10.6   Delta Reserve Credit Card "Invitation"

(continued)
surveys. Ask them explicitly: Do you have a blog? If they do, document the URL and research the blog. From this, you'll gauge direction, theme, and more important, tonality (the snark factor). Using this lens, you'll be able to more effectively service three types of customers: loyal, valuable, and loud.

This isn't rocket science. The simplest of Google searches can be conducted while talking to customers. In addition, most companies have expensive and sophisticated CRM systems and databases. Make sure your customer-service agents have full access to the full wealth of data available.

Do your research, be proactive, and for heaven's sake, when loud-mouthed influencers volunteer their social calling cards, take them seriously!

CUSTOMER SERVICE IS NOT ONLY ABOUT SOLVING PROBLEMS

The other day I called Starwood Hotels's customer loyalty program, Starwood Preferred Guest (SPG), with a routine query: I wanted to add my SPG number to two upcoming hotel reservations. As a keynote

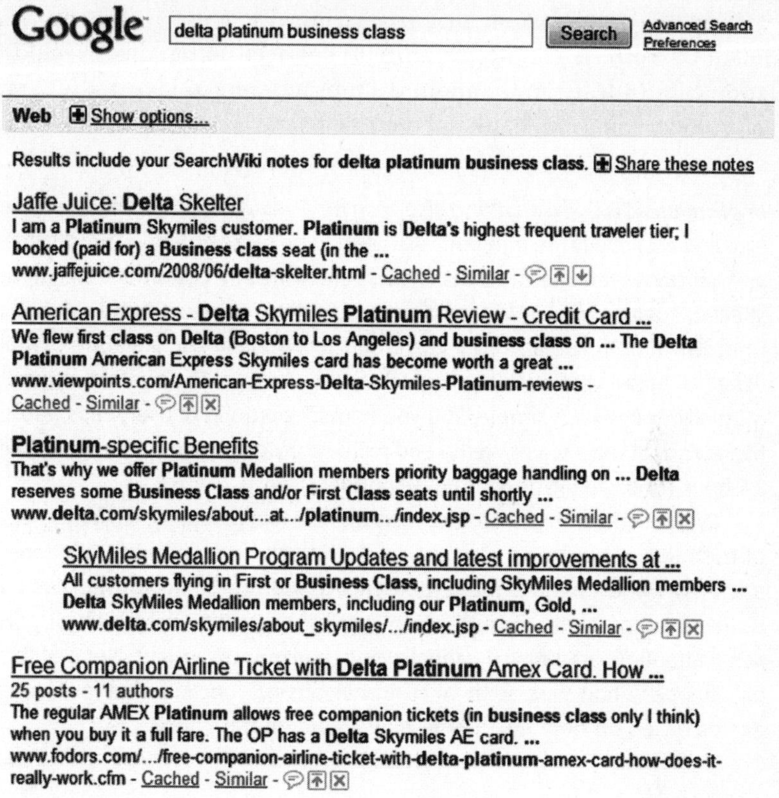

Figure 10.7   Google Search Results for Delta Business Class Platinum

public speaker who constantly travels around our wonderful planet, it is wonderful to be able to add up all those hotel, car rental, and airline miles and use them for future family vacations. The Starwood person I spoke to not only took care of my request, but—completely un-prompted—proceeded to look into getting me *better rates* on my reservations.

I was blown away. Was this an example of a rogue employee, a company with a sick masochistic tendency that got off by lowering profits or, in fact, a rare selfless organization? The answer is most likely none of the above or possibly some triangulated point in the middle. Either way, here was a gesture that's being acknowledged and recognized in this book and rewarded with future business from me and now, quite possibly, you. See, customers aren't always flipping the bird right back at companies. Sometimes they'll flip the funnel and return the love.

Every single time you make contact with your customers, it's a moment of truth. It's an opportunity to connect, to build or rebuild the relationship, to learn more about each other, and to invest a few more loyalty dollars in your bank account or trust.

Implications: "*Is there anything else I can help you with today?*" has become rote and essentially meaningless. We need to be more proactive, productive, and efficient with the precious time spent with our customers. Be more specific, suggest ideas, offer information of value, or recommend solutions from which both you and your customers will benefit. Use any form of real estate to upsell your customer on value, not revenue. The two are also not mutually exclusive. A simple "did you know?" portfolio of useful tips, tools, tricks, and tutorials is a powerful and painless accompaniment to your usual 24-hour (or hopefully less) auto-responder.

Every single time a customer talks directly to a company, it's a moment of truth that is becoming increasingly fleeting and rare in today's cluttered and busy world. So make these moments count! Times of confusion can be turned into moments of truth—even magical moments—with a bit of personal attention, empathy, personalization, and empowerment. None of this will happen, however, with a customer-service function that penalizes agents based on how much time they spend on the phone.

CUSTOMER SERVICE LIVES IN THE NOW

I'm not sure how else or more conclusively I can stress this next point, except possibly TO WRITE IN CAPS, but here's the thing: **You simply MUST figure out how to compress and reduce the time that elapses between identifying, communicating, and solving a problem.**

We can thank Bill Gates and his cohorts for turning our computers into perfect pieces of spying equipment. I'm actually not being sarcastic—well, perhaps a little. Your PC's registry is analogous to a restaurant kitchen, in that if you knew what went on there, you'd probably never eat in a restaurant again. it is literally *at this moment* sending information back to the geeks in Redmond—supposedly about your computer's performance, conflicts with software, identification of bugs, and other logistics. It's all in the name of continuous improvement, which is allegedly going to make everything better in the process. I guess it will translate into a 0.111 percent reduction in blue screens of death or a 0.3131 percent decrease in the number of malicious worms wreaking havoc with my address book and sending reams of porn to my network of contacts (you're welcome). Ultimately, however, we know this is a vital piece of Microsoft's valiant attempts to prevent Google from taking over the world. In reality, it's a free-for-all. Google's taking the same information from you via their various plug-ins, downloads, deskbars, widgets, and accounts. Apple's not far behind with its army of i-software, and HP reels in its rod of continuous data from the safety and comfort of your printer.

But how exactly is any of this helping ME? How do I benefit? What happens if all of us simultaneously switch off the one-way data flow back to the various mother ships?

This equation is missing better communication—and service—in return. This process represents an entire flipped funnel that puts the customer—as opposed to the corporation—first. **Acknowledging** the receipt of information is the first step. Updating (**dialogue**) customers on what became of that information—what it was used for and how it helped—is the second step. Offering some kind of benefit (**incentivization**) in return is the third. And over time, the ability to be part of an exclusive community (**activation**) of alpha and beta testers or prosumers comes with a long list of tangible and intangible (status) benefits.

Not for one second do I buy any argument that this level of participation is part of the rules of engagement; nor will I swallow the satisfaction of working with a more stable operating system or software package. I bought an operating system and I expect it to be stable. Period. Not more stable. But stable. And if you can't guarantee that, give me my money back . . . or at least part thereof. I don't want to play my part in the bigger picture—especially to a for-profit corporation, which should be on top of its game at all times by providing me with flawless products, service, and experiences. I'm a customer, dammit! I expect that what I've already paid covers the costs of past, present, and future R&D.

Contrast this with Dell's massive upgrade in customer service and experience commitment over the past years to include service elements like a Dell technician, with permission, taking over your PC to immediately zone in on the problem and attempt to find a solution there and then.

The ability to solve problems in real time is the consummate difference maker. The more time that elapses between problem and solution, the greater the risk of that problem ballooning out of control. Going back to the PC example, various gates or trigger points alert the parent company immediately when a problem arises. Shouldn't it come, then, with an accompanying solution other than a "thanks for sharing . . . sorry about all the lost data, bucko"?

The good news is that this is exactly where everything is going, largely thanks to technology. If you have OnStar[3] in your car, you practically have a call center at your beck and call, only a proactive and actionable one. For example, if you're in an accident and your air bags deploy, OnStar is immediately alerted and initiates a call to the driver to check that they're okay and prepares to outreach to the local authorities—police, ambulance, fire department—if needed, to deploy accordingly.

The Home of the Future will have similar checkpoints in place, largely due to radio-frequency identification (RFID) and Internet connectivity. When your water filter is low on your refrigerator, General Electric will either send you a new one automatically (assuming you chose this option) or send you a notification for express permission or approval.

These examples represent situations where the identification, communication, and solution of the problems at hand are almost instantaneous. How about your business? Are you following suit or languishing hopelessly behind?

In these examples, automation is a boon. However, for the most part, it's a challenge or even a curse for companies attempting to increase short-term efficiencies and pressured to deliver short-term results, while simultaneously trying to balance longer-term imperatives such as servicing customers. Having the foresight to invest long term in systems designed to accelerate the ability to solve problems is the ultimate challenge, but the problem is still that companies look at automation as a denominator cost-saving function.

What's worse is that most don't even know it. Playing dumb is one thing. *Being* dumb is another. It's critical for companies today to fight the urge to dehumanize their businesses. Depersonalizing a company can instantly transform a brand into a commodity.

---

[3] An in-vehicle diagnostics, navigation, and security system available to General Motors cars in the United States and Canada via subscription.

Web forms and e-mail are definitely the worst culprits in this egregious behavior. Calling them impersonal is the understatement of the century. Depth of understanding and empathy are pretty much nonexistent. Directing people to FAQs might as well be the same as a giant FU! And then there's the standard default response time of 24 hours. Let me be clear: A 24-hour turnaround is *unacceptable*. I don't care if it's a hedge or safeguard to ensure you don't break a promise. The promise itself was deficient to begin with, and the attempts are nothing more than a weak CYA (Google it). When your customers see this, they're not secretly hoping you surprise them with a response in half the time. They're resigning themselves to wait the full day to be accommodated, and that's the best-case scenario. Here are four other things that actually make the situation worse:

1. You take longer than 24 hours to respond. Promise broken.
2. When you do respond, you don't actually solve their problem. Instead, you offer them a one-size-fits-all template answer or ask them another clarifying question. E-mail is by far the biggest culprit in this category. "I'm sorry . . . are you on Mac or PC?" which leads to the third and fourth problems.
3. Hitting the reply button doesn't work half the time; in fact, customers are expressly instructed not to reply directly. In the other cases, the actual rep, John L. or Cathy S., cannot be contacted directly anyway, and so the response goes back into a (cess)pool, which is like *Groundhog Day* for morons.
4. Assuming you get this far, after you respond back to the customer-service person's clarifying question—you guessed it—another auto-responder and another 24-hour (or more) hellish wait.
    Perhaps you have experienced this vicious cycle yourselves. Or perhaps you're doing this to your customers.

United Breaks Hearts (and Guitars)

Delaying the solving of a problem merely delays the inevitable outcome, and it's increasingly becoming tantamount to viral Armageddon.

A band called Sons of Maxwell was flying from Halifax, Nova Scotia, to Omaha, Nebraska, for a tour performance with a layover in Chicago. As they were preparing to deplane, a woman behind them said: *"They're throwing guitars out there."* The instruments being thrown about by the baggage handlers indeed belonged to the band. However, when band member Dave Carroll pointed this out to a flight attendant on the plane, he was cut off with: "Don't talk to me. Talk to the lead agent outside." When he talked to an employee at the gate about how the instruments were being mishandled, he was told: "But hon, that's why we make you sign the waiver."

They landed in Omaha at 12:30 A.M., and there were no employees around. Carroll found out during the band's sound check later that day that his $3,500 710 Taylor was smashed at the base. After six months of literally being *bandied* about like a pinball from Halifax to Omaha to Chicago to India (via the call center) to New York and from United to Air Canada (United's Canadian partner), Carroll repaired the guitar himself for $1,200.

In good faith, Carroll continued to press for resolution, but after yet another two months, one Ms. Irlweg in Chicago finally denied the claim on the following grounds:

- He didn't report it to the United employees (who weren't present when he landed in Omaha).
- He didn't report it to the Omaha airport within 24 hours (despite the fact that he was driving to places that weren't Omaha).
- Someone from United would need to see the damage to a guitar that was (already, after 6 months) repaired.

Realizing that he was fighting a losing battle, Carroll decided to channel his energy toward what he does best: writing music. He wrote three songs about his experience with United, produced music videos of the songs, and uploaded them to YouTube and related sites. His original goal was to reach 1 million views (think big!) by the end of the year. The first video, uploaded to YouTube on July 6, did that before the end of the week and three weeks later had already registered 3,250,996[4] views. As of November 2009, it had racked up 6 million views . . . and counting.

To view the video, just search for "United breaks guitars" on YouTube or follow the links on www.flipthefunnelnow.com under "enhanced content." You'll also get to listen to my conversation with Dave.

---

[4] As of July 17, 2009 www.youtube.com/watch?v=5YGc4zOqozo.

This story shows just how important it is for companies to develop a streamlined and easy-to-use customer complaint or claims process. The system, as Carroll calls it, as well as many others, always seems to be built to discourage people from challenging it because it is so burdensome, complicated, and deflating to work with.

Furthermore, it shows how, sometimes, too late is too late. United eventually offered Carroll $1,200 cash and $1,200 worth of travel vouchers. Carroll rejected this offer and told United to put the money toward a charity of their choosing. They choose the Thelonius Monk Jazz Institute.

But the damage was done. Carroll has since appeared on the early show on CBS, NBC, BBC, Sky, *Rolling Stone* magazine, *USA Today*, *Newsweek*, the *Wall Street Journal, Consumerist*, "Boing Boing," every major Canadian television, radio, and print outlet—and the list continues.

Even worse was the ambitious and highly speculative observation via Chris Ayres from Times' Online[5] that within the first three weeks of the song's release, United's stock price had dropped 10 percent, the equivalent of $180 million in market capitalization. For what it's worth, 0.001 percent of this amount equates to $1,800, which is roughly the same as the damages associated with Carroll's broken guitar.

> *Implications:* Undertake an internal exercise and audit where you gauge your specific turnaround times for problem ID, communication, and effective closure. Set benchmarks and desired performance goals against which to measure and deliver. And of course, work toward reducing the lag or lapsed time between problem and solution. Begin to investigate how technology can help speed you up through various automatic alerts, reminders, and triggers. This kind of innovation will dramatically boost customer experience scores.

CUSTOMER SERVICE CAN BE A REVENUE GENERATOR

Building on several of the earlier new rules is one fairly counterintuitive one: Service can actually become a source of revenue for companies—not just directly (i.e., new business from old customers) but also indirectly (i.e., new business from *new* customers).

I've mentioned Apple's introduction of Genius Bars in their stores several times already in this book, but now I'll expand on this genius

[5] http://www.timesonline.co.uk/tol/comment/columnists/chris_ayres/article6722407.ece

measure. In an otherwise unexpected move—namely, investing in humans over and above technology—Apple they delivered on the in-the-now rule. In doing so, they earned the opportunity to charge a premium for personalized and personal expert service.

The Genius Bar isn't small print, nor is it a term or condition buried in a massive contract or operating manual. On the contrary, it becomes a primary selling point of the overall Apple value proposition, retail, and ultimately customer experience. This flies in the face of the current status quo, with all its bogus warrantees, guarantees, and on-site service solutions that come from the PC manufacturers and electronic retailers that we've been trained to instantly waive off.

In addition, the word of mouth is off the charts. Speaking as one constantly faltering PC user looking for an excuse to make the switch, I am tempted because of the Genius Bar, and if only I had an Apple store a little closer to me, I might be their best (or worst—I'm needy) customer.

To be clear, it is free to visit the Genius Bar, but to secure additional hours, there are premium fees. It also can be argued that the cost of this service is built into the purchase price of the hardware itself. I don't see anyone complaining. Either way, it's one very real reason why people choose Mac over PC.

PREMIUM SERVICE IS NOT ALWAYS INCREMENTAL

Another example is Netflix, which has essentially built an entire business (model) on service. No more trips to the store (sorry, Block-buster). No more limits on how long you can keep DVDs. No more late fees. Return packaging and postage are included in the price. I pay $16.99 per month (including the Blu-Ray premium) for two concurrent rentals. I don't think it's an obscene amount of money by any stretch, especially when I compare it with the $100+ I typically pay for a crappy Saturday night movie after babysitting, stale popcorn, and tickets have been factored into account. It's a win-win, as Netflix secures recurring revenue and a pretty impressive barrier to entry in the process.

Implications: Customers will pay a premium for higher perceived value. Charging a premium for enhanced services that offer tangible and substantial value is not necessarily going to be frowned on. It might even be

> embraced. If there's one thing that's in really short supply today, it's time, and when we can save our customers time, who knows—maybe there's some money in it for us. At times, you might want to bundle in a premium service to your most valuable customers as a perk, whereas at other times, your power users may very well want to ante up for key services.

CUSTOMER SERVICE LIVES IN THE PUBLIC DOMAIN

"This call may be monitored to help improve customer service." I'm not exactly sure what that means, but I can tell you that as far as I'm concerned, it's like waving a red flag in front of a bull. For starters, why *may* and not *will?* Why take a chance on service and inject randomness or serendipity into the picture? I get why I'm being informed of this (corporations aren't exactly sponsors of the Patriot Act) for litigious reasons; or perhaps it's more for the customer-service representative than for my benefit, meant to deter them from (further) disappointing me.

Either way, I have a standard comeback now for these occasions. I inform the customer-service agent that *I, too, "may" choose to record the conversation for my own purposes.* This is often where they flip out and tell me it's not possible, they don't feel comfortable, or it's not allowed. Sometimes they'll even put down the phone. Guilty consciences, indeed.

Whether you like it or not, bad service will find its way to the public domain. So why delay the inevitable? Or why avoid it?

Bottom line: Mess with your customer, and they'll let everyone they possibly can know about it. Or as author Pete Blackshaw puts it in his book, *Satisfied Customers Tell Three Friends, Angry Customers Tell 3,000.*

> You can hear my podcast conversation with Pete on www.flipthefunnelnow. com. Just click on "enhanced content."

I don't know about you, but being exposed in the public domain is pretty much the biggest deterrent I can imagine. It certainly makes the random monitoring of a call seem understated and almost insignificant in contrast. These kinds of isolated incidents tend to be microcosms that hold the entire company and all of its associates responsible.

Implications: Allow your customers to record your phone calls; even encourage it. Honestly, they're going to do it with or without your permission. Responding to consumers publically via blogs, podcasts, social networks, and twitter-like platforms is admirable but a learned art. You'll need to be adept at knowing when to open up a conversation, pull it in, and/or close it down. When a conversation escapes into the ether of public domain, don't fight it; rather, address it head-on—quickly, decisively, comprehensively, authentically.

CUSTOMER SERVICE NEEDS A MEMORY; IT IS A COMMITMENT, NOT A ONE-OFF HAPPENSTANCE

This rule draws on the need for integration and interdepartmental cooperation and collaboration. If "marketing is not a campaign; it's a commitment", then there's no more important commitment than that which we make to our lifeblood—our customers.

It's all well and good to talk about this, but the proof of the pudding is in the eating. We need to visibly demonstrate our commitment to our customers in practice and in action. They need to explicitly feel its effect and benefits.

One of the best ways to activate a long-term promise is to move from a goldfish approach to the elephant ninja stance. Earlier, I made the point that our customers have long memories. **Now we need to show them that we do, too.**

How many times have you made that fateful call to a service center where you're asked to say or key in your 16-digit account number, only to have the agent on the line immediately ask you for your account number? In my case and with my accent, I typically have to repeat it several times! Once you've managed to clearly convey this all-important number, the agent will typically proceed to ask you a series of probing questions for even more information, including date of birth, Social Security number, mother's maiden name, and where your first pet was buried. Only then do you get a chance to share your problem, upon which the agent tells you that you've reached the wrong department and he needs to transfer you, after which the call gets disconnected. #FAIL.

The game of pass-the-buck continues as you're thrust from one person to another, who clearly has no clue who you are and, in order to get up to speed, proceeds to ask you the same series of insane questions. This behavior is unproductive, frustrating, and extremely detrimental to the customer experience.

I would challenge all of us to ultimately transform the very manner in which calls are qualified and routed. I don't think we should ask our customers a thing, except perhaps their name, so that we can address them properly. I would let *them* ask the first questions or make the opening statement, get whatever they need off their chests, and only *then* ascertain whether they're in the right place. Contrast this with the status quo of forcing the issue before we have any clue what's eating Gilbert Grape.

We have to get smarter each time we deal with the SAME PERSON—specifically in terms of how we treat them AND in general as a company so we can learn, evolve, and improve on the whole. The simple ability to take notes and share them can help move this forward tremendously.

INTEGRATION IS INNOVATION

We live in a multichannel, multiplatform world. Our customers purchase from us in a variety of ways: in-store, online, via phone, catalog, iTunes, iPhone apps, and via third-party platforms like Amazon's Kindle or Nintendo's Wii. By the same rationale, customer service needs to mirror or reflect the same spirit and diverse approach.

If this book had been written 10 or more years ago, I would be focusing on telling you to integrate your customer-service channels, specifically your call center. I'd be talking to you about inter-departmental cooperation and advising you to ensure that every call from every single customer was connected. If this book had been written five or so years ago, I'd expand this thought to include a variety of new, digital channels including, but not limited to, e-mail and web site queries.

However, this book is being written (or read) now, which is why I need to extend your scope to a third world, namely, the virtual world (but not the one you think). (See Figure 10.8.)

My definition of the virtual world includes the obvious virtual reality, the maligned Second Life, MMORPG experiences like World

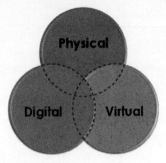

Figure 10.8   Three Dimensions of Service
Source: ©Joseph Jaffe.

of Warcraft, and more kid-friendly environments like Club Penguin or
Webkinz. But I would argue that it also includes blogs, podcasts, presence applications like Twitter, wikis, and social networks. In fact, my
definition of a virtual world is *any environment that utilizes avatar- and/or
profile-based participation with the option or possibility of anonymity.* In short,
it's a place or space where people can interact with one another in
ways they could never do in the real or digital worlds, a level playing
field where everyone is equal until they prove otherwise.

Our challenge is two-pronged: we need to deploy a deep and
meaningful capability across this third dimension (in addition to the
other two, of course) and also connect the dots *between* the respective
worlds, channels, or environments: physical + digital, digital + virtual,
physical + virtual, and physical + digital + virtual.

In my conversations with many of the world's largest companies,
I've scored companies' level of understanding, competence, investment,
and performance in the worlds as shown in Figure 10.9. I'm probably
being a little lenient, so why don't you tell me how you would score?
Send me a tweet to @flipthefunnel.

Implications: Numerous. Practical. Tactical.

- Take notes and document every single call and conversation.
- Integrate systems to make sure all conversations are documented
  accordingly.

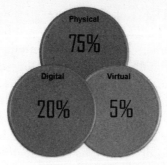

Figure 10.9   How Would You Score?

Source: ©Joseph Jaffe.

- Think personal journals or lifestreaming (the technical term for aggregating disparate pieces of multimedia content in chronological order to tell a story) meets customer service.
- Immediately ask for call-back numbers, e-mail addresses, and/or preferred means of contact and communication.
- Use case numbers to keep track of customers.
- If your customer-service agents are prevented from dialing out, change that. *Now!*
- Connect with customers by referencing previous conversations as a means of demonstrating you're paying attention, as well as following up on a progress or status report.
- Inform customers of any internal action that was taken from previous encounters especially if it has been incorporated into future business processes.
- In these cases, think about rewarding the customer for their contribution (see incentivization).
- Don't measure calls based on length of time but rather on quality of dialogue.

CUSTOMER SERVICE NEEDS TO BE PROACTIVE AND ANTICIPATORY

Customer service can be proactive, that is, originate from the company.

Yes, I'm sure you believe you're already doing this, in which case, good for you. However, I'm talking about something much more strategic, genuine, and far reaching. Too many companies operate on the level of don't ask, don't tell and assume that just because the phone isn't ringing, their customers are satisfied and content. Not surprisingly, the same companies are equally shocked when they open up the customer cupboard to find it bare. Instead, why not make a concerted effort to earnestly probe customers to find out how you rate and stack up against their high standards—and hopefully yours as well.

Old customer service spoke when it was spoken to. New customer service anticipates requirements, listens attentively for customers in need, and proactively searches for problems to fix. Part of this process is an engaged listening strategy designed to identify opportunities, spot problems before they balloon, and surprise (and hopefully delight) consumers by making an unexpected move in the form of responding to them.

In a perfect world, when a customer complains about a company to 1,000,000 of their closest strangers (i.e., they blog), before they know it, someone from the company is already reaching out to them to try to solve their problem. In fact, the sooner there is first contact, the quicker the problem can be addressed before it festers or erupts.

A vocal customer is our best friend (albeit in disguise). The real enemy here is silence; our failure to respond or inability to address a murmur before it becomes a shout—at which point we become defenseless to defection, misinformation, rumor, and lost patronage.

The notion of "silence" is not necessarily a new thought. It is well documented that vocal customers are in the minority, and silent ones in the majority. This changes, however, in the peer-to-peer word-of-mouth space. Today we can intercept various complaints, cries for help, or suggestions—whether they're one-to-many (a blog post or tweet) or one-to-one (a personal conversation). The virtual world (as I have defined it) is without question the catalyst that has catapulted customer service from the back office to the head of the class. We are slowly but surely waking up from a marketing coma to realize that just because our customers aren't calling on us doesn't mean they're not calling us out! The sounds of (our) silence and inability to join the conversation are terrifyingly deafening.

We don't need to be invited to the table to be useful and valuable in solving problems. Would you turn a blind eye if you came across a small child crying who'd lost a parent in the middle of the road? Of course not! How about this scenario: You work for General Motors and, at a cocktail party, overhear a conversation where a partygoer is expressing concern about buying a new vehicle from GM based on its solvency and life expectancy. Wouldn't you interject, especially if you could allay their fears (before they're convinced to go Japanese)?

Proactive or reactive? Both are fine, as long as you *act*. Whether anticipating next steps or responding to a clear and present complaint, as long as there's action, there's the potential to turn a negative into a positive and even to capitalize on a speculative opportunity.

A Word to the Wise: Don't Forget the Real World

You hear the term "social media" a lot these days. While this is thought to be synonymous with what I call "virtual," it truly is not. I'm not sure it's accurate, realistic, or even smart to restrict connections between consumers and the brands that court them. Peer-to-peer interaction belongs right in the middle of this framework; not only does it merrily exist in all three of the worlds, it acts as the glue that unites them (Figure 10.10).

Even though virtual tends to be the difference maker these days, don't lose sight of the base: the physical world where a frosty cold beer still tastes better in a glass than in an e-coupon or virtual gift via Facebook.

Implications: Solving problems, surprising or delighting your customers, and/ or capitalizing on opportunities to move a customer along the A.D.I.A. spectrum are the reasons you're in business and have a job. By deploying a commitment-to-conversation process—which incorporates both a listening

(*continued*)

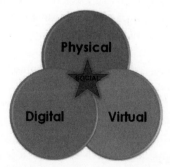

Figure 10.10   Social = Peer-to-Peer

Source: ©Joseph Jaffe.

(*continued*)

and a response strategy—you'll be able to spot problems before they spiral out of control. You'll also gain valuable insight that will help you do business better, cheaper, faster, and smarter. Understand the dynamics of how your customers live, act, and interact within the three worlds; in particular, determine how you can move them from one dimension to another. For example, Blockbuster could offer their customers something Netflix could never: the opportunity to return faulty DVDs to a brick-and-mortar store. Of course, Netflix can counter by making sure their DVDs are never faulty!

CUSTOMER SERVICE IS ALIVE

The final new rule is an obvious one. It essentially highlights or mirrors an organization with an entirely new set of criteria, beliefs, and characteristics that reflect a company truly in touch with its customer base.

If a company can see their customer service as a perfect chance for them to deeply connect with and evolve alongside its lifeblood, it becomes a cultural obsession instead of a mere department. It's a vital point of differentiation that propels innovation and creates new revenue streams, products, and barriers to entry.

The pursuit of cutting-edge lessons, insights, and ideas from the inside out cannot occur accidentally. There has to be a direct pathway back to the nerve center of the organization, and where better to begin than customer service? I cannot tell you how many suggestions I've given to customer-service agents. I have no clue (or faith) as to whether any made it back to the company's decision-making units. Even if they did, they probably fell on deaf ears . . . as opposed to actually incorporated and acted on.

Regardless, it's time to transform customer service from a one-dimensional, one-off, and transactional-based exchange into a fluid and integral part of doing business. Combining all physical or store encounters, live chat, and e-mail exchanges—and most recently, social media or virtual conversations—in an evolved Voice of the Customer program is just the beginning. Incorporating this feedback into the very engine of the company—AND communicating progress back to the point of origin—is equally, if not more, important.

Implications: Ten steps you can take to close the loop and use customer service as a live source of ideas, recommendations and productive feedback:

1. Make sure that all customer conversations can be entered into a report and feedback system, which probably means a literal and figurative systemwide upgrade.
2. Foster a culture that values constant customer response.
3. Incentivize customer-service agents to bring them into the ecosystem.
4. Communicate progress frequently back to *both* agents and customers.
5. When executing customer service in the public domain, for example, via Twitter, use keyword tagging or hashtags to catch significant words and phrases.
6. Just because customers don't volunteer suggestions doesn't mean they don't have them. Explicitly seek suggestions on matters from product development through positioning to service. And when unprompted suggestions are made, close the loop with your customer in terms of follow-up and follow-through.
7. Commit to acting on these ideas. Begin by implementing at least 1 customer-initiated suggestion per month, 12 in the first calendar year, 24 in the next, and so on.
8. Conceive tangible ways to build this service into your value proposition and make your customers (and prospects) aware of it. If necessary, communicate using formalized or paid methods (advertising, collateral) or through informal or nonpaid approaches (word of mouth, seeding).
9. Increase the amount of money in your budget allocated toward human resources and technology. When it comes to customer service, talent is going to prove as important as systems integration, empathy as important as scale, and human labor as important as automation. And as you'll soon read, this was a trap into which Target Corporation fell, hook, line, and sinker.
10. Measurement is fundamental, so constantly track, evaluate, and tweak a work in progress to ensure that you're getting the most out of the pathway to your customers. Reconcile medium- to long-term benefit from the implementation of ideas with the investment that was once incurred to produce them.

11

The New Channels of Customer Service

Much of the material in the previous chapter is built on a shifting landscape of increased choice, fragmented media platforms, consumer empowerment, infusion and adoption of technology, and common-sense evolution. This set of new rules comes with an array of new channels (blogging, twitter, search, live chat, crowdsourcing) through which to deploy customer service 2.0 as a bridge to superior customer experience.

On-demand customer management solutions provider RightNow uses the image in Figure 11.1 to show what the expanded contact management solution set looks like for customer service 2.0.

It's a pretty good summary of how customer service has evolved to become a truly dynamic, organic, and human ecosystem of peer-to-peer conversations (where the word "peer" can mean employee, customer, consumer, or influencer). But if you overlay this (or replace the "social web" node) with the conversation wheel or prism, the number of listening outposts, response mechanisms, or experience platforms *skyrockets*.

And you need to be *there*—and by "there," I mean *everywhere*.

Many of these new channels exist in the virtual world, what you might call social media or Web 2.0. And social media isn't just a "new channel," but arguably the 11 secret herbs and spices that have essentially transformed customer service into an entirely new category altogether.

In this chapter, I'll walk you through some of these "herbs and spices" in more detail, give you examples, and lead up to a revelation that might surprise or even shock you.

How's that for set-up?

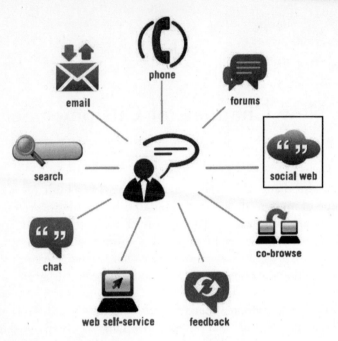

Figure 11.1   Expanded Contact Management Solution Set
Source: RightNow.

BLOGGING

Perhaps you've heard of this new trend called blogging?

It seems like blogs are almost taken for granted nowadays, appearing to be yesterday's news, even subservient to the rise of *microblogging* applications such as Twitter. That's a big mistake, though; blogging's death has been greatly exaggerated. Blogging—underpinned by its skeletal infrastructure, nerve network, and blood flow—is still very much the foundation on which most consumer-generated content lives. It is also still the number one favorite food of the Google spider or the main ingredient in the all-power antioxidant, Google Juice.

In 2008, 4 of the top 10 entertainment sites were blogs. Consumerland's number one blog is called "The Consumerist," and if you work in any kind of senior corporate position and receive a memo on your desk titled "Re: Consumerist.com," you'll probably want to start updating your resume. By virtue of the written word and the ease of publishing, commenting, sharing, and linking, blogging remains the simplest and most powerful way to express oneself or an idea, make a statement, and get noticed. Big time.

> If you want to hear my conversation with Consumerist's co-managing editor, Ben Popken—whom I liked so much I asked him to pen this book's foreword— take a stroll down to www.flipthefunnelnow.com and click on "enhanced content."

Keeping up with what's being said, when, where, and by whom is pretty easy to monitor; as is understanding the critical aspects of these conversations, including the likes of sentiment, influence, and authority. As I often tell marketers, step 1 is for you to set up a simple Google Alert (or the equivalent) to stay close to the marketplace. This is your Sam Walton equivalent of walking up and down the Wal-Mart aisles.

You'll also want to invest in some kind of monitoring tool or software that helps you filter, aggregate, and evaluate accordingly. I've put up a list of companies in the game at www.flipthefunnelnow.com/monitor.

In terms of organizational structure, you'll likely outsource this capability externally or, more likely, attempt to build out this capability with the help of a partner or specialist firm that does this for a living.

And it doesn't end there. A listening strategy without a response mechanism or function is like window-shopping without the ability to go inside the store and wave that credit card around. So unless your thrill comes from leaving your oily forehead print on the windowpanes, you'll probably want to take this a lot further. I like this metaphor as it illustrates the notion of being "shut or locked out" from where the real action is taking place. Until now, we've never really had the ability to be on top of customer sentiment, feedback and conversation about our performance, service, and experience—in real time and with scale, no less.

As I wrote in *Join the Conversation*, you need to familiarize yourself with the one-two punch of response and responsiveness. In other words, respond quickly, decisively, and comprehensively. This is not the time or the place to drop in a clichéd, automated, and/or *templatized* "Thank you for your blog post . . . someone (probably our lawyers) will be responding to you within 24–48 hours" standard response.

In 2009, P.R. firm MS & L conducted a corporate social media survey and found that one-third of companies were not currently incorporating social media tools as part of marketing efforts. However, of the 63 percent that were using social media, a full two-thirds had not made changes to products or marketing based on customer feedback received.

When you do respond, respond smartly, strategically and consistently. Don't fall into the trap where "the worst defense is offense." Your customers' blogs are their personal spaces that you need to respect. Just because there is the ability to leave a comment does not mean yours is welcome. Defensive, aggressive, or stiff responses can actually make the situation worse. Sometimes customers are venting, sharing their frustration, or even inviting others with similar experiences to share their stories or pile on the pain. Just not you.

It's like walking a tightrope, but that doesn't mean it's impossible to get to the other side.

BLOGGING BELONGS TO YOUR CUSTOMERS

In the olden days (meaning 10 years ago), companies and their customers really had no direct link to each other's respective worlds. Contact was sporadic, labored, and typically on an individual basis. Customers literally had to write a letter to a company in an attempt to get their attention, which was never guaranteed. Today, however, it's a completely different ball game. Blogs have given the meek (or is it geek?) the ability to inherit the earth, and the strong the ability to rule it. Not only can customers communicate very clearly with companies, they can connect with each other, often bypassing the middleman (that would be you).

BLOGGING BELONGS TO YOU

The good news is that you're not completely shut out. You *do* have the ability to join your customers' conversations—with consideration and permission, of course. And there's no reason you shouldn't establish a direct dialogue with your customers in return. A 2008 Burson-Marsteller study revealed that only 15 percent of Fortune 500 companies corresponded with their customers via blogs. That's a disgraceful 74 out of 500 that made any kind of attempt to establish an open line of communication with their most prized possessions.

Although this number is somewhat dated and will no doubt continue to rise exponentially, it does give you a pretty revealing snapshot of corporate fears, reluctance, and inability to meet customers halfway or on their own turf.

There's a noticeable imbalance when it comes to using the same tools that have become second nature to our customers; in fact, there are countless *individuals* with more subscribers or communities than billion-dollar global multinationals. Case in point, it's bizarre that I have more people following me on Twitter @jaffejuice (approximately 14,000) than are following Motorola's @MotoMobile (2,892), Super Bowl advertiser, eSurance (684) or Anheuser-Busch's @budweiser's (338), but then again, it also confirms the problems plaguing corporations today:

- Companies' "virtual" presences can be (ironically) highly fragmented. When you take the number of brands under their corporate umbrella and multiply them by the number of geographies, ongoing initiatives or campaigns, as well as the number of departments that lay claim to this precious virtual cargo or "real estate"—it's no wonder there is so little coordination, momentum and integrated, unified and holistic voice.
- Customers, on the other hand, have a very unified view of life, the world, and specifically, your company. They go straight to the source and look for *one* URL, telephone number, mailing address, blog, or Twitter account to make contact.
- *Nobody wants to have a conversation with a shoe.* When I talk about the fact that marketing can be a conversation, I'm not suggesting that consumers want to chat with a pair of Nike or Adidas sneakers. They do, however, want to talk with the human beings who design, manufacture, promote, distribute, service, and support these shoes. They do want to discuss working conditions, environmental commitment, and common passions, beliefs, and ideas.
- *The seeds of conversation are not magic beans.* There's no panacea when it comes to earning trust, rapport, and the right to build community. Companies are still way too focused on short-term quick fixes and instant cure-alls. There are little to none.

The good news is that several companies are getting in on the act with their own customer-service blogs. Some, such as tech or Web '2.0' companies, find it a lot easier (especially with less infrastructure and budget) to keep customers updated via an RSS feed or the like.

Here are 10 reasons why you might want to think about initiating a customer-service blog:

1. A direct and transparent dialogue or link with your customer base keeps them updated and in the know.
2. If nothing else, you're projecting a commitment to service, which—depending on your competitors' levels of activity—helps you stand out from the crowd.
3. It's a necessity if you have frequent service interruptions (such as lightning- or squirrel-induced power outages), constant updates, or a stream of announcements. Domain or hosting providers like GoDaddy or cable providers like Cablevision or Comcast need to provide real-time explanations when there is scheduled maintenance and when the service is down (or back up again).
4. Customers can subscribe to your feed or stream via RSS, which gives you a direct gateway into their daily dose of news, blog updates, and permission-based sources of information, education, and entertainment.
5. Communicating this resource to your customers (via packaging, e-mail, in-store signage, and even advertising) will help sell through this one-stop destination to your base. Once people know there is a single location to visit, you're going to see exponential decreases in frustration and increases in efficiency, satisfaction, and savings.
6. During challenging times (crisis communication), this becomes the go-to source for customers. Conversely, you now have an outlet to get out *your* point of view and side of the story in seconds. Domino's was reluctant to devote any of its Web homepage real estate to its problem. Perhaps they wouldn't have needed to in the first place if there had been an established resource in place at the time. And for now, a Facebook Fan Page is a pretty good placeholder.
7. If there is misinformation or misperception in the marketplace, this will allow you to easily address and discuss inaccuracies.
8. On the flip side, it's a great way to let your customers know about new product introductions or innovations, patches or downloads, tips or tools, announcements, and the like before anyone else.
9. Having a blog means acting like a blog(ger), which means remaining open to comments and customers' debates, disagreements, and even venting. While you'll be able to screen for obscenities and egregious slams, screening cannot be a crutch or safety net. For the most part, you'll need to accept the bad and ugly with the good in order to make it in this space.
10. Your blog is only as good as your last post. If you're going to commit to a customer-service blog, you'll need a dedicated, empowered, and

experienced person or team staffing and running it. Frequent, up-to-date, and timely entries are not a perk; they're a necessity.

Of course, direct rapport between brand and customer base does not have to be solely focused on customer service, although it more often than not will need to address these matters, or at least be prepared to.

Take Chairman and CEO of Marriott International Bill Marriott. It's no coincidence that Marriott has a consistent reputation of delivering an above-par experience to its multitude of customers around the world. In fact, it is ranked ninth on Forrester's 2009 Customer Experience Index. The hotel chain's blog wasn't created for the sole purpose of servicing customers. Rather, it gave Bill Marriott a voice, a chance to show that he's a human just like everybody else. It also doesn't necessarily follow what is considered to be SBOP (Standard Blogging Operating Protocol). Case in point: Marriott doesn't actually type the blog posts; he dictates them into a recorder, and someone transcribes them and posts them online.

The impact, however, has been outstanding.

Marriott has made more than $5 million in bookings from people who clicked through to the reservation page from Bill's blog (as of a *Washington Post* article published August 25, 2008). So while Bill is not dedicating himself to answering customer questions per se, he has had a tremendous effect as a brand ambassador on customer engagement.

TWITTER — FOR THE BIRDS OR TWITS

If you haven't heard about Twitter by now, you probably don't watch enough CNN. Here's your crash course if you're still relatively in the dark (it's okay not to know): Think instant messaging meets social networking. That's about it. Need more? How about the notion of a virtual watercooler and the ability to connect to every single office watercooler in every single country. That's Twitter. Some people call it microblogging (the text-messaging part), as its communiqué is done in 140 characters or less. I refer to this category as the presence space, the ability to be out there, connected, and conversing with friends, fans, followers, and even friendly stalkers in real time.

Time will tell whether Twitter becomes what Xerox, Kleenex, Hoover, and TiVo were to their respective categories. Most likely they'll get bought (if they haven't been already) by one of the Godzillas (used to be Gorillas before Google came along) out there, dismantled, integrated, reengineered, and relaunched. But that's incidental and even irrelevant. What is interesting is how Twitter has incited a tidal wave of innovation, creativity, and business-changing practices—some of them even best.

> By the way, I'm @jaffejuice and @flipthefunnel. The first account (@jaffe-juice) is the one you really want to follow as it's my primary account. The second one (@flipthefunnel) may be used exclusively for book-related promotions, communication, announcements (such as signings, meet-ups, webinars, and some surprises), and the like. I'm on a mission to build more followers than @oprah, so indulge me, won't you?

There have been countless stories concerning Twitter in a variety of categories. For example, charity: water (@charitywater)—a not-for-profit organization dedicated to bringing clean and safe water to developing nations—raised more than $250,000 on Twitter through a worldwide "Twestival" in 202 cities in February 2009. That's 55 water projects in Ethiopia, India, and Uganda or clean water for more than 17,000 people—if you're keeping score.

And from the sublime to the ridiculous, celebrities like Larry King (@kingsthings) or Ashton Kutcher (@aplusk) have kept themselves relevant by actively using Twitter to maintain an ongoing dialogue with their respective fan bases. Some companies have even managed to sell stuff on Twitter, such as Dell (@delloutlet), which as of June 2009 had already netted more than $3 million in sales.

But all of that pales against what I think is one of the most profound uses for Twitter: customer service.

CUSTOMER SERVICE HAS A NAME, AND IT IS FRANK

This is the story of Frank—Frank Eliason, Director of Digital Care at Comcast, to be specific. Frank's job is to serve as brand ambassador in the social media space. However, his journey to this point was seren-dipitous in many ways.

Frank began in his original capacity by simply identifying those seeking help online and, if possible, reaching out to solve their problems. His approach was somewhat different than most: He was both fishing where the fish are—namely, speaking to them using the same channels they were using—and utilizing a decidedly social toolkit, led by Twitter.

People—in particular bloggers and social media natives, but soon enough mainstream media outlets—started noticing what Frank was doing. They began drawing attention to his efforts, which caused the company to suggest Frank do the job full-time.

If success begets success, then proactive and social customer service is both self-fulfilling and addictive. So when TechCrunch's Michael Arrington took notice and reported on Frank's Twitter presence, it inspired or motivated Eliason to begin tweeting regularly. Over time, Frank began to highlight repeated, recurring, and/or relevant customer questions in a regular newsletter and continuously looked to find new ways to serve customers.

Comcast: The Un-Obama

While President Obama's social media success was predicated on the critical foundation of a great product (as validated by both Electoral College and popular vote), Comcast seemed to be coming from the exact opposite end of the spectrum (if not from a product perspective; certainly from a service one)

Both, however, were able to flip the funnel—tapping into passionate customers (lovers and haters for Obama and Comcast, respectively) and acknowledging, dialoguing, incenting, and activating them in a personal, meaningful, and impactful way. Whereas Obama received attention for all the right reasons, Comcast received much attention because of its legacy history of poor customer service. (Remember the poor technician who fell asleep on a customer's couch because he was left on hold on the phone by *his own technical support department?*)

Ultimately, the lesson here is that a negative can be turned into an overwhelming positive. Here are 10 ways to manage it:

1. **Putting the YOU in cUstomer service.**
   Eliason believes that the key to being successful in this space is simply being yourself. Those engaged in customer service have to let their own personalities shine through, and their companies need to empower and allow them to do just that.
2. **Measuring the unmeasurable.**
   Comcast management hasn't been all that concerned with Eliason finding hard metrics to justify his efforts, which frees

him up to focus on key corporate strategic drivers and provide great service within the company's internal and external communities. In doing so, he's dramatically changed public perception of the company. This stance is highly atypical of companies in the space who are either deploying similar programs with superficial follow-through and/or applying unrealistic, short-term expectations on its ability to drive cold, hard "results".

3. **One customer at a time.**

Eliason stresses the need to focus on one customer at a time. While many companies continue to automate, scale, and standardize customer service, the Frank solution is somewhat manual, time-consuming, and extremely labor-intensive. It's about humans helping humans.

4. **Integrate to innovate.**

Frank's ride has been pretty smooth, something he attributes to a close working relationship with his internal communications and public-relations teams, especially as it relates to various outreach efforts and relations (blogger, media, corporate, etc.).

5. **Always be learning.**

Stressing the *D* of Dialogue, together with new rules about customer service not being necessarily about solving problems, Frank has been listening and learning. He has become a valuable part of his customers' daily conversations and lives. Part of this process has been receiving predominantly constructive criticism on how to conduct himself in the social space, or *Internettiquette* (as Air Tran would call it). Frank's advice to newcomers is to not take anything personally and, of course, to listen. He recalls an instance where he was criticized for being too buttoned up when he used the word "perception." Put differently: *Corporatese* unwelcome. *Humanese* welcome.

6. **It's not who you bring to the party, but who you leave with that counts.**

Know when to take a conversation out of the public domain. Or offline. Or both. Eliason strongly believes in interacting with customers through the right medium at the right time. He might begin troubleshooting with a customer on Twitter but choose e-mail instead if it makes more sense to do so.

7. **Some scalability is possible.**

Although customers are serviced one at a time, they are all part of a growing Comcast community. This is the *A* of Activation.

Despite popular belief, Eliason believes it is possible to achieve a degree of scalability, but only to an extent, and only if you are realistic about the degree of help you can provide. As he cannot clone himself (yet), there has to be Life after Frank. Multiple people with individual yet related accounts, such as "Comcast_George" or Comcast_Sharon," is one viable solution, but people ghosting or masquerading as Comcast_Frank (i.e., @comcastcares) is not.

8. **Live in the now, but don't forget the then.**

According to Eliason, tracking conversation threads is a vital way to see the customer's true voice. Looking at the entire "conversation log" of the exchange over time helps to paint a clearer picture of total experience. This draws on the new rule of customer service: having a memory. And in the case of so many social media tools, you don't even *need* a memory, just the ability to hit the "back" button or scroll down a page.

9. **Customer triage.**

Eliason documents a very visible blog posting titled "Comcast Doesn't Care." In this case, Frank decided not to respond, believing that he wouldn't have been able to add any value. He clearly couldn't impact an impractical if not impossible situation (a customer wanted coverage in an area that Comcast did not service) and therefore diverted his attention elsewhere, where he could be of greater support.

10. **The blurring of personal and professional.**

It's taken him a while to grow comfortable with it, but Frank has become increasingly personal with people and, in doing so, has shared many details about his own life. This resulted in his community's decision to give him the day off in one instance, turning to one another to help troubleshoot their issues. Pretty amazing, huh?

Frank and I had a terrific telephone conversation. If you'd like to listen in, head to www.flipthefunnelnow.com and click on the "enhanced content" link.

BLURRING PERSONAL, PROFESSIONAL, AND PRIVATE

If the thought of three worlds—physical, digital, and virtual—wasn't daunting enough, let me take it one step further. Not only are there

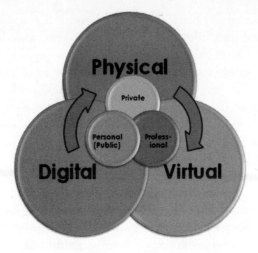

Figure 11.2   Shifting Persona Set
Source: © Joseph Jaffe.

essentially three platforms where peer-to-peer connectivity takes place
and where you'll likewise need to interact with your customers, you'll
also need to consider that every customer has three primary personas
that they draw from across these three environments (Figure 11.2).

The personal and professional components of this framework
seem simple enough to understand, except for the fact that our personal
and professional lives today blur together radically; nowhere is this
more evident than with the millennial generation.[1] In fact, a Pricewa-
terhouseCoopers study released in 2009 documented 88 percent of
respondents from this segment, who stated that they sought employers
(professional) with social responsibility values that reflected their own
(personal). This represents another kind of "flip"—our ability to
attract and retain the best and the brightest is no longer solely in
our control. I believe that companies that do not respect, empower, and
allow their employees to freely blog, upload, share, create, comment,
and moderate content are going to find it increasingly difficult to win
the talent war. Your IT and legal departments are groaning even as
we speak.

---

[1] Those born between the early 1980s and the mid-1990s.

Another major nuance here is the difference between personal and private. What many of us once considered to be private to us is now public to our kids. From vacation photos to articulating feelings and emotions, it's open season on Facebook! In fact, the phrase "personal life" might as well be synonymous with "public life." This goes a long way toward explaining the new rule of customer service, namely, existing in the public domain (new rule). At the same time, we're also seeing the very primitive beginnings of a countertrend: the private life, the equivalent of taking various conversations offline. On one level, this might seem to be a sort of backlash; on another, it's just a new form of intimacy, which can and will exist simultaneously with the various other personas. In fact, many younger consumers have two Facebook profiles to avoid their potbellied, balding, and awkward boss from getting a little too close for comfort. It's why on the likes of Twitter, users have the ability to protect their updates and/or direct message people. It's also why pretty much all the major social networks have varying levels of privacy and disclosure on permissions and access. We are living in an amazing period of evolution where the very words "friends" and "family" are taking on new meaning.

So what does this mean for you? Actually, a whole lot.

For starters, you'll need to invoke the new rule of "customer service lives in the public domain" and combine it with "some are more equal than others" in order to do both due diligence and even some investigative reporting to assess every aspect of future customer encounters. With a bit of research, you may be able to ascertain if your customer has a history or record with your company (or others). Are they habitual complainers or impossible to please? What are their trigger points that might make it exponentially easier to relate to and connect with them?

And be warned, when you think you've mastered the public persona, don't be too surprised if your customers take their conversations offline or private. If and when this happens, you'll need to be a friend or in their inner circle of their velvet rope social networks, or you're back to the sounds of customer silence. Can we really be friends with our customers? And if so, what does it take to cultivate this relationship?

Perhaps the answer lies in the professional persona, specifically, how this relates to your employees and *their* ability to engage with customers as (theoretically, real) friends. Ultimately you'll want to start thinking about how much access, transparency, and disclosure your employees, customer-service agents, and representatives have in terms of *their* public-facing lives. Just as easy as it will be to Google your customers, so, too, is it for them to Google *you!* Sooner, rather than later, you should be thinking about the following questions:[2]

- To what extent should your frontline staff have professional (corporate) Facebook profiles, Twitter accounts, or blogs?
- What about their personal equivalents? Can the company reasonably control the level of access and detail of information on these sites, especially the personal ones?
- Should they be one and the same?
- Should employees be allowed to exchange profiles with their customers?
- Should employees be allowed to share links, content, and web sites with a customers?
- When are they acting as official agents on behalf of the company?
- Can employees "friend" customers?
- Is sharing photos okay?
- Under what conditions should conversations be public versus private?

SEARCH (AND RESCUE)

All roads lead to, from, and through search—organized (search engines) and disorganized (Twitter conversations); structured and unstructured; organic, natural, or paid. It's a customer's version of *A Hitchhiker's Guide to the Galaxy* in the form of a blueprint or map of the entire information superhighway (or nearest mall) and it's all just a click away.

Being easily discoverable today is almost a minimum cost of entry in order to efficiently match brand solutions to customer problems.

Companies' ability therefore to accurately slice, dice, tag, and tag again every single bit of pertinent information is beyond critical in terms of helping customers find them at their time of need.

Help a customer today and you're helping countless customers tomorrow.

---

[2] Some of these insights are credited to RightNow's "Customer Service Meets Social Media" white paper.

"Cross" or hinder a customer today and you're creating an array of headaches for yourself in the future.

Every single nugget of content is another piece of an ever-expanding work-in-progress puzzle that is going to become an impossible labyrinth or breathtaking mosaic of inspiration and illumination.

In which direction are you currently heading?

LIVE CHAT—THE FUSION OF HUMANS AND ROBOTS

Let's go back to the iconic "markets are conversations" assertion. In the ancient bazaars of the past, the marketplace was teeming with life. All five senses were in full effect: You could smell the endless varieties of food being cooked, and taste it as well; you could see snake charmers, fire breathers, sword-swallowers; you could touch and inspect the merchandise firsthand; you could hear all sorts of music and, in particular, the constant haggling and ensuing negotiations. People were excited to buy and sell stuff. But today, the marketplace is serene, sterile, silent. The shopping malls are so clean you could eat off their floors.

And web sites are not much better—in fact, they're decidedly worse.

There's no music. No greeters. No buzz from the presence of online shoppers. Nothing more than a one-dimensional cover page. It's a shame, really.

Whether browsing, buying, or trying to log in a problem, there's really not much in the form of service or support that adds any depth or emotion to a fairly cold transaction. Finding the right FAQ is tantamount to finding a needle in a haystack and is no guarantee of success. And more often than not, using the search functionality to find a solution results in answering the question "Did this solve your problem?" with a big, fat "No."

That's where live chat comes into play. Companies like Liveperson are using predictive modeling mixed in with actual customer behavior to force the issue. They're connecting live service agents to customers via a variety of techniques, including live chat, telephone callbacks, and even remote access and/or control of machines (I see what you see). The ability to interact with a live person who is both up to speed and able to hit the ground running turns a one-size-fits-all contrived solution into a fully customized and personalized one, *without necessarily losing on the efficiency side*. In fact, this perfect marriage of technology and humanity is actually going to save the company money and/or result in higher sales down the road.

According to Liveperson, success metrics using predictive and proactive live chat include:

- Average of 20 percent increase in conversion rates/purchases
- Average of 35 percent increase in average order size/value
- Significant reduction in abandonment rates during online application and shopping cart processes
- Extremely high customer satisfaction ratings (based on surveys)
- Increased brand loyalty (based on surveys)

Liveperson also shares these key insights/takeaways by means of best practices:

- **Personalized Attention:** Real-time human assistance bridges the gap between the convenience of the Web and the personal attention available in the brick-and-mortar or telephone environments.
- **Engaging Consumers in Their Medium of Choice:** Consumers are on the Web for a reason. Instead of forcing a Web-oriented consumer to a telephone or store, why not stick within the medium of choice?
- **Reassurance of Human Contact:** Consumers often need reassurance or further information. Just because they're on the Web doesn't mean they're autonomous and self-sufficient.
- **Anticipating Needs:** Unlike the physical world, real-time analytics and technology overlaid on actual consumer behavior take the guesswork out of assistance and make any intervention as unobtrusive as possible.
- **Instant Gratification:** This is another point of differentiation that'not only emulates what is available in an analog environment but'also enhances it in unprecedented ways. No more telephone wait times, limiting or templatized FAQs, or long lines in a store.
- **Anonymity:** A key *virtual* attribute and differentiator, especially when compared with incumbent physical or analog encounters. By means of testimonial, retailer Backcountry finds that customers feel less embarrassed asking questions about new sporting equipment, whereas Overstock notes that customers feel less inhibited discussing clothing sizes via chat
- **Quality Matters:** Training and investment in talent remains a key priority. No amount of technology can hide inexperienced, unprofessional, or sloppy service.

CROWDSOURCING CUSTOMER SERVICE

The term "crowdsourcing" was coined in 2006 by Jeff Howe in a *Wired* magazine article. I spoke at length with Howe as he researched his article. At the time, I referred to it as "communal marketing"—a phrase I coined myself in *Life after the 30-Second Spot*. Jeff's term definitely stuck as a much sexier way to describe "leveraging the mass collaboration enabled by Web 2.0 technologies to achieve business goals" or summarize the union of cocreation and the wisdom of crowds.

Human-powered search (once again the balance between technology and humanity) has become increasingly popular in the crowdsourcing category. Companies like Mahalo are attempting to manually recode the search game. Yahoo! has led the way with its "Yahoo! Answers," which creates a platform for people just like you and me to ask questions, which other people (just like you and me) then answer.

Mixing all these ingredients together and then filtering them through a flipped funnel gives us a particularly unique and compelling value proposition: the ability to crowdsource customer service, aka community self-service. And if you think this is still out there on the distant horizon, think again. It's here right now (at least at an infant stage).

Manufacturer of unique and visually striking liquid soaps (in bright colors and nontraditional packaging or bottles) Method Products (www. methodhome.com/) utilizes a strong base of loyal fans and customers (or advocates) to spread the word about the brand. So much so that they have a rather unique problem (one that most companies wish they had): they receive more in-bound questions, feedback and *suggestions* from their base than they have dedicated resources to deal with. The first step to address this was an updated list of FAQs in an authentic brand voice that was decidedly "Method":

Does Method contain parabens?

No. Method doesn't contain any parabens. They are on our Dirty Ingredients List and therefore are never considered as formulation ingredients.

to the outright ridiculous:

Method's co-founders are cute. Are they single?

Yeah. We get that one a lot. Sorry. Both our co-founders are happily married; but feel free to print this out and pin it up on your wall. Or cubicle.

Figure 11.3   Method's Co-founders.

How can I unsubscribe from Method's mailing list?

Want to clean up your inbox? We get that. But we're sorry to see you go. You can unsubscribe in one of two ways: either click on the unsubscribe link at the bottom of any of our method emails or write to info@methodhome.com. Please state that you would like to unsubscribe from our list and include the email address you'd like to have removed from our database.

Method never sends unsolicited emails or shares our database with other companies.

Method then attempted to take this to the next level[3] when they looked to partner with a company called Get Satisfaction. They opened up the entire process to their community of customers and advocates (www.methodhome.com/PeopleAgainstDirty/), who in turn were able and empowered to add, modify, and essentially curate the work-in-progress database of questions and comments.

In many respects, crowdsourcing is just another name for what happens when consumer-generated content meets community and social networking in somewhat of a brand-flavored context. It's a terrific way to deliver against the following value statements:

- If we don't know the answer, we know someone who does.
- Nobody knows our brand better than you, our customer.
- We're only as strong as all of us together (the old $1 + 1 = 3$ equation).
- Collaborating with our customers opens up an entirely new set of possibilities.
- Our future livelihood depends on the degree to which we relate to, rely on, or resonate with our communities.

PUTTING IT ALL TOGETHER

When I picked up my new iPhone 3GS from the Apple store, I headed back home, and—upon backing up and restoring my data—found that none of my 17,000 applications made it to my new phone. I submitted a query to Apple's customer-service center and got the 24-hour autoresponder (on Friday at 2:16 P.M.) indicating that the turnaround clock has begun.

Here's where it gets interesting. It dawned on me a few hours later that there was a better way; and so I tweeted my problem. Within seconds, I had the solution at hand—not from an Apple representative (although theoretically it could have been), but from the crowd. I also Googled the problem and got the same solution within seconds (admittedly, many results were from the Apple forum).

Apple responded to me on Saturday at 12:08 P.M. with what can only be described as a terrific response:

---

[3] www.businessweek.com/smallbiz/content/sep2007/sb20070910_313949.htm.

Hello Joseph,

Thank you for taking the time to contact us. I am sorry to hear that after updating the iPhone software your apps are no longer found. I know it is important to you to have this issue quickly addressed, my name is John and I am glad for the opportunity to take care of this for you.

Good news Joseph, App Store purchases may be downloaded again at no charge, either from your device or using iTunes on your computer. Be sure that you are signed in to the same iTunes Store account that you used to shop from the App Store, and follow the steps to purchase any missing content again. You will be notified that you have already purchased the App and can download each missing item again for free.

For more information, please visit:

App Store FAQ: http://phobos.apple.com/WebObjects/MZStore.woa/wa/ApplicationsFAQPage

If you have difficulty downloading any applications, please reply to let me know or consult this article: *Troubleshooting applications purchased from the App Store*http://support.apple.com/kb/TS1702

Joseph, I trust the information and steps I have provided are of help. I will be checking in with you shortly to make sure that everything is in order with this matter. In the meantime, let me know if I can still help, thank you for your support of the iTunes store and take care.

Sincerely,

John

iTunes Store Customer Support

I then got *another* response from them on Sunday at 3:17 P.M.

Hello Joseph,

This is just a quick follow-up. I hope that you received my email with steps to help you recover at no cost all the apps you had previously purchased. I trust the information provided was useful but let me know please if I can still be of help with this issue. Thank you for your continued support of the iTunes Store and take care.

Sincerely,

John

iTunes Store Customer Support

The old Apple customer service might not have been this responsive, personalized, or persistent. Still, the wisdom of crowds easily beat out the wisdom of Jobs in this particular case. There's a lot Apple can learn from this example, and there's a lot other companies can learn from it as well. Suffice it to say, the ability to integrate additional new forms of customer-service channels into an existing solution will only help brands become more responsive and efficient, not only at solving customer problems, but in moving customers along the flipped funnel as well.

In this particular case, the formal and informal—or official and unofficial—solutions worked neatly side-by-side, but can you imagine how powerful it might be if they were somehow connected—or even interconnected? That's the kind of integration worth banking on!

THE REAL ROLE FOR SOCIAL MEDIA

In 2009, a company called Knowledge Networks published a fairly unpopular piece of research, which stated that while "social media has reached critical mass, with 83 percent of the Internet population using it—and more than half doing so on a regular basis . . . the genre has failed to become much of a marketing medium, and in [their opinion], likely never would."[4] The report—titled "How People Use Social Media"—concluded that social media had become a profound way for people to connect with other people but not a meaningful way for people to connect with companies, brands, or promotions. The study continued to assert that social media was not necessarily a very compelling or effective advertising medium and would ultimately find its place somewhere "down the road," that is, downstream in the consumer behavior process.

Little did they know that they were 100 percent correct, if *for all the wrong reasons*. In a clunky and flawed manner, Knowledge Networks focused their methodology on social networks like Facebook or presence applications like Twitter as replacements for web portals (Yahoo! or MSN) or even television networks (CBS or NBC)—in other words, high-reach vehicles. In doing so, they pretty much ignored 95 percent of the rest of the space. They also separated word of mouth from social media, when, in effect, the two are inextricably linked.

---

[4] www.mediapost.com/publications/?fa=Articles.showArticle&art_aid=106445.

Unbeknownst to them, Knowledge Networks was literally inches away from a fairly stunning epiphany about the *role* of social media: **that it is almost exclusively a retention imperative or capability, not an acquisition one**. Human beings want to have conversations with other human beings. They don't want to have a heated debate, passionate conversation, or intense verbal love affair with a can of soda, flat-screen TV, or extra-crispy piece of chicken. This is one of the basic reasons that so many companies found out very quickly that fake or even character blogs fell flat. What people *do* want, however, are solutions to their problems, elucidation on their questions, and assistance in making informed decisions. Does it really matter whether this comes from another person "just like you or me" or a credible, trusted, and committed person from a company hoping to make a sale, keep a customer, and/or expand their base? I would categorically argue, "No, it does not!."

Perhaps you're already utilizing this suite of new tools, channels, and techniques to deliver an expanded, evolved, and superior service to your customers, in which case, "As you were!" However, if you've been racking your brain to figure out how to crack the code of social media, you might want to reconsider and realign your thinking.

Section III

Making It All Happen

12

Transforming Mouths into Megaphones

The final part of this book focuses on the "so what?" or the "now what?" of flipping the funnel. We all understand deep down that we should treat our customers better. We all buy into the theory that more loyal customers will stick around longer and buy more in the process. And despite how hard we try to deny it, we all probably feel that we spend too much time and money courting imperfect strangers when we could be doing so much more (and for so much less) with our existing base.

So what's new?

Well, on one level, nothing, and on another, everything.

It's time to take the customer experience conversation to the streets—parlaying retention together with word of mouth to pave the way for retention to become the new acquisition.

Many people claim that word of mouth is nothing new. It's been around since the days when primitive men used to scrawl drawings on cave walls to recommend a good hunting spot, or perhaps to warn that potential hunters needed to look elsewhere. While that may be so, what is entirely new is an unprecedented set of accelerants, magnifiers, and amplifiers. These have propelled the speed at which content is spread, the number of people who are connected or affected, and the distances covered in the process to unimaginable levels, heights, and echelons.

If the cat's out of the bag in terms of recognizing that not only are our customers talking, but they're doing it on a platform—the likes of which we never imagined in our worst nightmares or wildest dreams—do we embrace this or fight it? What *exactly* should we be doing about it? And more interesting, how can we turn an otherwise-perceived weakness into a tremendous strategic strength?

In fact we have a profound opportunity to flip this on its head. Instead of viewing it as a one-way street or an uncontrollable and unfriendly phenomenon resistant to brands, companies, and corporations, we could instead embrace it by specifically and overtly arming our customers with megaphones, amplifiers, and platforms to spread the word.

So why *wouldn't* we encourage our customers to talk—a lot? To tell it like it is and to share, warts and all, everything there is to know, like, or dislike about their personal experiences with our company? Why wouldn't we want the truth to come out and set us free? To quote Jack in *A Few Good Men*, it's probably because we can't handle the truth. Any word-of-mouth program is predicated on a few baseline assumptions that underlie confidence, self-assuredness, and an unwavering belief that the product, service, and overall experience can stand on their own, prevail against the test of time, and withstand the scrutiny of consumer nation. In other words—not suck.

It might sound daunting, but is it? Aren't we in the business of producing great products that exude quality, consistency, and superior delivery? We *should* be, but in reality, we often have to turn to the crystal meth of sales—advertising and promotion—to misdirect or dupe our savvy customers into giving us a try or a second (or even third) chance at redemption.

By not only joining our customers' conversations (with permission, of course) but actually catalyzing (making them better) them by promoting, distributing, or even sponsoring (rah-rah-rah) them, we can shape or channel the buzz about our brands to new heights, audiences, consumer groups, or segments. What we *cannot* do at any stage is to attempt to manipulate, fake, dominate, or control this conversation. We also have to be ready to take it on the chin; glass jaws or houses need not apply. As the saying goes, *"if you want to run with the big dogs, you can't pee like a puppy."* In other words, be prepared to take the bad and the ugly along with the good if you want to arm your advocates with megaphones.

That might sound risky to you (remember the section on boldness), but I'm not really sure it is. Again I ask you: "Would you rather someone talked about you behind your backs or to your faces?" Sounds like something you'd say to a child on a playground and yet it applies not only to life, but most certainly to business as well. This—coupled with the reality that our customers are already talking and are going to anyway—should be enough to motivate us to develop a new operating framework in which we will be better off if we attempt to be masters of our own fate, versus putting it in the hands of others—even, or perhaps in this case especially, our customers.

Weird thought, I suppose.

Let me take this one step further. It's commonly documented that *most* peer-to-peer conversations happen offline—face-to-face in the physical world. These conversations are difficult, if not impossible (not to mention illegal), to monitor or comprehensively measure. So why even try, and instead, why not just dial up the inevitable digital—and in particular, the virtual? There's no way to police tens of thousands of inquiries every day (you'll recall USAA fields more than 55 million calls every year or 150,000 daily), but what if we allow the community to police itself? By giving our customers social megaphones in the net-worked public domain, we're actually encouraging organization-wide transparency that prompts a completely different scenario. Remember that blog comes from the word "web-log" (e.g. *"Dear Diary, today I had coffee with a good friend and discussed brand X"*). Can you see what's happening here? We're actually helping to codify "offline" conversations in an always-on(line) environment.

In addition, instead of telling tales of nightmare encounters, why not consider the spreading of the good word about great customer experience examples? Of course, there will always be some bad or even ugly mixed with the good. How much, I guess, is one part calculated risk and one part safe bet (if you're doing your jobs well).

When we empower our customers with tools of *mass dissemination* and trust them to do the right thing, isn't it more likely they'll respond in kind and this will spill over into the physical world with an inevitable outcome—increased business?

The new customer-service channels mentioned in the previous chapter are the same ones our customers are already using. They don't ask our permission, nor do they need our blessing to reach out and touch us with their praise or criticism. In fact, one might even assert that these channels *belong* to our customers, that we're just guests, hoping to join in all the fun and games.

We just need to jump on the carousel already in motion.

Just look, for example, at all the major info-mediaries (information intermediaries) in the social networking space right now: From Facebook to Twitter, or YouTube to Flickr, the goal has always been to attract consumers for free, but corporations at a fee. What does this tell you about who are the invited guests and who are the party-crashers?

I'll answer the rhetorical question: *When it comes to the game of life, corporations are, at best, guests and, at worst, intruders. We must never forget that our tenure in our customers' hearts and minds is based on our behavior, reputation, performance, and consistent ability to prove ourselves trustworthy, valuable. and relevant. Period.*

Well-known PR blogger Steve Rubel wrote a post in 2009 titled "Customer Service Is the New P.R." Of course, to a hammer, everything's a nail. So ostensibly, everything that builds in a decent mix of word of mouth, buzz, and ability to affect a company's perceived status or ongoing efforts could be considered PR or publicity, especially to a P.R. professional. Not so fast, Mr. PR professional; I'm not going to hand you the keys to the kingdom just yet. Your profession prematurely claimed social media not too long ago, but you're not going to usurp a pivotal strategic differentiator and anoint it with a PR label, when PR is just one component of this new commitment-based approach to customer relationships, community, and inside-out attraction. That said, I *will* give you full credit for nailing the direct relationship between successfully herding our customers through the flipped funnel and the benefits that accrue to us for doing so—in this case, earned media or impressions, credible buzz, and influential recommendations.

IT ALL COMES DOWN TO TRUST

In a world where consumers trust other consumers more so than corporate and government institutions, is it any wonder that the man in the street is more like Superman when it comes to persuading others from following their lead—or dissuading them from making the same mistake they did?

The 10th edition of the Edelman Trust Barometer, released in 2009, opens with this pretty grim executive summary of the State of the Trust Union:

> Government bailed out banks in New York and London. Melamine-laced baby formula rolled off assembly lines into the homes of Chinese parents. American auto executives descended on Washington hungry for handouts. An Illinois governor was led away in handcuffs. And as a $50 billion Ponzi scheme collapsed, an Indian tech mogul's fraudulent enterprise started to crumble. This year, the world had more reasons than ever before to suspend its trust—and for the most part, our data reflect this. Nearly two in three informed publics—62% of 25-to-64-year-olds surveyed in 20 countries—say they trust corporations less now than they did a year ago. When it comes to being distrusted, business is not alone. Globally, trust in business, media, and government is half-empty; and trust in government scores even lower than trust in business.

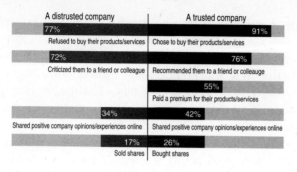

Thinking back over the past 12 months, have you taken any of the following actions in relation to companies that you trust? Have you taken any of the following actions in relation to companies that you do not trust?

Informed publics ages 25–64 in 20 countries

Figure 12.1   Deconstructing Trust in Companies

Source: Edelman.

As Figure 12.1 illustrates, trust itself is a barometer of sentiment and a harbinger of action.

Putting two and two together reveals a singular call to action for companies: Earn and build trust to your benefit; destroy or compromise it at your peril.

The further down the funnel customers find themselves, the more likely they'll be to trust that particular brand, and the more likely others would be to trust *them*. The longer their tenure, the stronger the relationship and, ultimately, the more frequent their purchases and tendency to advocate for the brand—and in doing so, invest their social capital in the process.

That's the good news. The bad news is that the bubble can burst at any moment throughout this process, when problems aren't solved, customer service is not living up to its potential or to our customers' expectations, and customer experience is underwhelming or disappointing.

A lifetime to build up and an instant to destroy. Forever.

We want our customers to trust us (and clearly they're doing so less and less), so why don't we trust them in return? They have powerful, passionate voices, but when we deny them the right to extol our virtues or vent about our inadequacies, we convey an acute lack of commitment, belief, and confidence in their merits. And when this happens, all the goodwill we've spent so long building up and consolidating can evaporate in a split second. It's the one chute in Chutes and Ladders you so much want to avoid, lest you find yourself sliding back to the start. It's quite regrettable to cascade back to a rerun of Groundhog Day (better luck next time), having expended tremendous, precious, and limited energy, effort, time, and budget in the process.

Back to square one.

Or perhaps your version of this popular board game is the Snakes and Ladders version, where the end of the tail has a fatal rattle waiting for you. In other words, if you've made—and subsequently—broken promises, whether in advertising, product delivery or even the beginnings of a flipped funnel process—either from lack of commitment, follow-through, or ability—you risk facing a worst-case scenario, which exceeds your safer middle-of-the-road scenario of status quo.

Customer #49281041, Pete Abilla, blogged about an unsatisfactory customer experience he had with Home Depot. No sooner had he griped into the public domain, he was contacted by a profusely apologetic corporate communications manager from the company, who asked him to send a detailed personal account of what transpired in the store and promised to follow up with a response. The catch? That was in March 2009, and Pete was writing this post in August! Pete calculated that his initial blog complaint reached about 2,935 people. (You can add to that the number of readers of this book, Pete.)

The lesson learned is a crucial one. Like *Delta Skelter*, if you're going to respond, you're in it for the long haul. In fact, responding half-heartedly or deficiently might very well be worse than not doing it at all. Sounds like a catch-22, and for the most part, it is.

Fact is, you can't be half pregnant; you either do this properly, or don't do it at all. Any superficial commitment or—worse still—attempts to lie to, attack, or reprimand customers can very quickly turn the tide against us. Blogger backlash is always just a post away. (I will say that these scenarios are, in fact, the exception, not the norm. It's just that we're much more likely to single out and recognize the horror stories versus the feel-good ones)

Often times, it's not our fault at all. After all, why would anyone do anything intentionally poorly or halfheartedly? The problems that arise result from poor departmental collaboration or integration or the inability of legal affairs, corporation communications, or strategic security to get out the(ir) way. Either way, it's unacceptable. If you're going to give your customers a voice, you can't treat them like puppets, censor them, or subjectively decide when what they say is in or out.

The takeaway is clear: Make sure that if you give customers a voice, you let them use it. If you give them an ear (yours), make sure you listen. If you give them an arm, you give them support (and don't let go). If you give them a leg up and empower them, you let them share—or even take—the spotlight.

BUILDING AN INFRASTRUCTURE POWERED BY WORD OF MOUTH

The idea behind flipping the funnel is that a company can grow its business and customer base by expressly concentrating on retention, customer experience, relationship building, *and* the networked effects of customer-originated word of mouth. Whereas the first three focus on maximizing value from a business's *existing* base (measured predominantly against tenure, frequency of purchase, and basket size), the final component emphasizes new introductions or connections formed with the outside world via insiders. In other words, it's about growing the customer base from the inside out.

There are five primary ways to harness the all-powerful community-powered word-of-mouth effects to achieve these worthy goals. I'll call them the five Rs (only because it *R*olls off the tongue and is easy to *R*emember).

1. Rants, Ravings, or Riffs
2. Response in Real Time
3. Reviews
4. Recommendations
5. Referrals

All five exist in an organic state—they happen naturally. However (and this is whole point, is it not?), companies can absolutely tap into and harness these efforts, parlay them on top of others, integrate them into existing systems or processes, and finally, propel them to even greater heights via explicit investment (buy, build) or implicit support (sponsorship).

RANTINGS, RAVINGS, OR RIFFS

People talk, now more than ever. They'll discuss the stuff they care about intimately, as well as the innocuous, mundane, and matter of fact. They'll often talk just for the sake of it. And in the center of these conversations are companies and brands, perhaps even yours.

In fact, according to 2009 research from Penn State, a full 20 percent of all "tweets" mention a brand name.

Give customers the slightest opportunity to share their love or war stories, and they will—prompted or not. At times, this input is so unstructured and unformed that it doesn't make much sense. But at some point, and after enough mentions it will begin to resemble reviews, recommendations, or referrals, and while there may be a semantic difference between "I'll never buy from company X again" and "don't ever buy from company X again," the result is ultimately the same. Either way, most rants, raves, or riffs are essentially open and urgent invitations that beg for real-time response to satisfy them or counter escalation.

Customer experiences are very quickly becoming public spectacles that are living out their voyeuristic drama in the public domain. All-powerful consumer blog "The Consumerist" was launched by the Gawker blog network[1] as the TMZ of customer service. However, it quickly became a weapon *against* companies to exacerbate their shameful shortcomings. Not only that, but it served as a tool to help them avoid further ridicule and, perhaps more profoundly, act as a catalyst for both internal and external transformational change.

Open displays of ranting, raving, and riffing have even become part of our culture. Tags or hash tags have become standardized markers, used across the virtual space to assign some kind of consistent identification. They're instrumental in terms of how content is categorized and subsequently searched for and found. Hash tag #FAIL has particularly become a central part of the new social lexicon.

Early in 2009, e-tailing giant Amazon.com encountered an "embarrassing and ham-fisted cataloging error" that conveniently deranked 57,310 book listings with gay or lesbian content or themes. What began as a public curiosity quickly ignited into an overwhelming outcry of anger and the birth of #amazonfail.

When these titles began disappearing from sales rankings, people started asking questions to which Amazon reps didn't have answers. Member services rep "Ashlyn D" told *The Filly* author Mark R. Probst: "*In consideration of our entire customer base, we exclude 'adult' material from appearing in some searches and best seller lists. Since these lists*

---

[1] The same company that launched Stalker (www.gawker.com/stalker), a blog to expose the locations of celebrities in real time).

are generated using sales ranks, adult materials must also be excluded from that feature."

Among those that lost their rankings were titles like James Baldwin's *Giovanni's Room* and Annie Proulx's *Brokeback Mountain.* It's uncertain as to whether what took place was truly a glitch in the system, but most people do not believe that this was done maliciously. When Amazon *did* release an apology, they clarified that the error wasn't limited to gay- and lesbian-themed titles and that it impacted "57,310 books in a number of broad categories such as Health, Mind & Body, Reproductive & Sexual Medicine, and Erotica."

For the most part, Amazon was forgiven for this short-lived fiasco that was resolved fairly quickly. But of course, there are always critics, like Kate Harding of Salon.com: "It's still not a real apology to all the authors and publishers affected, or the customers who had pretty good reason to wonder if Amazon had indeed instated a homophobic and misogynistic corporate policy."

It also doesn't help matters (in terms of credibility) that a few months later, Amazon founder Jeff Bezos had to issue a personal and contrite apology when his company—without any advance notification and without obtaining express permission—summarily removed legally purchased digital copies of George Orwell's *1984* from customers' Kindles due to "copyright infringement."

Seriously, you can't make this stuff up.

It's inevitable that at some point or other, your brand is going to #fail as well. To check your progress thus far, go to Google, YouTube, or Flickr and type your company or brand name, together with the word "Fail," into the search bar (example: company fail or "company fail") You might need to be sitting down when you do so!

Here are some random examples of Google results:

Toyota Fail: 8,480,000 (made even worse after the 3.8 million recall in October, 2009 – the largest in history)

Vodafone Fail: 728,000

Budweiser Fail: 197,000

Bank of America Fail: 3,530,000 (it's over 31 million without putting the quotes around "Bank of America")

Pepsi attempted to jump on the bandwagon when it proactively introduced #pepsifail to cope with a controversy surrounding their ill-fated Amp iPhone App. Unfortunately for them, this was like throwing gasoline over a fire!

While there are many interpretations—however subjective and diverse—of the word itself, when all is said and done, a fail is a fail in the eyes of consumers. From a cultural standpoint, associations like these are only going to be increasing in incidence. By the same token (I'm the eternal optimist), we may also see a positive counterbalance to the word "FAIL"—but I wouldn't hold my breath. In the interim, if you're in the mood to crow or croon, might I suggest the following words to add to our social lexicon, and let's see if any catch on:

- #WIN
- #SCORE
- #SUCCESS
- #GREATSUCCESS (in honor of Borat)

RESPONSE IN REAL TIME

Many of the new rules of customer service directly dial into this word-of-mouth herald. Companies like Dell and Zappos actively participate in many social forums and are therefore acutely aware of these conversations as they unfold. There is no room here for a "not my job" mentality. With emotion on the line, you can't waste time trying to find the right person, department, or division to act accordingly. Empowerment is the order of the day.

As are initiative and ingenuity. When a customer's loyalty—and a company's honor—is at risk, is it *inconceivable* for an independent contractor, employee, or vendor's spouse to jump right into the fray and offer some assistance? Based on the way we currently approach business, it might as well be. A royal headache just waiting to happen. And while avoidance or doing nothing is a direct path to a throbbing migraine, so, too, is a chaotic free-for-all, which is what happens without a baseline structure or infrastructure designed to react. Whereas too many people responding at the same time can be tantamount to harassment, the absence of any reply—due to the naive assumption that someone will be or is already on it—is equally hazardous. Either way, I'd still recommend pursuing a flatter, democratized, and empowered methodology that supports an adaptive, responsive, and connected system—active with the pulse of life and customer conversation.

When Is the Right Time to Respond?

Real-time response implies reacting in the now. Still, it can be a little uncomfortable when this time is measured in seconds versus minutes. Why not take a deep breath and who knows? Perhaps someone from the community—maybe even one of your customers (see: crowdsourcing customer service)—will step in for you on your behalf. That's *always* going to take first prize. For everyone else, you're on the clock. Your problem isn't associated with eavesdropping à la Big Brother, but rather being associated with pure and simple neglect.

If you'd like to read an article I penned for one of the industry trades on the idea of waiting for the community to respond (and rescue your honor), please visit www.flipthefunnelnow.com and click on "enhanced content"

One way to avoid being sucked into the black hole of indifference or ignorance is to integrate both maximum and minimum acceptable response times associated with dealing with real-time conversation. Stop-gap or interim acknowledgments with personalized messages to the effect of "I'm looking into getting this addressed for you as soon as possible"—and, if need be, periodic updates to reflect progress or updates—are quite effective at staying on customers' radar screens and reminding them that they are priorities.

Find out what works for both you **AND** your customers, and then execute against it.

One of the most important reasons why proactive listening and response strategies are so important is so that queries, comments, or issues don't snowball out of control. Conversely, when it comes to positive sentiment, it's a perfect opportunity to seize the moment and help spread the flames of positivity and goodwill in the process. When Oprah announced on her show that she was giving away free KFC grilled chicken to her viewers, there were literally riots at several KFC stores that failed to deliver drumsticks on demand. Popeye's Chicken was quick to pick up where KFC dropped the ball by offering to honor the deal on which KFC was #failing to deliver. This shows how real-time response can be both speculative and opportunistic—and does not even necessarily need to originate from the brand itself but can instead be a *gift* from a competitor.

TWO-FOR-ONE SPECIAL

Most companies are still trying to both effectively harness word of mouth and separately deliver against customer retention, loyalty, and customer experience. But what if you could do both at the same time? That's what happens with peer-to-peer or many-to-many conversations where customers are involved. And the truly sublime insight is that by doing one part particularly well (a renewed focus on retention and customer experience), you'll get the networked benefits of social media and word of mouth at negligible to no cost. That's just another way of conceptualizing the flipped funnel as part of a logical, systematic, and ordered process.

Are *you* a buyer?

A one-two conversational punch is exactly why we need to make sure that we can handle and expertly address customer conversations *as they happen*. And it's not just about *responsiveness*, it's as much about quality of response as well.

Take the folks over at Target. In 2008 Amy Jussel, founder and executive director of Shaping Youth (a nonprofit consortium of media and marketing professionals concerned about harmful media messages to children) felt that a Times Square billboard from cheap chic discount retailer Target contained a little too much sexual innuendo for comfort. If you'd like to see the "offensive" billboard in question, please visit the "enhanced content" section of the web site for the link.

Jussel sent a letter to Target, and this is what she got back in return:

Good Morning Amy, Thank you for contacting Target; unfortunately we are unable to respond to your inquiry because Target does not participate with non-traditional media outlets. This practice is in place to allow us to focus on publications that reach our core guest. Once again thank you for your interest; have a nice day.

Not only was Jussel being told that neither she nor any of her readers were Target's customers but moreover, they weren't important to the company (at least relative to the readers of traditional publications like *Modern Bride* or *Gourmet* magazines, which — oops — no longer exist). By inference, Target was also "target"-ing all blog, podcast, video blog publishers and their readers as well!

The blogosphere blew up with disbelief and anger toward the nonresponsive brand, and Amy Jussel subsequently became frustrated that Target's arrogance was being given priority over the real issue at hand: the billboard (not to mention the fact the store sells Toddler Tees that read "Hooters Girl in Training" or Infant shirts that read "Playground Pimp").

Target finally took its one foot out of its mouth, only to insert the other one in its place by explaining that the *reason* they don't respond en masse to any inquiries from nontraditional outlets (bloggers, blogs, and the like) is because they just don't have the manpower/human resources to do so. So let me get this straight: They have enough money to invest in Times Square Spectaculars and a seemingly endless supply of 30-second spots, but when it comes to allocating budget toward human-to-human interaction, the cupboard is bare? Do me a favor.

Why Respond at All?

Reading this book should make it patently obvious why responding to customers is not just a good idea; it's a vital aspect of any company's modus operandi.

As mentioned previously, customer service absolutely needs to be (and is becoming) a strategic imperative within the organization. It must move from the dusty, musty broom closet in the back office to the wall-to-wall windowed corner front office.

The very advent and proliferation of social media and social networking forced our hand, so to speak. Remaining on the sidelines isn't an option any more. Marketing is no longer a spectator sport but rather a contact sport, and to prevail, companies need to suit up with the appropriate equipment and padding. Listening and responding are your equivalents of gum guards and helmets.

Once you're properly attired, here are four pages from the *responder's playbook* that run the gamut from the routine to the ultimate Hail Mary:

1. **S**atisfy Curiosity and Confusion — Flip the passive phrase "customer satisfaction" and you get an active one, "satisfying

customers." When a customer makes a brand-related comment or asks a question via a blog post, or any other social medium for that matter, it's a prime opportunity to add value by responding. In these cases, there isn't really any sentiment other than minor intrigue. By joining the conversation, you're able to surprise your customers with an unexpected move.

2. Address Concerns, Issues, and Questions—When customers have a problem, you need to come up with a solution. Just because the question might not be specifically addressed to the company (for example, appearing in a Facebook status update) doesn't mean you aren't expected to respond and dedicate resources against resolving it. Unlike the first point, now there is emotional skin in the game and higher table stakes.

3. Festering—Leaving something out there for too long can have drastic repercussions. Typically, customers tend to resolve issues privately before taking them public. A first port of call is to contact the company before blurting out a rant. However, this soon changes as customers become increasingly frustrated with companies' service inadequacies and shortcomings and/or when they see the rewards of the one-to-many megaphone. A public-facing expression is typically a time bomb waiting to explode, as well as the best tasting juice for Google. In other words, the longer it hangs out there, the more likely it'll come back to hang you.

4. Escalation—This is the worst kind of scenario to find yourself in and one that has to be avoided at all costs. Any grievance or issue that festers for too long is likely to escalate. And this takes many forms—from the passive aggressive "give peace a chance" United Breaks Guitars, to the vengeful Dell Hell crusade, to pretty much anything that hits "The Consumerist," to Twitter (a fleeting heads-up, albeit a harbinger of things to come). When a complaint becomes a religious mission, a company is in full crisis communications mode. At this stage, your best-case scenario is to minimize damage. Stopping it is pretty much off the table.

Put it all together and, yes, it spells S.A.F.E., because when it comes to responding, 'tis better to be S.A.F.E. than sorry.

REVIEWS

The tendency to distrust governments, corporations, and brands is increasing. In fact, people are more frequently turning to one another for advice in the wake of a void of credible advice. The simple ability to review a possible purchase on a site like Amazon.com is the difference between ignorance and informed decision making. Whereas a handful of reviews are directional at best and unrepresentative at worst, a critical mass of reviews creates the perfect vetting process to help prospective buyers make a decision that's the result of considerable help from *the* community. It might be a chicken-egg debate in terms of whether Amazon.com's installed base of customers helped scale its ratings and reviews' competitive advantage or whether the customers' ability to rate and review helped Amazon.com grow its customer base. Regardless, there's no debating how powerful this functionality is in terms of integrating a powerful system of inside-out buzz.

With more than 61 billion reviews, stories, and answers generated through their system and various products, consumer response site BazaarVoice (www.bazaarvoice.com) is at the center of this customer-driven phenomenon. They've witnessed firsthand the power of both positive and, in particular, negative personal accounts, endorsements, and testimonials.

As a fun yet extremely pretty powerful demonstration of this point in action, take the Three Wolf Moon T-shirt phenomenon.

A while back, manufacturer The Mountain Company uploaded an apparel item, a T-shirt depicting three wolves howling at the moon, onto their Amazon.com storefront. For some reason, the image was intriguing enough to one or more individuals that they started leaving somewhat zany reviews like these:

> When my order arrived, I was not disappointed. As the UPS truck was driving down the street with my delivery, my female neighbors began opening their doors and stepping outside. I suspect the Three Wolf Moon T-Shirt contains powerful lupine pheromones.
>
> The shirt is made up of soft cotton. I was grateful to see this as it flexed as my muscles grew after donning this garment.
>
> The Three Wolf Moon T-Shirt gave me a +10 resistance to energy attacks, +8 Strength, and added 30 feet to my normal leap. I cannot list the specific

effects involving the opposite sex as I am still discovering these. And they are many.

Since owning the Three Wolf Moon T-Shirt, I have successfully solved 7 crimes in my city, including 4 cold case murders. The local police force is currently wishing to retain my services.

I do have one complaint, and that's that I must stay indoors on windy days. Last fall we had a windy day and I received notice that hundreds of women were suddenly pregnant, carrying my offspring, up to 12 miles away.

—**Lupidorr Theopian**

I accidentally spilled a glass of Tuscan Whole Milk down the front of this shirt, and my soul was torn from my body and thrown into heaven by a jealous God.

—**Chaon**

Even the 1-star reviews were positive:

So I got this wolf shirt because of, you know, the sweet wolves on it.

However, having owned this shirt for three weeks now and having tried it out in a variety of situations, both formal and informal, I'm beginning to believe that some of the benefits—as described by other reviewers—are exaggerated. For example, not ONE supermodel has approached me. Some of you may be used to having supermodels approach you on a regular basis but, believe me, I am not: I would notice one should she appear in my vicinity.

Similarly, I have not been invited to a vision quest, even though I wore my wolf shirt in New Mexico.

There is one thing, though, and that is that whenever I wear the wolf shirt I have a lot less issues with involuntary urination. I have not studied it long enough, however, to establish a cause/effect relationship.

Once, however, while wearing the wolf shirt I was mistaken for Schneider, the building superintendent on "One Day at a Time."

So I guess the jury is still out.

—**Go Down, Moses (clearly his real name)**

There are also countless customer-uploaded images—including ones with Steve Jobs and President Obama donning the garb that clearly proves it has magical powers—as well as mashups of popular memes such as the infamous keyboard cat (see Figure 12.2).

Figure 12.2   Three Wolf Moon Meets Keyboard Cat

Oh, and by the way, as of writing this book—the Three Wolf Moon T-shirt had 1,483 reviews on Amazon.com and was #1 in Apparel (Figure 12.3).

And in true form, I just ordered my own T-shirt as I typed these words. Look out for me, won't you? I'll be the one surrounded by the supermodels.

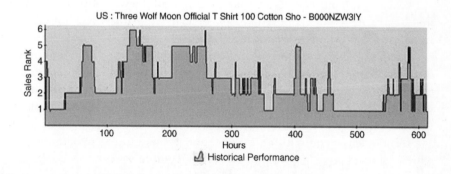

Figure 12.3   Tracking Three Wolf Moon' Sales Ranking

When Is a Review Not a Review?

A word of caution: Reviews are not always as helpful as they seem. Though often wonderful, they also need to be viewed with a very sober dose of reality. People lie. People have agendas. Under a veil of anonymity (there's that virtual world rearing its head again), things are not always as they appear.

It's vital to open our systems to customer contributions, but we must be wary of opening ourselves to abuse in the process. It's not disingenuous to take precautions in order to apply a degree of quality control and due diligence to the all-powerful process of customer-generated reviews. For starters, make sure that they're coming from *actual* customers who made *actual* purchases. Second, apply real names or, failing that, some kind of "verified by Visa" program, where their identities and intent are manually vetted and approved by a board of independent human beings (like Wikipedia, only objective). Amazon .com applies a lot of these safeguards, including the sparkly Real Name badge, which is there to give shoppers a little bit more confidence in their evaluation process.

Another shortcoming is almost counterintuitive: It's now so easy for people to give their two cents that they're not always thinking things through along the way. They tend to be a lot more critical in a digital or virtual environment, compared with what they might say to your face. For this reason, we're also creating an entirely new layer of hypercritical commentary. Along the way, we're going to need to educate our customers and prospects to be a little more discerning and perhaps even a little less gullible when taking what they see, hear, and read at face value.

Once again, our friends at Amazon.com lead the way with the "Was this helpful to you?" contextualizing or clarifying question, but it's a small step down a very long rabbit hole.

I actually think we should ban 5-star ratings or at the very minimum discount them. I'd go so far as to say that a 1-star review is more helpful than a 5-star one, provided it is constructive, accurate, thoughtful and well intentioned. Perhaps we should do what they do in the Olympics and omit the highest and lowest scores.

Let me leave you with an experiment: I'd like to try something or which I'll need your help to pull off. I'd like you to review this book on Amazon.com, or whichever online bookstore you frequent or even your blog. While I won't say no to an empty 5-star review I'd prefer a 4-star one that helps a future customer decide on purchasing this book: not binary as in YES or NO, but rather WHY they should purchase this book. After all, they're there because they're interested in the book in the first place. All things being equal, why shouldn't I be able to receive more reviews than 3-Wolf Moon, *Good to Great* (770 reviews) or ultimately, even *The Da Vinci Code* (3,955 reviews)?!

RECOMMENDATIONS

I chose to separate recommendations from referrals. Though they probably could be grouped together, the distinction helps segment customers into two groups: one that signals intent a little more passively but makes a statement nonetheless, and one that deliberately tells people their point of view regarding a brand, product, or service and is potentially vested in the process (directly or indirectly with respect to credibility, integrity, and even some kind of reward).

Satmetrix's Net Promoter Score is based on the response to this simple question: "To what extent would you recommend product or service X?" On a scale of 1 to 10, a 9 or 10 would indicate a promoter, a 7 or 8 an indifferent, and 6 or below a detractor. I've always loved the fact that 5 or even 6 out of 10 is actually considered to be negative or even detrimental to the brand at hand. On a typical scale of 1 to 10, a rating of 5 might typically considered to be average, satisfactory, or just okay. Using Net Promoter as a benchmark, however, it is a glaring indictment of why the term "customer satisfaction" is fundamentally flawed in terms of its *INability* to create the kind of loyalty that prompts future purchases—from the individual at hand and/or his or her circle of friends.

Recommendations are typically sought by those in need of credible advice. Our networks have traditionally been pretty self-contained, manageable, and controllable: our friends, family, and/or coworkers. Today, however, we are connected by *six pixels of separation*, as my friend and co-author Mitch Joel—who penned a book of the same name—might say. The same rationale that separates us from Kevin Bacon by a mere six degrees also connects us to one another.

And that's just the beginning. Our search for recommendation enlightenment is unpredictable, inconsistent, and almost irrational. Not only are we linked in to a network of friends or followers that can hit the 7- or even 8-figure mark but, more often than not, we trust the opinions of strangers that are vetted by the social currency of community.

When searching for a new product that we're considering purchasing, we'll typically click on a result that appears above the fold on the first page. Here's the rub: Google lists or ranks these pages based on relevance and doesn't necessarily discriminate as to whether the page comes from a multinational corporation or Joe Smith's blog.

So when I'm purchasing something on a whim, I might turn to Twitter, where I can get instant responses on what to—and not to—buy. I'm not spending time vetting responders based on their level of experience, their expertise, whether they own the product or not, or whether they're being rewarded to recommend (though perhaps I should). In many cases, I don't even know the people I'm blindly trusting. There's an innate and inherent faith in the crowd, and until I'm disappointed, I—and many of your customers—will continue down this path.

In other words, the ship has sailed on corporations owning or controlling the ability to influence—credibly or otherwise—future purchases of their products. Relying on (and trusting) your customers to represent your value proposition is your only hope.

One final point: Customers are engaging in (volunteering) peer-to-peer recommendations with increasing frequency, without necessarily being requested, and without anyone in particular in mind.

Think about your customers who are blogging right now. One thing's for sure: There are more of them today than there were a couple of years ago, and there will be even more of them in a couple of years' time than there are today. A blog is an amazingly powerful platform for harnessing the power of word of mouth. It's a public-facing diary, personalized and decorated with various buttons or badges that give its readers a chance to see who the author of that blog *really* is, what motivates them, and the people, places, or brands with which they surround themselves or affiliate. Consumers nowadays are quick to share their personal accounts, viewpoints, or recommendations with their community. How many of your customers are outwardly demonstrating a sense of pride and preference with regard to choosing *you?* And no, being a "fan" of yours on Facebook doesn't count!

REFERRALS

If you think about it, a referral is a kind of *personal* recommendation that carries a corresponding social currency. *"Tell him Mo sent you"* is the physical version of a referral; in the digital space, Amazon.com has one of the most robust affiliate networks that build referring sites in to a purchase process. In a virtual or social environment, GB1, GB2, and GB3 are the codes Cali Lewis, the host of the popular video tech podcast Geek Brief TV, uses when registering a domain from GoDaddy. And although a referral doesn't have to involve some kind of compensation plan, it usually does.

I believe that these kinds of systems will be deployed across the board at an accelerated pace in the months and years ahead. It's an inevitable response to the continued explosion of choice, fragmentation of traditional promotion and distribution channels, and adoption of social networks as a more efficient means of spreading the word. I also think there will be a Pandora's box of missteps, controls, rules of engagement, rebukes, regulation-versus-deregulation disputes and deliberations, and more that will come along for the ride.

In the next several chapters, I will elaborate on how companies are formalizing or can formalize this practice *without* muddying the drinking waters. It's surely going to be a heated topic for debate going forward, so we might as well tackle it sooner rather than later.

13

To Incent or Not to Incent: Is That the Question?

Actually, no. I don't think the question at all is *whether* to incentivize our customers who spend more money and/or help us grow our business through positive ravings, reviews, or referrals. The real question is HOW we do this in a way that frames our customers in an unprecedented new light as vital business partners—and rewards them in the process.

Personally, I think it's selfish and incredibly shortsighted to believe that our customers help us entirely out of the goodness of their hearts. Certainly there are going to be times—probably quite a lot—where intentions are pure. However, is this enough to sustain—or accelerate—the potential impact of these organic efforts?

The primary reasons that people spread the word about brands really have nothing to do with the brand itself. It's a genuine attempt to help someone else make an informed decision, a little bit of self-validation (*"I have an iPhone, so you should have an iPhone"*), or both.

We should probably butt out of their lives and leave them to do whatever they were doing in the first place. Why would we even dare taint the drinking waters of natural recommendations with our flavor of marketing manipulation? Isn't this supposed to be all about authenticity?

But these questions beget another: *If you knew that a customer was outwardly dissuading others from purchasing you or spreading negative sentiment about the brand—wouldn't you do something about it?* If the answer is even *remotely* yes, wouldn't the converse be equally true? Wouldn't you do something about it if customers were promoting you like crazy? Why on earth would you take this for granted? What if someone else— let's say your competitor—approaches them with a more attractive offer? What if your customers wake up one day wondering what you've done for them lately? Why would you give them even the slightest reason to doubt all the altruistic pitching they've done on your behalf?

All of these questions and scenarios suggest a need to formalize a process to determine how we work with our customers as partners, especially when they're out there pounding the pavement for us. Fortunately for you, I've done just that.

ARE WE SELLING OUR SOULS TO THE DEVIL?

The term "authenticity" is bandied about pretty liberally these days. Everyone wants to be authentic—oil companies, tobacco companies, power-hungry dictators, even toothpaste manufacturers. It's a free-for-all that would make sense if the companies and individuals doing the *authentication* were in any way honest, upfront, direct, and real. In addition, I'm not sure it's necessarily a fait accompli that our customers are anywhere as honest as we purport them to be. Beating the system is often the name of the game.

The million- (even billion-) dollar question is: *What happens if customers are rewarded for promoting word-of-mouth on behalf of the brand? Are they going to make recommendations just for the hell of it—or specifically, just because they're getting compensated? Are they going to recommend products, goods, or services that they don't necessarily believe in merely because they're getting something back in return—and in doing so dispense bad intelligence to their personal or professional networks?*

And we're back talking about trust again—mixed in with a healthy dose of integrity, ethics and common sense. It's a proverbial minefield to be sure, but that doesn't mean that we can't successfully navigate it with the right tools, roadmap and process.

It's perplexing to me to see the Federal Trade Commission (FTC) wallowing around in such a nascent space when, to date, there are so many bigger issues being willfully ignored in the process. Specifically, the FTC had been hinting at updating its testimonial guidelines to require bloggers and the like to disclose any connections they had to marketers. Doing so when money crosses hands is a no-brainer (bravo!), but it's never completely black and white, is it?

I'm a big believer that markets will inevitably police themselves and self-regulate. Consumers are smarter than we give them credit for, and ultimately, the social capital that we spend lifetimes accumulating is priceless. Why on earth would we destroy that in the form of misrepresented recommendations?

This is why the "Mothers that Blog" community—under the leadership of Liz Gumbiner—astutely launched a version of the Good Housekeeping Seal called "Blog with Integrity" (www.blogwithintegrity.com) in 2009 as a proactive counter to the FTC bravado. None of this, however, stopped the FTC from updating their "Guides concerning the use of endorsements and testimonials in advertising" in October of 2009 for the first time since 1980 to address this growing space. Here is one excerpt as it relates to bloggers and "sponsored conversations":

> The revised Guides also add new examples to illustrate the long standing principle that "material connections" (sometimes payments or free products) between advertisers and endorsers—connections that consumers would not expect—must be disclosed. These examples address what constitutes an endorsement when the message is conveyed by bloggers or other "word-of-mouth" marketers. The revised Guides specify that while decisions will be reached on a case-by-case basis, the post of a blogger who receives cash or in-kind payment to review a product is considered an endorsement. Thus, bloggers who make an endorsement must disclose the material connections they share with the seller of the product or service.

I applaud the move, which essentially does nothing more than state the obvious: disclosure and transparency are critical. I certainly wouldn't want to be in the FTC's shoes when it comes to auditing and policing this, but I guess that's why they get the big bucks.

Marketers should be rejoicing in this decision, which helps sort the wheat from the chaff. It should also reassure and give you confidence to no end that you are operating in a family-friendly, well-lit and safe environment. This should be no different from a celebrity who endorses a brand in a television commercial, sponsorship, live read on the radio, or Web-based testimonial. And apparently the FTC agrees:

> Celebrity endorsers also are addressed in the revised Guides. The revised Guides also make it clear that celebrities have a duty to disclose their relationships with advertisers when making endorsements outside the context of traditional ads, such as on talk shows or in social media.

I'm overjoyed. I've always thought that emerging media should not be held to a higher and/or unfair standard compared to the rest of the incumbent mediums. We carry massive labels on cigarettes today saying, "SMOKING KILLS," so why aren't we slapping giant disclosures on every shred of product placement on television?

In truth, this "woe is us" argument is both irrelevant and fallacious. The idea is not to hold ourselves accountable to the same low standards as the rest of the world, but to raise the bar across the board. The real issue has always been about trust and credibility.

And now my B.F.F., the F.T.C., has donned the "Sheriff' badge for all to see. Scumbags and celebrities be warned. You're on notice!

DANGER: CHARLATANS AHEAD

Put aside any personal discomfort you might feel toward this new form of human-based affiliate marketing. That uneasy feeling is less about doing the wrong thing and more about doing something new and different. I'd go as far as to say it's normal, natural, and even healthy to be a little uncomfortable. It's what will keep us humble and honest.

Then again, it's not you or me that we have to worry about.

Enter deception, manipulation and, opacity, which have reared their ugly heads in every single industry, format, or new approach since the dawn of time—from the snake-oil salesmen of the distant past to the telemarketers of the (hopefully) near past to the combination of entre-preneurs, opportunists and mad programmers of the present who are just looking to make a quick and fast buck (Tony Robbins, I'm talking to you). It's still the earliest days in both the digitally and virtually enabled word-of-mouth eras, and the industry is struggling to deal with a rapidly evolving space. The infamous and maligned pay-per-post or Blogola debates rage on. The FTC has attempted to shine some light on this category; however, the mighty Google is still not amused and has pub-licly grumbled its disapproval of content that has been incentivized, sponsored, or paid.

This seems somewhat like taking the goose that laid the golden egg and barbecuing it. My hope is that the cream always rises to the top or in this case, the spoiled milk curdles and is thrown out in the trash! The market tends to expose both unethical companies *and* customers and relegates them to integrity purgatory. Remember the companies who partook in fake blogs?

I would challenge the notion of the natural search result versus the sponsored or brand-affiliated post (which I guess would be considered unnatural). What is unnatural about sponsoring a rising star; an up-and-coming weblebrity or member of the emerging creative class? And on the flipside—why is it okay to consider an obtuse and bankrolled corporate web site with unlimited funds and resources invested in its search engine optimization (SEO) any more "natural" than a lowly blogger's post? Finally, doesn't this lead toward a very slippery slope in terms of bias associated with evaluating these posts (let alone the tremendous manual labor and impracticality of auditing and compliance)? What if Joseph Jaffe's unbridled love for Charmin is mistaken for a sponsored review of the ultrasoft tissue's performance compared to the leading brand?

And if positive posts that come via sponsored programs end up being excluded—will there be equal pressure from corporations or the associations that represent them to "remove" select negative ones? If the answer is "no," expect a huge imbalance of representative sentiment. If the answer is "yes," say good-bye to "Here Comes Everybody[1]" and hello to 1984 (unless it's been removed again)—corporations regaining the upper hand of information control.

The conspiracy theory is now complete.

SPONSORED CONVERSATIONS ARE HERE TO STAY

What some might call "influencer outreach," analysis and research firm Forrester calls "sponsored conversations." Contrasting sharply with paying people to explicitly write positive posts about brands, sponsored conversations leverage the new generation of content creators and, with a few key provisos, recognize their ability to create content for their respective readers, viewers, listeners, or community. On one level, it's no different than the *New York Times* tech journalists receiving loaner products of the latest releases to review in their upcoming columns. On another level, it's completely different because the people in question are not journalists at all.

Content creators are not usually on staff, nor do they have salaries, perks, or other incentives considered to be standard operating procedure in the corporate world. Under these conditions, should they not get paid? And is it really such a travesty for them to at least get to keep the product?

[1] A book of the same name authored by Clay Shirky.

You'll hear the words "disclosure" and "transparency" used in conjunction with one another these days when it comes to sponsoring or sponsored conversations. There are already several key best practices when it comes to sponsored conversations. For example, content creators are not necessarily obligated to blog, post a video, or create an episode of their show about their product or brand experience. But if they do, they *absolutely* must share basic details of their situation with their community: *I received product X from company A for a six-month loan. I am under no obligation to blog about this, nor am I excluded from being critical and even negative about the product in question.* This was already happening as a norm rather than an exception way before the FTC updated their guidelines.

In some cases, content creators are asked to indicate in the very first line of the post *"This post has been sponsored by company A."* I'm not so sure I like this approach, as it implies an explicit obligation and comes with a degree of compromised subjectivity.

Renowned blogger Jeremiah Owyang breaks down sponsored conversations into the following eight categories:

1. **Access:** Blogger is sponsored; a brand sponsors a blogger trip or conference. *Example*: Wal-Mart sponsored Mommy bloggers to visit HQ, but did not pay them to do so.
2. **Incentive:** Discounts and other incentives are offered to bloggers to get them to buy. *Example*: A friends and family code or discount to readers, listeners or viewers.
3. **Thank you:** Brands sponsor influencers' blog, podcast, or video show, a conference or an event, and the blogger or organizing body thanks them in the editorial stream. *Example*: Mashable thanks its list of sponsors at its various events.
4. **Product Demo:** Bloggers are loaned products over a period of time. *Example*: Nikon's blogger program (written up in *Join the Conversation*), where bloggers are treated with the same rules of engagement as journalists. Bloggers may or may not write about their product experience and almost always will be free to write anything they choose to.
5. **Advertorial:** Bloggers embed a brand or sponsor into ongoing editorial. A little too close for comfort in terms of ensuring that a line is not crossed in terms of compromised integrity and perspective. Debate varies based on one's stance as to whether bloggers are considered to be journalists. Clear and present disclosure is mandatory.

6. **Paid Reviews:** Bloggers are compensated in some way, shape, or form: cash (like when Google hired bloggers to review widgets products) or kind (such as a gift voucher which K-Mart and Sears gave bloggers) in exchange for an honest, authentic review.

7. **Junket:** Bloggers are treated to a special dinner, event, trip, or lounge at a conference, event, or other venue. *Example*: Blogger trips like the one organized by the Israeli Foreign Ministry or blogger lounges at events like SXSW (South by Southwest).

8. **Payola:** Bloggers are paid to blog but are not mandated to disclose or be authentic. This part of sponsored conversations needs to (and most likely will) be eradicated soon enough as part of the natural succession and evolution of the space. Good riddance.

So how do we apply this thinking to our customers? A lot of influencer outreach is targeted at content creators, who usually have fairly large audiences or communities, who may not necessarily be customers of the brand sponsor in question. Isn't it time, though, to think about explicit ways to involve our active, engaged customers in addition to the unaffiliated influencers—especially when they're already feeding back insight, suggestions, and positive word of mouth that is actually and already driving tangible business?

Here are a few ways (there are many more) to do just that.

SURVEY SAYS . . .

Let's start with the simple survey. For no other reason than the fact this appeared in my e-mail in-box, I'd like to single out Hertz Rental Cars as my test subject and deconstruct this colossal waste of my time. Please find my colorful commentary in caps.

Ref: Rental Record 169257082

As a valued customer **MY NAME IS JOSEPH JAFFE. WOULDN'T YOU KNOW THIS ALREADY, CONSIDERING I'M A "VALUED" CUSTOMER?**, we would appreciate your taking a moment to complete this brief Customer Satisfaction Survey regarding your recent rental at Dallas–Ft Worth AP. Your comments will help us gauge how well we performed on your rental and will enable us to enhance your rental service.

CAN YOU BE MORE SPECIFIC AND/OR PROVIDE EXAMPLES OF HOW PREVIOUS CUSTOMERS HAVE HELPED ENHANCE THEIR SERVICE? HOW ABOUT PROMISING TO FOLLOW UP WITH ME ON EXACTLY HOW MY FEEDBACK HELPED LEAD TO ENHANCED SERVICE FOR ME?

If you have already completed this survey by calling the telephone number, or accessing the website noted on your rental receipt, we thank you. **ER, SHOULDN'T YOU KNOW THIS ALREADY? BESIDES, DO YOU REALLY THINK I WAS MOTIVATED OR THAT BORED TO READ THROUGH MY RENTAL RECEIPT?**

Use the following link to complete the Customer Satisfaction Survey: www.yaddayaddayadda.com.

Please do not reply to this email since such responses are not reviewed. **THAT'S JUST GREAT. YOU CAN E-MAIL ME AND INTRUDE IN MY IN-BOX, BUT I CAN'T CONTACT YOU DIRECTLY. AND WHY ON THIS EARTH WOULD YOU NOT BE REVIEWING RESPONSES WHEN THIS ENTIRE SURVEY IS ALL ABOUT RESPONDING WITH A REVIEW?** *If you need customer assistance, you may contact us by using the "Contact Us" link on hertz.com.*

Thank you for giving us the opportunity to serve you.

Sincerely,

Joseph R. Nothwang

Executive Vice President and President

Vehicle Rental and Leasing

The Americas and Pacific

The Hertz Corporation

JOSEPH, MAY I CALL YOU JOSEPH? THAT'S ONE HELL OF A LONG TITLE. YOU MUST BE VERY IMPORTANT. DO YOU EVEN EXIST? HOW ABOUT SUPPLYING AN E-MAIL ADDRESS SO I CAN CONTACT *YOU* DIRECTLY? DIDN'T THINK SO. OH, WAIT A SECOND—YOU DID. IT'S "THE HERTZ SURVEY." NO DOUBT YOUR REAL NAME!   [TheHertzSurvey@hertz.com]

Clearly, a #fail or #hertzfail in my book.

To be fair to Hertz, they're most likely the norm as opposed to the exception. Many companies throw in something bland like an offer to one lucky responder for the random chance (as in one of 10,000) to win something ridiculous like a $10 Amazon.com voucher. This, after they've spent 15 minutes of their valuable time giving the company invaluable feedback and insights. Clearly not cool.

The only suitable approach in my book is to give a customer a guaranteed win or benefit. Perhaps $5 off their next purchase (or rental, in the case of Hertz); or a follow-up to share results or specific actions that have been taken by the company on account of consensus feedback from customer surveys.

Banana Republic does just that with a specific code, entitling customers to a 20 percent discount on a future purchase, given out AFTER a customer completes the feedback survey.

Retention is the new acquisition. Indeed.

TELL THE WORLD: THE SPONSORED REVIEW

Take the lease or purchase of a new vehicle, for example. What would happen if the dealership or manufacturer in question *specifically* asked for a review of the purchase process as well as an account of the actual consumption experience? What if the purchaser was specifically asked if they had a blog, a Facebook profile, a channel on Youtube, an account on Flickr, or the like? What if they were asked to cross-post this review on the brand's web site, blog, or message board as well, and incentivized with some kind of value added for their review?

Where's the offense that comes from the lead sentence, "*I was specifically asked by company B to talk about my experience buying this car . . . so here goes.*" What's the worst that could happen? They give a negative review and *you're* responsible for it? Is that *really* what we're so scared of? And if so—why are we producing products and delivering service in the first place that yield detractor-type results? What about the flipside? What if the review is positive? Hey, it could happen . . .

The *sponsored review* is a powerful and direct method to produce as many reviews as there are customers—in other words, to obtain a critical mass of representative and accurate reviews. It's a surefire way to generate an entire layer of content that will help future customers make informed decisions and make existing customers feel like they matter to the brand and its ultimate legacy.

Of course, it's not for everyone. It takes a special type of company to face the music and deal with the reality that they might not be as good-looking or sing as well as they thought they did. There's a Simon Cowell that exists in every single one of our customers just waiting to utter the fateful words, *"If I'm being honest. . . . "* In these cases, take solace in the fact they're just trying to help us be better marketers.

You Scratch My Back, I Give You Free Stuff

Content creation aside, what should happen when our customers are responsible for actual sales? The answer? Pay it forward. Spread the love. Figure out a way to reward customers for driving your bottom line. However you cut it, a customer-initiated sale is going to be ridiculously more efficient and will yield an off-the-charts cost per acquisition compared to your company or industry norm.

We need to create some kind of infrastructure or methodology that delivers the consummate win-win-win scenario: You win through increased sales, your *new* customer wins both directly (by buying a great product) and indirectly (with a possible additional benefit), and of course, your *existing* customer wins intangibly (goodwill from sharing their positive experiences with another person, as well as the recognition from your company acknowledging their contribution) and tangibly (some kind of offer, perk, or incentive).

No longer should any customer have to feel underappreciated or rebuffed.

Incentivization Does Not Always Have to Mean Compensation

I think it's important to stress that incentivization itself is multifaceted. It doesn't always require a tangible reward to provide some kind of acknowledgment to customers for their content, referral, or loyalty.

Figure 13.1 breaks out two types of incentives — tangible rewards and intangible recognition — across both repeat purchases and successful word-of-mouth referrals.

Are you able to document the ways you're currently rewarding — let alone recognizing — productive dissemination of word of mouth? How about the same for repeat sales? Or — taking a giant step back — to what extent are you even aware of the current level and state of customer-initiated word-of-mouth and sales referrals?

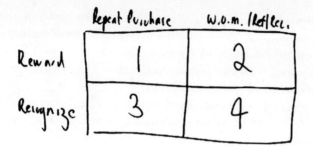

Figure 13.1   Recognize and Reward Matrix
Source: © Joseph Jaffe.

If you can fill out the below grid, you're probably in a good place. Regardless, I'd strongly recommend that you think about formalizing four distinct strategies and corresponding tactics to deliver against these four quadrants.

Strategies and Resulting Tactics	Repeat Purchase	Word-of-Mouth Referrals
Reward	:	:
Recognize	:	:

To help you with this process—and with apologies *to* and inspiration *from* Maslow—I've come up with two hierarchies (see Figure 13.2.) that illustrate basic to complex levels of both incentivization and compensation.

Incentivization can take the following forms (from bottom to top):

1. **A chance to win**—This is the weakest of incentives, wherein customers have a minuscule chance to win an otherwise indifferent prize. Largely used for surveys and refer-a-friend tactics to capture an e-mail address. Customers approach these with the same degree of indifference, increased skepticism of whether the incentive is even real, and for the most part—garbage in, garbage out.

2. **Guaranteed win**—There's a reason "everyone's a winner" kiosks at carnivals do better (and have less kids bawling in the process) than the stalls dangling the 800-pound green gorillas as the elusive jackpot. Several years back, Amazon.com passed on the savings from eliminating television advertising to their customers in the

form of free shipping. Now they do the same in the form of Amazon.com Prime, which—even at $79—still pretty much gives tremendous value to customers in the form of FREE two-day shipping, with no minimum order size. This is a great way to boost referrals and repeat purchases.

3. **Universal currency/marketplace**—This produces an infrastructure to recognize customer contributions, conversations, content, and commendations where customers can essentially buy, sell, barter, and *redeem* points or miles for additional product, accessories, and offers—and provides an advanced form of *Activation*. I''ll expand on this in a moment.

4. **Experiential rewards**—Providing exclusive content, access to information, executives, behind-the-scenes footage, tours, first-looks, and pre-sales, are all ways to activate this form of incentivization. This layer of reward or recognition can easily layer over the universal currency/marketplace solution. (From a redemption perspective.)

5. **Customer actualization**—At the top of the shop is the least tangible of ways to make the best customers feel incredibly satisfied and motivated in return for their contributions. Naming a new product after a customer, for example (it works for comets) is likely to provide indefinite and never-ending goodwill, uber-loyalty, not to mention, buzz.

Encouraging customer contributions with a variety of incentives is often enough to motivate them to act, stay engaged, and remain active customers. These incentives can be one-off or ad hoc, promotional by nature, or ever-present, consistent, and ongoing. Whereas incentives go a long way toward fostering goodwill—that is, are as much capable of building the brand as they are able to generate additional sales—it is occasionally advisable to literally compensate customers for their business. As an easy way to differentiate between the two, *incentivization is indirect, and compensation is direct*. They can also be one and the same; that is, one person's incentive is another's compensation (a simple thank-you is enough).

Compensation itself can be broken down into five categories (following the same hierarchical pyramid format; see Figure 13.2):

1. **Money**—Hard cash or cash back on credit card purchases. Simple, crude, effective.

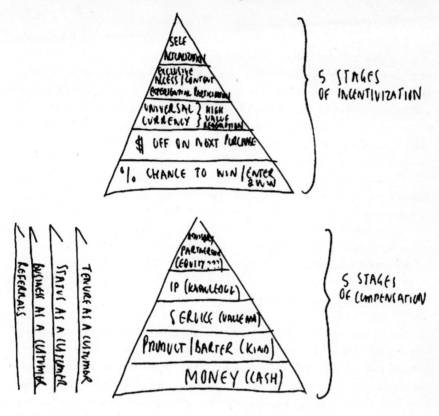

Figure 13.2 Incentivization and Compensation Hierarchies
Source: © Joseph Jaffe.

2. **Kind** — Bartering product in exchange for patronage is the foundation of most loyalty programs. Example: exchanging miles for free tickets.
3. **Service** — Added value in the form of intangible reward, such as faster check-ins or member lounges.
4. **IP** — An intangible form of reward that pays customers with the most exclusive knowledge or information.
5. **Advisory** — When customers become actual partners, they are tantamount to strategic advisors and should be treated as such. In the extreme and rare case in which a customer is essentially sitting on a board (not a focus group, but what we at crayon call, a Prosumer Advisory Board), why not put equity on the table?

QUALIFYING AND SEGMENTING CUSTOMERS

It's both an art and a science to determine which customers should be eligible for which forms of incentives. Of course, this can (and probably should) also have a subjective level of evaluation to complement an otherwise objective and formalized process. Judging situations on a customer-by-customer or case-by-case basis and empowering frontline staff and/or executives to make these calls is a more advanced form of prioritization and selection.

To assist you with this due-diligence discovery process, I'd suggest quantifying and weighting customer actions against the following levels of submission:

- Referrals from a customer—indirect value
- Actual business as a customer—direct value
- Status as a customer—loyalty
- Tenure as a customer—longevity

Based on the weighting and prioritization you allocate to these respective categories, you'll also want to think about what kind of reward you attach. Market Research from both Visa and MasterCard concluded the following: When rewarding people for a job well done, use cash; when recognizing specific behavior or achievement, use noncash. Ultimately it's a combination of the two; however, the rule of thumb is to favor noncash rewards for longer-term performance versus cash for shorter term performance (easy come, easy go).

As you can see, this isn't a one-size-fits-all approach. And while you may still not be 100 percent comfortable with this yet, there are a wealth (pun intended, I guess) of different combinations and possibilities to explore and experiment with—any of which may very well be within reach for your particular scenario.

14

The New Customer-Activation Model: Content, Conversation, Commendations

With more proactive, integrated, responsive. and accessible systems designed to move customers along the flipped funnel, companies put themselves in a better position to foster a customer culture built on a platform of customer experience, loyalty, and an inside-out approach to marketing.

By tearing down the walls that prevent employees (team members, as Virgin America would call them) from openly conversing with customers (or guests to Virgin America), companies become that much more human, approachable, trustworthy, and engaging to the various communities they serve.

And all the while, the inevitable by-product is a customer who spends more frequently and more money—and one who is more likely to tell others to spend, too.

As mentioned in Chapter 13—to incentivize or not is less the question than *how* to do so in a manner that is transparent, authentic, credible, and trustworthy.

I've developed a model that fills in the final part of the flipped funnel with a bridge of partnership between company and customer. It provides a win-win-win scenario by extending an arm beyond: the segment that—for the longest time—was the target of the spray-and-pray approach of the holey net of acquisition marketing.

UNIVERSAL CURRENCY

The much maligned world of Second Life introduced a virtual currency that had very real and tangible economic value. In fact, as of July 2009, more than $1 million worth of value was being exchanged daily. The real commodity in this virtual environment is time (itself the only meaningful scarce and precious resource), and the work product of this time—virtual goods such as a designer house or services such as a classy escort—is, in fact, a real service—in the form of intellectual property (IP). Either way, this time has a price that is either based on a deliverable, hourly rate, or whatever the market will bear.

Universal currency is a great playing-field leveler—especially when those playing fields span nationalities, geographies, languages, and audience segments.

Yahoo! Answers is a terrific example of universal currency. It's an IP marketplace where people buy and sell solutions to problems, with a point system as a method of payment. How does it work? Turns out the answer is already in the Yahoo! Answers database:

You lose 5 points for every question you ask.

You earn 2 points for every answer you post.

Yes—if you continue asking questions without answering you will run out of points and will no longer be able to ask questions.

So as to be able to ask more questions per day, all you need is to get to higher levels by earning more points.

At level 2, you will be able to ask up to 10 questions a day (level 2 starts at 250 points).

Starting from level 5 and up, you will be able to ask an unlimited number of questions per day (level 5 starts at 5,000 points).

For more details about points and levels: http://answers.yahoo.com/info/scoring_system

According to Yahoo! the reward for accumulating more points and reaching higher levels is *"our special brand of thank you's!"* an intangible recognition that seems to be working. The system has natural extensions for brands to help catalyze this process. For example, purchase a tub of Philadelphia Cream Cheese and earn 50 Answers points. Of course, by the same token, there's no reason Philly Cream Cheese wouldn't build or white label their own type of IP marketplace. Perhaps they already have . . .

One of the best example of building a universal currency solution is The Coca-Cola Company's MyCoke Rewards loyalty program. You can imagine the complexity of setting up a system for a company that operates in more than 200 countries. However, the standardization and simplicity of a code on every bottle or can sold offers sublime potential. While I'm not sure this program has lived up to its potential yet; at its core it is a simple and effective retention and loyalty program that is built on a powerful proof-of-purchase premise.

The best part about universal currency is that every single business or industry has either an obvious unit of exchange based on existing frequent flyer or purchase programs—such as British Airways Miles or American Express Rewards—or, if not, can very easily deploy a standardized one using a generic points system.

THE THREE PILLARS OF ACTIVATION: CONTENT, CONVERSATION, AND COMMENDATIONS

By establishing a universal currency system of reward and recognition, brands can begin to leverage the natural loyalty and innate desire to spread positive news about personal purchase, consumption, and service experiences.

I'm going to outline the three pillars that support this offering. Only one of them is obvious, whereas the other two are relatively new thoughts. However, I first want to recap on the 6-C model I introduced in *Join the Conversation*—as it provides both context and framework for this dynamic interplay and incentive methodology.

THE 6-C MODEL: A CRASH-COURSE RECAP

The traditional 4-P marketing model is outdated and commoditized (Figure 14.1). The notion that we can build entire brand platforms—and tangibly differentiate and sustain the brand from its competitors by using a one-dimensional framework of product, place, price, and pro-motion—is both limited and passé. Success stories today on any of these levels have been few and far between; and are truly exceptions to the norm and *outliers* in and of themselves.

Product = the iPhone or Wii

Place = the Kindle and its WhisperNet, and WhisperSync technology

From 4 P's to 6 C's

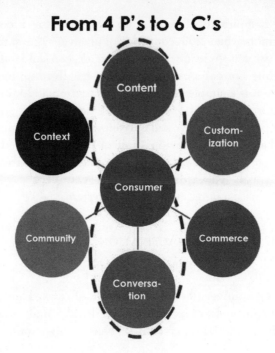

Figure 14.1   From the 4-P to the 6-C Model

Source: © Joseph Jaffe.

Price = Priceline.com, Coldplay, or Radiohead's honor system

Promotion = Tourism Queensland's "Best Job in the World"

In a three-tiered, physical, digital, and virtual world, there is a new foundation on which to substantially and authentically create meaningful departure or arrival points that demonstrate real differences—as opposed to perceived or artificially created ones:

Content	}	
Commerce	}	The classic Web 1.0 formula (Digital)
Community	}	
Context	}	
Customization	}	The emerging Web 2.0 formula (Virtual)
Conversation	}	

Our role as marketers is to decipher connections between the six categories, not only how one might influence another—for example: *"What is the impact of content such as consumer-generated content on commerce?"*—but also how they affect the consumer, in this case, our customers.

I won't expand on these categories in much more detail (you'll need to read *Join the Conversation* if you want an overview and explanation of this model), however, I did want you to think about Content and Conversation—two of the three pillars of the customer incentive activation model—overlaid on the strategic framework of differentiation as outlined in the 6-C model.

CONTENT: THE BACKBONE OF THE 6 C MODEL

The following is excerpted from an article I wrote for the U.S. trade publication *Adweek*, an introduction to the concept of "hubs", and specifically, content hubs. (For the full article, please visit www .flipthefunnelnow.com and click on enhanced content.)

What Kind of Future Do Web Sites Have?

Web sites are not ends unto themselves; they are simply a means to an end. You don't want your customers to move into your stores—you want them to buy into whatever you're selling and take it with them into their own homes, where they consume it, share it, and tell their friends and families that they enjoyed it. So why should you expect something different from the Web? Consumers' digital homes are their Facebook profiles, blogs, and custom-created communities. That's where they "live" in the digital world, and that's where we need to be invited to hang out from time to time, not the other way around.

Think of a web site like a hub or a train station; it can be a point of origin or a destination. Some people begin their journey there while others are ending it; some are just in transit, or meeting someone, or taking refuge from the storm—you get the picture.

Hubs need to be open, fluid, and infused with "sociability"—teeming with life and alive with conversation. They are decidedly nonlinear and diverse by nature, and they need to be loaded with content, information, and features.

In a world of RSS feeds, embeddable HTML, and links, hubs reign supreme. In a world of multiple personalities and personas, the key to

(continued)

(continued)

digital success is not a one-size-fits-all approach—the "or" approach—but rather an "and" approach. The goal is to coexist in multiple places at any given time. With a bit of effort, determination, and luck, consumers will hopefully get in on the act and take us with them to their homes, communities, and meeting places.

Consumers live their online lives in a distributed fashion (feel free to substitute the words "fragmented," "disjointed," or "frenetic," if you like). It's incumbent upon us to play into that, be where they are, and—most important—give them a way to take what we offer them back to their digital or virtual "homes."

Figure 14.2 is an illustration of a fictitious travel brand, represented as Ⓡ. In this example, the brand has spent a substantial amount of money to build a destination web site, to which it might even direct people occasionally. The site itself is overloaded with corporate-vetted,

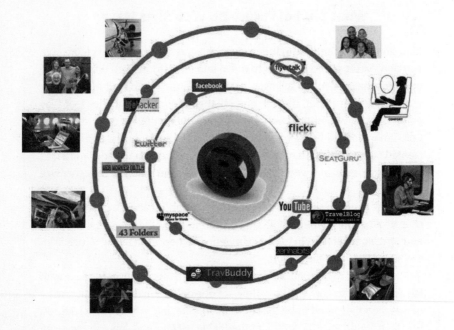

Figure 14.2   Content Hub—Messaging

Source: © Joseph Jaffe.

brand-friendly, controlled content. Perhaps it's even fairly easy to find your way around there. But is it realistic to assume the Field of Dreams scenario, that is, if we build it, they will come? Have we not learned from the mistakes of the dot-com boom and bust? What would happen if the brand released its stranglehold on content and let it freely swim around the wide world of the Web?

The reality, of course, is that the walled garden of corporate web sites is a drop in the ocean when it comes to the number of viable—even competitive—alternatives for an average consumer to choose and visit. As the illustration suggests, there are several layers of content categories that ripple out and away from the brand nucleus. What's interesting about these layers is that the further away they move from the center, the less controlled, less formal, more authentic, and more credible they become. As they fan outward, the brand also becomes less able to influence or filter what is being said and who is saying it.

The first layer represents the best-in-class social networking and content-sharing hubs—each of which is individually stronger and more powerful than the brand could ever hope to be. In the video category, YouTube prevails. In photos, Flickr lives large. In social networking, Facebook outshines MySpace (until the next one comes along). In microblogging or presence, Twitter rules the roost. In each of these networked hubs, brand content enjoys a rich and relatively social existence, able to rank, rate, review, comment, and share accordingly. In many cases, brands have carved out specific channels or *content hubs*—such as www.youtube.com/nike or www.facebook.com/pepsi (which redirects to www.facebook.com/refresheverything). In others—such as www.youtube.com/bankofamerica[1]—zero videos and a solitary comment reading, "lolz fuck ya!" greets the brand enthusiast and/or Bank of America customer! In all cases, companies have a far better chance of seeing and being seen by a larger base of prospects and customers by establishing an ongoing, active, vibrant, and current presence accordingly.

The second ring represents blogs, sites, message boards, communities of interest, and associations that are influential on their own because of either their reach or their composition (category relevance). For example, airline CEOs are nowadays more likely to be lurking on the Flyer Talk site than reading the pages of the *Wall Street Journal* for feedback (which typically reports on Flyer Talk anyway). In this world, the brand has very

---

[1] I'm assuming by the time you read this, someone will have advised our conservative friends at America's bank to rectify this disconnect.

little control, and in some cases —like with the traditional "cease and desist," or what I call "sue and rue," such as in the case of Engadget and T-Mobile (just Google "T-Mobile Jaffe" to find out more)—it's probably better to stay as far away from them as possible. Members of this category typically act as accelerants and disseminators of content, as well as connectors that offer a two-way bridge between consumer and corporation.

The third ring represents you and me, the average Joe or Josephine, the individual blogger, photographer, or activist who is increasingly creating content. And when they do, they're smart enough to be doing exactly what *you* should be doing: posting it on their blogs, alerting the community hubs, sharing it on the networking hubs, and uploading it on the content hubs (and in case you didn't know, they have their own channels—mine are www.youtube.com/jaffejuicetv, www.twitter.com/jaffejuice, or www.facebook.com/jaffejuice). For the most part, however, they're *carriers* in the germ (i.e., viral) sense, by referencing other people's content and *curating* it for their own communities. Often times, it's *your* content, though not coming directly from you. On some occasions, it appears alongside questionable content (such as *lolz fuck ya*) or is framed in commentary, criticism or conversation. But for the most part, the choice to create or curate brand-centric content is exceptionally positive and immensely valuable for brands.

The ripple/hub diagram works equally well to illustrate the way the brand advertises or communicates its messages. The center of the diagram represents traditional media outlets, which are exceptionally controlled and theoretically most capable of reaching the largest number of people at the same time. As people move further away from this center, however—be it watching a 30-second spot on YouTube, creating a video response to it, talking about it to a friend, or commenting on its merits (or demerits) on a blog—the message itself becomes less moderated and therefore less persuasive from a blind perspective than it once was. In addition, the number of people exposed to it are extremely staggered, fragmented, and spread out. The result is extreme dilution of impact (at least across a small, concentrated window)

SO WHAT CAN YOU DO ABOUT IT?

There are two (though not the only two) interconnected approaches for companies to adopt when thinking about integrating content into a customer activation model.

1. **The rabbit approach**—as in multiply, multiply, multiply. Congratulations: You're now in the import-export business and need to act accordingly. Duplicate, distribute, and seed your content to the nether regions of the Web and wherever that conversation exists. Let your content be transported, accompanied, and shared by—and with—any and all.

2. **The gold rush approach**—Source and select new content from your customers. When it comes to original content creation— that is, MESSAGING—you're no longer calling the shots. The discovery of brand-relevant and -resonant content is like sifting for gold. Though there's going to be a lot of dirt along the way, one thing's for sure—*there's gold in them thar hills*. Who knows— it could be your next 30-second spot or purpose-based call to arms.

Deploying a robust content-hub strategy gives the brand an unlimited number of opportunities to seed the kind of content that carries a commensurate amount of buzz and influence. By creating a two-lane superhighway of content flow—and rewarding and recognizing creators and their content—companies can activate customers' engagement and explicitly amplify a very credible body of creativity, perspective, and knowledge.

And for every bit of content that is sourced, acquired, and curated, universal currency is bartered in return.

CONVERSATION: A PERFECT MARRIAGE OF CONTEXT + COMMUNITY

Whereas the brand is strongest in the center in the messaging world of content, it is effectively vanquished from the conversational arena—it is, essentially, on the outside looking in. In the world of conversation, the key ingredient is influence, dominated by the army of Davids[2]—a collection of like-minded individuals. Look closely and you'll see yourself as an individual frolicking somewhere in the middle.

This is where the ordinary become the extraordinary, where stay-at-home moms become all powerful Mommy bloggers. This world is a parallel universe where a brand is not just foreign; it's positively alien.

[2] http://armyofdavids.com/.

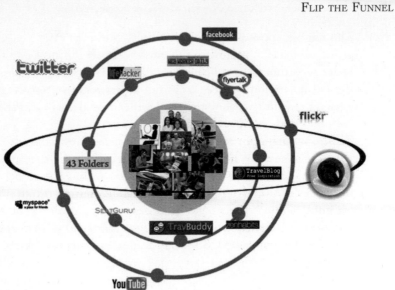

Figure 14.3   Conversational Hub—Influence

Source: © Joseph Jaffe.

Here, the brand orbits around the stratosphere of conversation on a continuous and at times desperate mission to gain new insights and entry points into the strange and seemingly angry local residents (Figure 14.3). And separating the brand from its consumers are rings of resistance that become harder to penetrate the further in they go. Think fan pages on Facebook if you need a reminder as to what is cool and what is not.

Of course, the same scenario is a lot less daunting when we're talking about current customers (especially the loyal ones) versus prospective ones (consumers). That's the whole point of establishing a flipped-funnel approach: in an ongoing dialogue between customers and the people representing the brands they purchase, companies exponentially increase their ability to participate in conversations. They can address concerns before they become raging forest fires, and capitalize on suggestions, ideas, and insights as part of a real-time and representative R&D process or focus group.

In the conversational hub of influence, people are talking continuously, often unprompted; sometimes prompted. Either way, a brand's best-case scenario is to be a satellite, monitoring and responding to conversations as they happen and when it (the brand) is invited to do so.

So What Can You Do about It?

- In three words: *Join the Conversation*. In a few more words:
- Adopt a listening strategy, or "commitment to conversation". Perhaps you call it something else, but the idea is to develop a culture centered on response and responsiveness. Be warned though: A listening strategy is not a license to eavesdrop on your customers or an invitation to dominate their conversations with your futile protests.
- Segment customers into three simple categories, corresponding to positive, neutral, and negative sentiments.
  1. **Positives** are your lowest-hanging fruit; they are typically loyalists, enthusiasts. They're going to sing your praises, so you need to give them a megaphone and then get out of their way. Reward your raving fans by bringing them back for more.
  2. **Neutrals** are, sadly, the majority of consumers, but less so in more high-involvement and emotional categories. Look to proactively establish relationships, thereby insuring against future negative reactions. Help find reasons for people to care; offer up low-risk means to induce them to join the conversation, without the effort and the fuss.
  3. **Negatives** are inevitable. Though in the minority, they carry a disproportionate amount of clout. Always anticipate backlash from a number of various possible scenarios; be swift and decisive by listening (identification) and responding (effectively). Avoid frustration festering, or escalation; ignorant, inaccurate or speculative commentary can become perceived de facto truths.
- Encourage reviews of the product, either informally (an open invitation to leave a review on Amazon.com or iTunes, for example) or formally through a transparent and fully disclosed program; perhaps even a "sponsored conversation.".

And with every unit of conversation created, curated, and catalyzed comes some kind of compensation—cash or kind—often in the suggested form of universal currency.

Commendations: The Direct Path to Commerce

By integrating the content and conversation hubs, a new center emerges: the community hub (Figure 14.4). I call this the epicenter, but it really

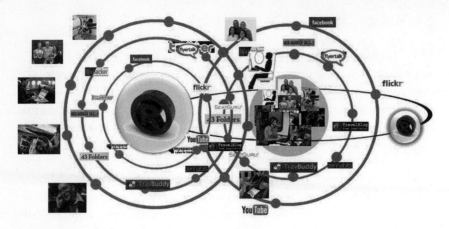

Figure 14.4   The "Epicenter": Community Hub (Activation)

Source: © Joseph Jaffe.

represents equilibrium, a middle point between inside-out and outside-in marketing. At this point, a true partnership-based or win-win outcome represents possible: commerce.

In this shared space, the final piece of the puzzle resides, namely peer-to-peer (one-to-one) and/or community (many-to-many) recommendations, specifically in the form of referrals. Somewhere in the epicenter of content creation and peer-to-peer interaction (the conversation) is the place where word of mouth and brand marketing peacefully coexist to produce a mutually beneficial result.

On the most basic level, a commendation is a modern-day version of affiliate marketing, in the physical world, represented by the familiar Tupperware party or, on a much more organized scale, multilevel marketing as made famous by Amway. Affiliate marketing is even more pronounced in the digital world, where an explosion of banners, buttons, and text links appear to promote individual authors, manufacturers, and entrepreneurs—but really just make Amazon.com, eBay, and Google very, very rich. Even in the emerging and nascent virtual space, an array of experiments and innovations have emerged, including widgets; blog, podcast, and Web video sponsorships; and reincarnations of the neighborhood five-cent lemonade stand (www.lemonade.com).

Whether implied or overt, endorsements are another powerful way to demonstrate an affiliation with a brand. With or without compensation, they carry huge weight in terms of their potential impact and influence. This all falls flat, however, when there is manipulation, coercion, opacity, or incomplete disclosure. Even so, it is becoming increasingly easier to smell a rat and uncover a less-than-kosher player among an expanding cast of characters. The *New York Times* refers to this phenomenon as online sleuthing; it's the same communal behavior that identified the Domino's offenders and exposed some very famous brands' infamous attempts to dupe consumers via fake blogs.

Maker's Mark (my ambassador's number is #621161) has long been harnessing the network effects of their passionate customer base. Bose radios gave their purchasers unique, customized business cards, through which to pass along referrals. Many moons ago, Palm created Palm Champions to set up a win-win scenario where referrers and referees both benefited from a formal transaction between old and new customers.

For the most part, we've not seen this kind of formal and scaled referral program in the marketplace of late, at least not in the form outlined in this book, under the protective umbrella of a flipped-funnel commitment to existing customers' value to the company.

THE ECONOMICS OF REFERRALS

If you're wondering why any customer would participate in a referral program for a third-party company, the answer is that they're already doing it. They're just not necessarily getting credit for it.

The other day my wife and I were watching the reality program *America's Got Talent* (don't judge me). She was questioning why the judges were so liberal when it came to sending—questionable at best, and bizarre or even obscene at worst—performers or entrants to the next round of auditions in Las Vegas. I explained to her the very simple economics of advertising-subsidized or supported television programming. To begin, we were looking at between two and four hours of this show every week during a summer hiatus when there was pretty much nothing else to watch (which is not to say that AGT's any better). Multiplying this across 10 weeks of masochistic pain, extrapolating the total revenue the show received from advertising, and offsetting this against the $1 million prize and the judges' (The Hoff, Sharon Osborne, and Piers Morgan), host (Nick Cannon), and crew fees would net out a pretty healthy bottom line P&L. Calculating the incremental cost (round-trip coach and a couple of nights of—shared—hotel fees) of

sending 50 made-for-TV" heartstring or freak-show no-hope acts to
Vegas barely makes a dent in the show's profit. And there you have it.

Ultimately, it all comes down to economics, and as the next chapter
will reveal, the economics of customer experience are staggering. Overlay this with the ability to activate and scale loyalty (why should this be
happenstance?), and the numbers are going to be even higher.

When you compare the cost of acquiring a new customer via
advertising (or other forms of paid media) to that of a referral from
an existing customer, the results are otherwise undefined because—for
the most part—the existing investment into customer referrals has until
now been essentially zero. Isn't it time we changed this, especially when
the devil we know—namely, the wasteful costs of acquisition—is the
current working benchmark?

So What Can You Do about It?

Here are a handful of ways you can jump start the power of customer
"commendations" or referrals:

- Create unique customer or ambassador profiles, as well as referral
  codes based on content creation, conversation, referral behavior,
  and activity to match to the profiles. ("Customized" and "customer" are almost the same word; need I say anything more?)
- Harness and activate a passionate, distributed *sales force* by creat-
  ing a community of like-minded, energized, and appreciated
  customers.
- Using barometers and other standard sales-tracking tools, intro-
  duce tiers of performance and reward accordingly.
- Why not create a customer salesperson of the year?
- Create widgets, badges, stickers, and buttons for web sites that
  endorse, recommend, or just acknowledge an existing affiliation
  with a brand:
  - I am a customer.
  - I own this.
  - I love this.
  - I'm satisfied.
  - I'm a promoter.
  - I'm an affiliate.

PUTTING IT ALL TOGETHER

Formalizing a customer-driven word-of-mouth network that acts as a credible way to build the business via content creation, conversation, and commendations (referrals) is the kind of long-term thinking that has the potential to deliver consistent, sustainable results. By operationalizing and scaling a process that gives customers a suite of tools to use to share their passion, personal experiences and purchase advice with others, companies put themselves in a position to boost both their top-line revenues and bottom-line profits from the *inside out*. By maintaining a vigilant obsession with compliance and transparency, brands can partner with their customers—without overstepping their boundaries, compromising integrity, and muddying the drinking waters of disclosure.

It's a technique that sends out a series of compelling messages to the marketplace:

- We acknowledge the role our customers play in growing our business.
- We don't take this or them for granted.
- We're prepared to share our wealth with those customers who continue to support us above and beyond their initial purchase and with their continued loyalty.
- We're equally prepared to spread this wealth to new customers.

The end result is a transformative program that—using universal currency, community, and empowerment—rewards and recognizes *everything* good (positive), bad (indifferent), or even ugly (negative) that our customers do for the brand.

Yes, you heard me right; content is content, and in order to be credible, companies have to be truly democratic in the way they utilize their customer contributions. A 1-star review is a 1-star review, and really, without the bad, it becomes difficult to appreciate and fully evaluate the good. As with Three Wolf Moon, even the 1-star reviews were beneficial to the cult of T-shirt. Or in the case of constructive criticism, the operative word is "constructive." In other words, any customer insight that can help the company improve on its offering is invaluable, especially if the company responds directly to the commenter or their community—and acts on the advice.

With both of my first two books, I introduced an initiative called Use New Marketing to Prove New Marketing (or UNM2PNM for short). In a simple twist on the conventional, publicist-driven, no-strings-attached method for sending review copies to bloggers and the like, I attached very tangible strings. I offered a free book to anyone who *explicitly agreed* to review it and invited anyone to participate—that is, request a copy. What they said about the book, however, was entirely up to them and without any precondition or pretense. I'm doing it again with this book, except this time I'm using a retention lens; this time I'm focusing on my customers (readers) asking for a review and recognizing and rewarding this. Just go to www.flipthefunnelnow.com and click on "I've reviewed the book" for more information.

I banked on the all-important premise that the product was solid (that I'd written a good book). That's probably one of if not *the* key takeaway(s) associated with any know-control outreach efforts that are based on word of mouth, community pass-along, and honest feedback: the product or service in question needs to be superior. If the customer experience is a cut above the rest, activation programs become accelerants to the inevitable; they accentuate the positive with an essentially certain outcome. Sound like cheating? Not really. Its simplicity makes it appear to be like taking candy from a baby. The marketing equivalent of Occam's razor: The simplest solution is most likely the correct one. In other words: Design and manufacture best-in-class products (like the iPhone), distribute them with unparalleled class and distinction (Netflix), and sustain them with exquisite personal service and commitment (USAA)—and the result is a holistic customer experience that oozes infectious goodness and delivers consistent results.

It also makes way for a complete customer-centric ecosystem that rewards all customer creation, contributions, and collaboration along the three tracks of:

Content—Building a repository of multimedia contributions (videos, audio recordings, photographs, blog posts) that exist on the customer's personal blog or web site, various sharing hubs (like YouTube), and of course, the brand's curated web site and various distributed channels. Whenever the content is uploaded, shared, and duplicated by consumers or imported or exported by the brand, there is barter or exchange of currency. The more they create, the more they earn. Different forms of content may have different prices (e.g. organic home movie of a visit to an adventure park versus a specific account of a particular ride that is briefed by the brand).

Conversation—Every rating, review, or comment has a point value, a natural extension of the content-creation category. However, now it carries context, that is, sentiment and evaluation. In this category, brands work directly with customers as marketing partners. Outreach efforts with enthusiasts are designed to harness the power of social networking in general; in other words, introducing seeding programs that connect brands with communities via community leaders. Sponsored conversations create a structure that rewards peer-to-peer connections.

Commendations—The easiest to measure and track, since unique customer IDs can be matched and reconciled accordingly. Like the previous two categories, customers receive rewards for their ability to drive new business based on their own recommendations and credibility. Utilizing both explicit and implicit endorsements—from both direct and indirect means of referrals—customers and those they ultimately influence are equally compensated. Think match-making meets marketing (or even "match-marketing").

WHEN IN DOUBT, LEAVE IT IN

So where's the catch with introducing and implementing a customer activation program? There really isn't one, unless, of course, you doubt your own integrity or your customers' ability to self-police and regulate without being lured to the dark side of bias, manipulation, and coercion. Disclosure and transparency are not optional; they are critically vital components of any program that uses any kind of formalized financial or bartered compensation. There's an inherent danger to paying (pun not intended) lip service to both of these; they're almost becoming clichés in today's corporate environment. Clearly, any superficial understanding or execution against these core tenets is unacceptable.

For this reason, any program must be supported by vigilant compliance and auditing, including guidance and policing related to:

- Vetting of all guidelines under development
- Recommendation of new policies and policy revisions that conform the highest standards of transparency and disclosure
- Signoff from the legal department where and when necessary

- Real-time and intense feedback loops designed to integrate new learning into ongoing policies
- Contingency and scenario planning
- Course correction
- Policy training for internal stakeholders and/or outside moderation, using community management partners
- Dedicated (human) resources to monitor the program, with a zero-tolerance approach to abuse and fraud

You'll also want to introduce two more critical words into the mix and make certain that they are measured and incorporated accordingly. They are:

- Authenticity: the truth will set you free, and anything less will hang you—and
- Consistency: both in terms of how you conduct yourself AND how you expect your customers to act in turn

CASHING OUT

What ultimately protects the structure and longevity of a customer activation model is that this is really nothing more than a (highly evolved) loyalty program, with the inherent ability to very explicitly, tangibly, and publicly acknowledge the invaluable role customers play in furthering the brand's health and the business's growth. By utilizing a universal currency system, there really is no actual currency—that is, money—that changes hands, but instead a barter system of value exchange built on or around the product or brand experience itself ("on brand").

Miles or points can be traded for branded services or experiences, accessories, or upgrades and, in the case of an IP marketplace, status, social capital, or additional perks. Using a point system to arbitrate between action and engagement on the one hand and compensation on the other creates a buffer of protection that essentially insulates—and even strengthens—the customer community from outside or external pressures.

TRANSFORMATION

In Chapter 6, I introduced the distinction between enthusiasts (customers) and influencers (not customers). I broke this down further by

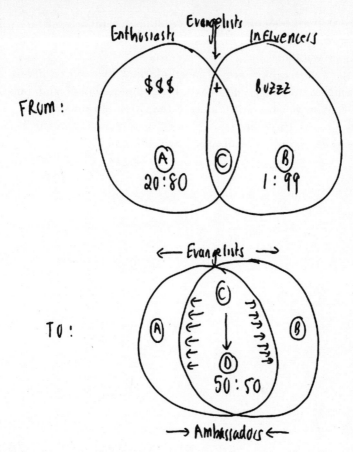

Figure 14.5   Merging Enthusiasts and Influencers

segmenting the disproportionate imbalances between the heavy buyers and/or loyalists (enthusiasts) and loud mouths (influencers). I also spoke about the need to treat influencers as customers and vice versa.

And now we get to put it together as Figure 14.5 outlines. This is the metamorphosis; the moment of transformation, where the long-term "commitment" bears fruit: this is where we're able to merge the two intersecting circles together . . . to the point where they theoretically become concentric. In other words, by flipping the funnel with our customers as the focal point, and in doing so, providing them with tools, incentives, motivation, community, and purpose, we transform our entire customer-force into a salesforce; an army of galvanized advocates or ambassadors for the brand.

This is partnership.
This is equilibrium.
This is win-win.

In its rawest, purest, and/or most informal form, we're talking about harnessing, activating, and maximizing the potential and impact of customer evangelists. But it's more than that. Brands have a unique opportunity to formalize this process and convert evangelists into ambassadors. Proud. Persuasive. Powerful.

15

The Economic Benefits of Customer Experience

It's been a long time coming, but there's an increasing amount of physical proof that validates what we've always known (but perhaps ignored) for the longest time about a flipped-funnel approach to business. *Investing in your customers pays tremendous dividends.*

Conventional thinking held that it costs roughly 5 to 10 times[1] the amount to acquire a new customer than it does to retain an existing one. With the advent of the Internet and other electronic forms of marketing, these numbers only skew higher in favor of retention. However, what these numbers *don't* take into account are the additional economic benefits that businesses enjoy from both repeat purchases and, more pointedly, new business via word of mouth from existing ones. It's a bit of a mouthful, but it essentially says, "Flip the funnel now!"

Here's a simple place to start. Fill in this grid please.

	Acquisition (First Purchase)	Retention (2 or More Purchases)
% Budget Spent		
Revenue Received		

My guess is that if you're relatively healthy and functional, you're going to see about 65 percent to 75 percent of your current revenue coming from returning customers. However, the dollars invested in this segment are most likely going to be the exact inverse, about 25 percent to 35 percent. What would happen if you changed that, if you flipped that

---

[1] eMarketer, 2005; Reichheld and Schefter, 2000. E-Loyalty: Your Secret Weapon on the Web, Harvard Business Review

equation and focused the lion's share of your budget on the people who *keep you in business?* What if you considered retention to be an offensive rather than a defensive strategy? What would happen if you altered your retention strategy to harness the network effects of word of mouth and, better yet, actually reward customers who bring in new business?

CUSTOMER EXPERIENCE PAYS

In 2009, Forrester Research released a report that put some juicy flesh on the bones of a customer experience hypothesis that attempted to connect loyalty and business benefits. By ranking Customer Experience Index (CxPi) scores of 113 organizations and segmenting them into quartiles based on their scores, Forrester could compare customer loyalty between the haves (1st quartile) and the have-nots (4th quartile). The results revealed double-digit differences:

- More customers willing to purchase: 14.4 percent
- More customers reluctant to switch: 15.8 percent
- More customers likely to recommend: 16.6 percent

Figure 15.1 shows the full hall of fame—or shame—depending within which quartile you find yourselves.

Applying these scores against a set of business and revenue assumptions revealed some staggering numbers when extrapolating a 10 percent CxPi shift (i.e., what would happen with a 10 percent improvement) against projected or extrapolated revenue change:

- Large firms[2] can gain $177 million to $311 million per year.
- Increased loyalty from an enhanced customer experience can generate more than $206 million per year from a combination of increased tenure (decreased churn or switching) and increased purchases.
- Word of mouth, on the other hand (highest levels of volume predictably among airlines, followed by wireless carriers), can net up to $118 million incrementally per year.

---

[2] On a base of $10 billion increments in revenues.

Firms were grouped by their CxPI score relative to the CxPI score for their industry.

Company (Industry)

Top quartile	Second quartile	Third quartile	Bottom quartile
A credit union (bank)	Anthem (BCBS) (health plan)	Aetna (health plan)	AAA (insurance)
A credit union (investment firm)	BJ's Wholesale Club (retailer)	Allstate Insurance (insurance)	Best Buy (retailer)
Alltel (wireless carrier)	Charles Schwab (investment firm)	American Airlines (airline)	Capital One (bank)
Amazon.com (retailer)	AT&T (wireless carrier)	An independent insurance agent (insurance)	Charter Communications (ISP)
American Express (credit card)	CVS (retailer)	Bank of America (bank)	Charter Communications (TV service)
AOL (America Online) (ISP)	DISH Network (EchoStar Satellite) (TV service)	Bank of America (credit card)	Circuit City (retailer)
Apple (PC manufacturer)	eBay (retailer)	Capital One (credit card)	Citibank (bank)
AT&T (ISP)	Edward Jones (investment firm)	Chase (credit card)	Comcast (ISP)
Barnes & Noble (retailer)	Gateway (PC manufacturer)	CIGNA (health plan)	Comcast (TV service)
BellSouth (ISP)	Holiday Inn (hotel)	Citigroup (credit card)	Comfort Inn (hotel)
Borders (retailer)	Holiday Inn Express (hotel)	Compaq (PC manufacturer)	Dell (PC manufacturer)
Bright House (TV service)	JCPenney (retailer)	Continental Airlines (airline)	Delta Air Lines (airline)
Costco (retailer)	Kohl's (retailer)	Cox Communications (ISP)	Farmers Insurance Group (insurance)
Cox Communications (TV service)	Lowe's (retailer)	Fidelity Investments (investment firm)	HSBC (credit card)
DirecTV (TV service)	Medicare (health plan)	Geico (insurance)	JP Morgan Chase (bank)
Discover Financial Services (credit card)	National City (bank)	Hewlett-Packard (PC manufacturer)	Liberty Mutual Insurance (insurance)
Hampton Inn/Suites (hotel)	Old Navy (retailer)	Hilton Hotels (hotel)	Medicaid (health plan)
Kaiser (health plan)	Sam's Club (retailer)	The Home Depot (retailer)	Merrill Lynch (investment firm)
Marriott Hotels & Resorts (hotel)	State Farm (insurance)	Kmart (retailer)	Northwest Airlines (airline)
MSN (Microsoft Network) (ISP)	SunTrust Bank (bank)	Macy's (retailer)	Office Depot (retailer)
Other cable TV provider (TV service)	Target (retailer)	Nationwide Mutual Insurance (insurance)	RadioShack (retailer)
Progressive (insurance)	T-Mobile (wireless carrier)	Other full-service brokerage (investment firm)	Sprint (wireless carrier)
Qwest Communications (ISP)	Toys "R" Us (retailer)	Road Runner (Time Warner Cable) (ISP)	Time Warner Cable (TV service)
Southwest Airlines (airline)	TracFone Wireless (wireless carrier)	Sears (retailer)	United/Ted (airline)
USAA (credit card)	TriCare (health plan)	Staples (retailer)	US Airways (airline)
USAA (insurance)	U.S. Bancorp (bank)	United Healthcare (health plan)	Wachovia (bank)
The Vanguard Group (investment firm)	Verizon (ISP)	Walgreens (retailer)	Washington Mutual (bank)
Wells Fargo (credit card)	Verizon Wireless (wireless carrier)	Wal-Mart (retailer)	Washington Mutual (credit card)
		Wells Fargo (bank)	

54750   Source: Forrester Research, Inc.

Figure 15.1   Industry CxPi Rankings

Source: Forrester Research, Inc.

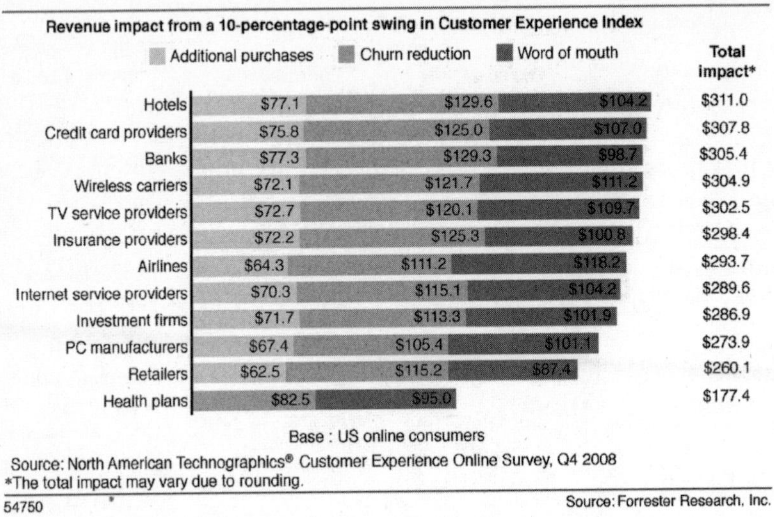

Revenue impact from a 10-percentage-point swing in Customer Experience Index

	Additional purchases	Churn reduction	Word of mouth	Total impact*
Hotels	$77.1	$129.6	$104.2	$311.0
Credit card providers	$75.8	$125.0	$107.0	$307.8
Banks	$77.3	$129.3	$98.7	$305.4
Wireless carriers	$72.1	$121.7	$111.2	$304.9
TV service providers	$72.7	$120.1	$109.7	$302.5
Insurance providers	$72.2	$125.3	$100.8	$298.4
Airlines	$64.3	$111.2	$118.2	$293.7
Internet service providers	$70.3	$115.1	$104.2	$289.6
Investment firms	$71.7	$113.3	$101.9	$286.9
PC manufacturers	$67.4	$105.4	$101.1	$273.9
Retailers	$62.5	$115.2	$87.4	$260.1
Health plans	$82.5	$95.0		$177.4

Base : US online consumers

Source: North American Technographics® Customer Experience Online Survey, Q4 2008
*The total impact may vary due to rounding.

54750   Source: Forrester Research, Inc.

Figure 15.2   CxPi Revenue Impact

Source: Forrester Research, Inc.; North American Technographics® Customer Experience Online Survey, Q4 2008.

The full extrapolations (shown in Figure 15.2) range from $177.4 million (health plans) to $311 million (hotels).

Deconstructing the methodology and the various assumptions and supporting framework of the analysis reveals even more useful insights:

- The analysis is done on a revenue base of $10 billion. Companies with even larger revenue bases (Lenovo at $16.8 billion in 2008 revenue is ranked 499th on Fortune's Global 500 list; Wal-Mart's annual revenue of $378.8 billion puts them in 1st place, Toyota's $230.2 billion puts them 5th, Bank of America's $119.2 billion is at 28, and AT&T's $118.9 billion is at 29) have even more to gain (or lose).
- A 2-percent influence rate from word-of-mouth referrals is exceptionally conservative (see the upcoming Satmetrix analysis or just apply your own personal logic when confronted with a recommendation from a friend or colleague).

Both of these caveats hint at even bigger upsides or downsides—depending on which side of the experience continuum your company falls.

From a simple what-if return on investment perspective, consider what it would take from a budget reallocation or optimization standpoint to realize these superior lifts. Now compare these levels against your company's current investment in customer experience versus traditional acquisition marketing and compound these metrics against long-tail investment (ongoing maintenance, staffing, operations, commitment to conversation) versus long-tail returns (a seemingly exponential network effect that comes from continued business and word of mouth, especially from pass-alongs, which are part of a process as opposed to an end unto itself).

We're not exactly talking about hemorrhaging the system in order to get to a very special place, are we?

SO WHAT'S A SATISFIED CUSTOMER WORTH?

Another consideration of customer loyalty and evangelists' economic effects is the comparison of promoters to their evil twins—the detractors—in terms of both repeat business (or lack thereof) and positive or negative referrals.

According to Satmetrix—creators of the Net Promoter methodology—word of mouth's incidence and impact on sales is on the rise. Promoter referral rates increased by 8 percent from 2006 to 2007, and by another 14 percent from 2007 to 2008. Based on the methodology, most self-reported referrals came in the physical world, that is, face-to-face, over the phone, or offline referrals. In other words, they did not factor in digital sites like Amazon.com and, more specifically, a social media lens, or multiple. If they had, this number would be considerably higher and not just the absolute number, but from the exponential number or networked community that it could potentially reach over time.

From a sociological perspective, there's a profound cultural shift taking place, wherein people are more apt and open to share than ever before. It's more than just having an expanded set of tools (megaphone); rather, it's about a renewed sense of connectedness and a genuine desire to share knowledge with and help others.

Satmetrix attempted to calculate total worth of a customer based on two prime variables: buyer economics (past behavior as a proxy for future purchases) and referrer economics (word of mouth) as they both related to customer experience. Using the oft-maligned wireless industry (with an industry net promoter score of 14 percent, i.e. 41 percent promoters less 27 percent detractors) and surveying the likes of Alltel, AT&T Cingular, Sprint Nextel, T-Mobile, Tracfone, US Wireless, and Verizon, they determined the following:

- To start, spend (previous 12 months) did not necessarily correlate with customer loyalty. On average, promoters spent $1,145; and detractors $1,155. This is easily explained by a highly commoditized industry that has undermined itself by carrying an unusually large base of customers who intensely dislike their provider (I'm pretty sure you're one of them), most of whom either feel it's a lesser of evils (they all suck) or are trapped in a contract (AT&T sucks, but they're the only provider tied to the iPhone). It's a recipe for disaster that more or less invites competitive conquest and constant churn—exacerbated by tremendous vulnerability from curveballs like being able to switch providers while keeping your number.
- Customer retention, on the other hand, was predictably a little higher for promoters than for detractors: 5.35 years versus 4.60, respectively
- Now, here's where it gets interesting: 75 percent of promoters made referrals (in the previous year), with an average of 3.24 referrals and a 23 percent success rate. This translated into 0.559 of a customer acquired for every 1 promoter "created" and an average of $639 incremental revenue generated from promoter referrals.
- Detractors, however, exhibited the following behavior: 32 percent generated 4.33 negative referrals with a whopping 92 percent customer loss rate or 1.275 customers lost (opportunity loss) for every 1 detractor created, translating into $1,459 revenue lost from detractor referrals.

So—combining purchase and referrer economics yielded a $2,088 differential between producing a promoter versus a detractor. Drilling down to the brand level—for example, comparing Sprint to Verizon—revealed a catch-22 of epic and dire proportions—especially considering the millions invested in acquiring customers yet leaking both actual *and* potential customers in the process due to poor (relative) customer experience.

Verizon's 2007 net promoter score (NPS) was 25 percent versus Sprint's *negative 18 percent*, which translated into a customer worth promoter/detractor differential of $1,916 versus $2,728 for the two brands, respectively. Whereas the promoter revenue for both companies was roughly the same, the biggest difference was in the detractor economics, specifically via the toxicity emanating from Sprint detractors versus their Verizon counterparts.

The Satmetrix study provided immediate insight into one of the central theses of this book: Not only is retention the new acquisition but also our failure to invest in customer experience as a primary driver of customer loyalty *adversely affects* the prospect and potential of future business growth via new customers (acquisition).

The implications for business at large are just as powerful:

- There's no point fishing with a wide net that is full of holes. Acquisition without a retention counterbalance is like flushing money down a toilet.
- The traditional concept of churn needs to be updated to integrate the opportunity costs of both buyer and referrer economics. In other words, the numbers are worse than we ever imagined. Churn itself is a vicious circle that hits us from both sides of the customer equation: It increases acquisition costs (from a relatively smaller pool of prospects) and decreases revenue from said acquisition.
- Therefore, companies need to increase their investment in retention marketing efforts (including, but not limited to, improving and even obsessing on customer experience) both in terms of current (future purchases) and future (referrer word-of-mouth) impact on customers.
- One obvious way to fund this increase is by optimizing or realigning the money spent between acquisition and retention efforts to align economic impact and importance to the business.

    In other words, reallocating dollars from one acquisition channel to another does not even begin to realize the opportunity at hand. So if you're currently agonizing over moving money from 30-second spots to prerolls (new media) or Facebook ads (social media), you're a lifetime away from getting in the game. What you really need is a complete overhaul of the marketing machine—in other words, a permanent flip of the funnel.
- One more point: In any industry of relative negative parity—such as airlines, cable, or wireless—the door is wide open for a challenger brand to literally clean up by doing one thing particularly well: delivering a superior customer experience.

- This means getting back to basics or slowing down (slow marketing[3]) and even becoming boring by returning to fundamentals. This flies in the face of flashy, glitzy, big ideas like incumbent brand marketing and marketing communications.
- And while we're on the subject of acquisition-focused "big" ideas, the whole concept of breaking through the clutter can actually be detrimental to the brand, especially when it draws undivided attention to the company's negative characteristics, service, and customer fulfillment. Promises broken versus promises kept. Visit www.flipthefunnelnow.com and click on enhanced content to view an episode of JaffeJuiceTV where I talk (rant) about why American Express should rename their small business program, "CLOSED" as opposed to OPEN and conclude that "advertising is going to become the noose that hangs us if we cannot deliver against our promises."

MEASUREMENT GUIDELINES

New paradigms inevitably call for new metrics. What we measure and how we measure it will determine short-term performance, medium-term direction, and long-term achievement.

For example, USAA doesn't just measure retention (they retained 96 percent of their customers in 2008; thanks for asking). They also track "retention for life" (95 percent of their customers plan to be lifelong members), which is pretty cool and enviable. Global information services corporation Experian uses 11 different key drivers to help determine various elements of customer experience and loyalty.

I'd like to suggest another more direct comparison. It's time to take on the big dog—*acquisition itself*—with all its bloated blubber and unnecessary padding of superfluous brand hyperbole and esoteric symbolism.

We must determine both the exact cost and the return on that cost to acquire a new customer using traditional acquisition channels versus acquiring a *new* customer *via* existing ones. We should also look at an apples-to-apples comparison of one additional (repeat) purchase from an existing customer versus a purchase from a new customer (singular) from a basket-sized perspective. Finally, look at the transaction value

---

[3] Based on a conversation between Pete Blackshaw and myself.

of a preferred customer. How do these three buckets compare to one another?

All you have to do is follow these simple steps:

1. Figure out where your business is coming from—that is, segment new (unaffiliated), referred (affiliated), and existing/returning customers.
2. Determine its cost—budget spent against the transaction.
3. Calculate its worth—basket size or transaction value.
4. Project or extrapolate how much it *could* be worth if it could be formalized, scaled, evolved, and activated.
5. Optimize and repeat!

Amid all of these calculations, you'll want to assign weights to tenure, loyalty, trust, credibility, influence, preference, and insistence, among other variables.

16

Cultural Sell-through and Organizational Sign-off

Flip the Funnel isn't a fleeting experiment or a fad. It's not the next shiny bright object or must-have of the new marketing season. Rather, it's a seismic and irreversible shift in terms of how companies conduct business, relate to their customers, and balance the mission-critical objectives of keeping the cash registers ringing and customers singing (their praises).

As simple and profound as this may sound, the very sad truth is that the entire marketplace is built around an acquisition-centric methodology.

But it's changing. When I visited Forrester's Customer Experience Forum in 2009, I couldn't help but think about another event taking place concurrently almost halfway around the world — the Cannes Advertising Festival. With a 40 percent drop in attendees and a 20 percent decrease in entries,[1] 2009's Cannes Festival seemed more like a wake. What made this navel-gazing spectacle even more intriguing was not even the fact that the coveted film category was won by a digital agency and a web video (as opposed to a television commercial) but rather that the real, big winner in the Titanium and Integrated categories, "Obama" — was a prime example of what happens with a flipped funnel.

At the time, I reflected on my decision to be at a customer-experience forum and writing a book about retention as the new acquisition, instead of getting a tan on the French Riviera, basking in the validation or affirmation of how right I was in my predictions from *Life after the 30-Second Spot*.

I was at peace.

More importantly, I thought about the two events' various attendees in terms of which executives would have a better chance of keeping *their*

[1] www.brandrepublic.com/News/914729/Cannes-attendance-expected-down-40/.

jobs in the years to come: the acquisition (Cannes/advertising) or the retention (customer experience/loyalty) ones.

Hopefully, you'll find yourselves setting up shop in the same camp that I call home. And if you're wavering in any way or doubtful about your ability to make this shift, my message to you is this: *yes, YOU can!* However, it won't be easy. Change never is.

What we desperately need right now is a complete reengineering of the corporate machine from outside in to reflect an inside-out approach to business. And while I'm certainly not an expert at organizational change, I have triangulated several ideas and approaches that may come in handy.

Flipping the funnel and creating a means to nurture and sustain a customer-centric migration path (A.D.I.A) is not achieved with a one-off pilot test, but rather with a commitment that is grounded in organizational change and supported by complete cultural buy-in.

My bias has always been strategy. I'm a *why* guy and feel that everything we do must deliver against this one-word question that is as much compass as it is roadmap; a seamlessly grounding force that marries vision with mission. Everything begins with strategy: This is where tactical game plans can be developed successfully and where frameworks of change can be constructed against a solid foundation of insight, vision, and mission. (See Figure 16.1.) Your starting point might be slightly different across the continuum of COST, but either way, it is imperative that commitment to change is championed by company constituents.

In various organizations, these agents of change are mapped quite conveniently against this four-phase evolutionary process:

Tactical — Anyone (as an individual) from a rogue employee to an intern, typically junior, often disconnected, under the radar, and unnoticeable unless their efforts are extremely well or poorly received. Biggest challenges are getting the funding, support, approvals, and commitment required to invest enough (both time and money) to maximize the possibility of success. On the flip side, less likely to succeed as efforts are detached from the core and integrated strategy.

Strategic — Someone with a degree of autonomy, authority, or credibility. Could even be an outsider like a freelancer or consultant; typically one-off or project-based investment. Biggest challenges are getting buy-in and collaboration from the rest of the department and

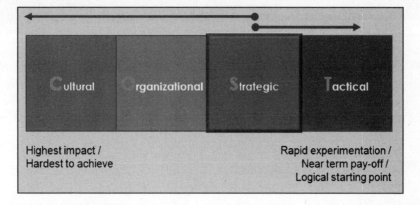

Figure 16.1   C.O.S.T.

Source: © Joseph Jaffe.

equivalents within other departments. These attempts generally do well but struggle to get mindshare and sustainability within the company beyond their project-based efforts.

Organizational—An entire department that works well within but not necessarily with other departments—for example, the digital department. Biggest challenges include collaboration and integration from other departments. Over time, getting the rest of the organization's attention becomes necessary, especially with sustained results.

Cultural—Everyone within the organization, from the CEO to the mailroom clerk. This is the organization that marches to the same drum and attracts like-minded customers like moths to a flame. Biggest challenges include eradicating bottlenecks that often come from middle management or cultural change that is dictated as opposed to arrived at via consensus.

Most companies seem to be stuck somewhere between strategic and tactical stages of change when it comes to adopting emerging, alternative, or lateral technology, methodology, or different practices. Finding a common entry point is often the best level-setting technique to set up the systematic and standardized process needed in order to evolve and integrate across the board. This place, more often than not, is strategic planning.

Beyond a common entry point, there also has to be protocol for championing change and, in this particular case, customer experience, retention, and activation. And while having *no one* to lead this charge is clearly not recommended (today), the opposite end of the spectrum is equally concerning: what happens when *everyone* runs the show (tomorrow) aka a customer free-for-all or land grab? Which begs the question . . .

WHO OWNS THE CUSTOMER?

Is it marketing? Is it customer service? Is it customer experience? (assuming there is even a customer-experience department in the first place)? Is it John, the CMO, or Jane, the assistant store manager who helped you out the last time you were in a pickle?

In *Join the Conversation*, I introduced the notion—and rise—of a conversation department and a chief conversation officer to run it. I'm still waiting. As *Life after the 30-Second Spot* taught me, change almost always takes longer than we think possible. Most companies are still on the outside, looking in on their customers' lives—at least when it comes to joining the conversation. Par for the course seems to be superficial monitoring with negligible or anemic follow-through; listening strategies are still—for the most part—anomalies.

Progress is slow, but perhaps your competitors' red flag or amber caution is your green light. Perhaps that's your cue and opportunity to be out there— in front. That's why they call it leadership.

My call for a conversation department and a chief conversation officer was perhaps a little ahead of its time. It still is. Establishing a specific capability and group to oversee all forms of conversation—whether they are customer, consumer, channel, journalist, influencer, or content creator-based—may yet be just around the corner; or it might be a generation away. Or perhaps this kind of department will be completely unnecessary due to the advances (being) made in the customer-experience space. Whereas chief conversation officers are about as commonplace today as Loch Ness monster sightings, many companies have already deployed chief customer officers and/or chief experience officers. I've even met some of them. For now, they less own and more champion the customer's experiences. Indeed, customer experience is (or should be) as horizontal as it is vertical and ultimately must be holistic in order to pervasively integrate and unify all the ways the company conducts business.

Going back to the COST analogy, the evolution of the customer ownership debate looks like the complete inverse of the earlier comparison:

Tactical = Customer-Service Department

Strategic = Chief Marketing Officer (or marketing department)

Organizational = Chief Customer Officer or Chief Experience Officer (and their departments)

Cultural = No one

At the lowest end of the spectrum, customer service remains siloed and is typically still viewed as a cost center. Satisfaction is the objective du jour, and raving fans are nothing but a pipe dream. In other words, maintaining law and order or the status quo is the primary goal. That's not to say that gains can't be made by adopting advanced technologies like live chat, for example; however, for the most part, progress is going to be fairly linear and incremental. In these scenarios, customer service is considered to be a defensive tactic.

Steve Smith, who spent more than 20 years at Enterprise Rent-a-Car, is a prime example of the *S* as in strategic solution. In his tenure as chief marketing officer, Smith had a long list of responsibilities from advertising to branding, from promotions to customer loyalty. Including loyalty under the same umbrella that stewards the brand's identity, health, and equity has obvious advantages from an integration vantage point. At the same time, it also risks relegation to the back of the line, especially in an acquisition-dominated organization.

There's absolutely no reason why marketing shouldn't oversee retention. In fact, most companies do exactly this—with CRM or customer-relationship management, one-to-one marketing, or even e-mail marketing. The challenges, of course, are the same that the CMO faces every single day of his or her endangered tenure: holistic integration, accountability, and privatization and allocation against scarce resources.

The traditional marketing or sales funnels are 100 percent focused on driving the purchase ("action") or closing the deal. Once that happens, there's a gaping void that represents an unmet need. Customers are either referred to an entirely different department or, worse, abandoned or forgotten. Against this logic, there needs to be a single point of contact—marketing—that accompanies customers who continue their brand journey.

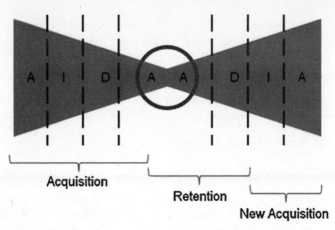

Figure 16.2 Closing the Loop: From Acquisition to Retention to the NEW Acquisition

Source: © Joseph Jaffe.

But what if there were a bridge—offering continuity and consistency between the chasm that separates acquisition and retention—a moment of truth where the classic (A.I.D.A.) and flipped (A.D.I.A.) funnels come together, as depicted by the bowtie diagram in Figure 16.2.

Smith offers up the following advice to individuals looking to change a company from the inside out:

- Learn the business.
- Become an advocate (support others; solve their problems).
- Build consensus (establish expectations).
- Be transparent.
- Meet expectations (keep promises).
- Communicate key, quantifiable results.

Smith's message is really quite simple: *You can't manage what you can't measure.* One particular metric speaks volumes about realizing success within Enterprise: Among consumers who were not predisposed to consider Enterprise (candidate for classic awareness-oriented advertising), the share of rentals was 27 percent; among those who were, the share doubled to 54 percent. However, among those committed to the brand, the share leaped to an impressive 71 percent. This customer commitment matched an internal commitment to those doing the servicing. Case in point: No one in the company is promoted unless her or his department has scores equal to or greater than the company's average for customer satisfaction.

If marketing is everything, then everything that touches a consumer—especially those who become our customers—should be a part of marketing.

ORGANIZATIONAL MELTDOWN

According to an August 2009 study from the CMO Council and the Customer Experience Board (CEB), *"free or low-cost interactive digital media channels, social networks, mobile messaging devices, online communities and other forms of content-rich engagement are permanently altering the communications marketplace and redefining customer experience."*

That's good news for anyone reading this book. As the reconciliatory mantra states, *"if you can't beat 'em, join 'em"*. In other words, don't fear the change; embrace it. Use, integrate, and benefit from it.

And just in the nick of time as more than 84 percent of respondents in the CEB study indicated that it's costing more to acquire and retain customers, and 63 percent reported seeing higher rates of customer churn and attrition. One of the biggest contributors to defection was inadequate customer service. Sound like déjà vu all over again? Consider yourselves on notice.

Realistically, however, that's easier said than done.

While 89 percent of the sample believed they need to get better at customer handling and response—which includes better listening—more than 50 percent felt their organization *"is not culturally or organizationally aligned around the customer."* This encompassed—among other things—business practices, billing policies, and personnel who were not "customer friendly."

Get busy living or get busy dying.

The sound you just heard is your number being called to investigate setting up a customer-experience department.

CUSTOMER EXPERIENCE IS BIGGER THAN MARKETING

What do M. Bridget Duffy, M.D., and Ingrid Lindberg have in common? Besides being women, they're also living embodiments of the *O*

(organizational) commitment to customer experience. Duffy and Lindberg are customer-experience officers at Cleveland Clinic and CIGNA,
respectively. Both are partly—if not wholly—responsible for transforming their organizations' approaches to customer service, loyalty, and
experience, which was convenient, since both needed changing.

Cleveland Clinic begins their annual statement with a bold quote:
"The patient is not only an illness. He has a soul." But it wasn't always like
that. In fact, Duffy had to deal with statements like *"Why do I have to be
nice to patients? I just want to get them off the table alive"* before she helped the
organization make over its business perspective and processes. This shift
wasn't grounded in intangible or feel-good spirit; the clinic was losing
potential business to competitors who were perceived to care more about
their patients.

Part of the problem came from the organization's structure. Every
physician on staff is under a one-year contract, which makes sense when
the stakes are so high and "average" performances aren't quite satisfactory in life-or-death situations. In the past, physicians were evaluated on
volume and safety metrics; patients were merely numbers. Now, customer experience has become a leading driver of quality and a variable in
physicians' scorecards. The result has been a renewed sense of respect
and proof positive that doing the right thing will ultimately lead to the
right result (the very same volume and safety metrics).

CIGNA operates in a space (health insurance) fraught with extreme
customer emotion. At a time when health care reform is at the top of
most political agendas, doing business is a catch-22 game where victory
is often about choosing the lesser of evils.

That hasn't stopped CIGNA from relentlessly pursuing attempts to
improve customer service. Over the past few years, the company has
won numerous customer-service awards and been recognized substantially for decisions to extend service hours to weekends (new rule alert),
introduce new service-enabling technology, and deploy fully integrated
service teams.

At the heart of CIGNA's commitment is their call center, which
makes attitude and personality traits such courtesy, concern, and
knowledge—as well as "timely resolution of problems"—entry-level
requirements. In order to be selected, representatives must pass a
certification program, which requires performance within the top 20
percent of scores, based on J. D. Power and Associates' multi-industry
benchmarks.

A key to success has been the ability to streamline customer
offerings using technology. Most notable is the member-facing health

management tool MyCigna—a personal intranet of sorts that provides access to various information and functionality about plans, coverage, tools, and potential savings. Through MyCigna, beneficiaries can find a physician, compare hospitals and prescription prices (brand name and generic) at more than 57,000 pharmacies nationwide, get quotes on medical and dental treatments, access articles covering more than 5,000 health conditions, and more. Using the *C* of customization, members receive targeted health messages and links that highlight clinical information, as well as tips regarding generic and therapeutic alternatives based on their profiles and search history.

The same access is provided to customer-service employees, who can retrieve all documents, notes, and information relevant to every customer. Being able to instantly log and aggregate every customer interaction—as well as any previously existing (open) or archived (closed) cases—has allowed CIGNA to not only resolve most issues with a single call but also save millions of dollars. In fact, printing savings alone (by eliminating burdensome interoffice correspondence, faxing, and duplication of multiple call notes) were close to $1 million.

CIGNA's own customer-experience maven Ingrid Lindberg has a unique approach to selling through a better way of doing business. She's a big believer in bottom-up sell-through, but warns against middle management mafia (the average tenure within CIGNA is 11.2 years). Part of her irreverent yet charming style is to force people to act, well, like people. She *charges* people who use acronyms—especially concerning customers—and challenges everyone to refer to customers by their given names. Like Smith, Lindberg uses data as her weapon of choice. She has a coffee mug that reads, *"Your opinion, although interesting, is irrelevant,"* which she conveniently positions to face anyone who attempts to perpetuate the status quo based on how things have always been done. Her philosophical approach is simple: *"What you did before is not necessarily wrong . . . but in order to get to the future, you have to do things a little differently."*

Lindberg has used this spirit to effect pretty substantial changes within the company, such as extending customer-service hours to weekends and holidays.

IT'S ALL ABOUT CULTURE

The will to change isn't an epiphany or revelation. Nor is it a scene from *Jerry Maguire* where a simple Manifesto (or memo) is going to transform a company overnight. If anything, it may get you fired.

Figure 16.3   I'm a Zappos V.I.P.!

Source: © Joseph Jaffe.

Do you know the difference between a chicken and a pig in a ham-and-egg breakfast? The chicken is involved but the pig is committed.

Like our poor friend Porky, *Change* is a commitment. It's an irreversible and irrevocable all-hands course correction that can have a profound impact on an entire organization and even the market in which it operates. Change is also conspicuous, and in a world of sameness and mediocrity, it sticks out like a sore thumb. It's also infectious and hard to ignore (or imitate) once a leader emerges from a pack of clones.

There's a reason the first four letters of "culture" are *C U L T*. Take the Zappos Experience—happening almost hourly at their corporate offices in Henderson, Nevada—and you'll see why. You'll meet Doctor Vik and get a Polaroid in their VIP chair (Figure 16.3). As you walk past each department, they'll all spontaneously and collectively whoop, chant, and play a musical instrument in an almost territorial and tribal way. It doesn't take too much of a leap to see how this translates to world-class customer service.

Travel web site Kayak.com, cofounded by the same Paul English from Get Human, proves the point in the most tangible way possible. Kayak doesn't have a single customer representative and yet it keeps millions of customers happy. How? By instilling the process and buy-in that EVERY SINGLE employee (including the founders) would spend a minimum of 20 minutes a day responding to customer issues and concerns. They even take it as far as to display all customer scores, inquiries, and responses in real time on large screens in their offices— clearly exposing employees falling behind their quotas in RED. Now that's commitment!

And then there's Virgin America. The challenge of launching a new brand into the already-challenged U.S. airline market might seem elementary or preposterous—depending on your perspective. Extending a larger-than-life brand with a global footprint into a market desperate for leadership is always a little easier when beginning with a clean slate, which includes zero legacy systems, union contracts, or ingrained attitudes. Conversely, well-established barriers to entry from mature loyalty and frequent-flier programs almost eliminate an entire segment of frequent travelers off the bat. Various other cost structures associated with a highly capital-intensive, competitive business make competitive inroads even tougher.

In an industry that scores lower in customer satisfaction than the IRS[2] or the U.S. Postal Service,[3] it seems that one would need to be very salmonlike (or just masochistic) to swim against the raging current of status quo. But that's where differentiation comes into play, and it certainly doesn't hurt to have a slightly affected leader like Richard Branson either! Besides, there was enough guiding inspiration in the form of Southwest Airlines and JetBlue to justify the rewards for another challenger to enter the ring.

Virgin America bypassed function and went straight to form in the "form" of an intangible and amorphous emotion—love—and proved that even in business, love conquers all. Except that the love shared was pervasive; it didn't just flow from employees (team members) to customers (guests), but rather came from within the company itself—common respect, a shared sense of purpose, and a community of genuine commitment to a single cause: building a *consumer-driven next-generation airline* essentially from the inside out.

A major part of this plan focused on customer experience. In fact, part of Virgin America's strategy was to keep costs low (there's nothing new there) by avoiding all expenses that did not directly improve customer experience (that *is* new). In other words, customer experience was an exception to the rule and thus was able to escape the clutches of the bean counters.

[2] *USA Today* headline, May 2007.

[3] University of Michigan American Customer Satisfaction Index.

Figure 16.4   Virgin America Check-In

Source: Virgin America.

Everything began with the workforce, or talent, by hiring and nurturing the kinds of people that had service in their DNA. Virgin recognized that for all the training in the world, people either get it or they don't when it comes to uniting under a common flag (in this case a brand logo) and working as one cohesive unit to achieve a common goal. None of this is possible in an organization that doesn't instill innovation, change, and purpose in its cultural wiring (Figures 16.4 and 16.5).

Figure 16.5   Happy Employees = Happy Customers

Source: Virgin America.

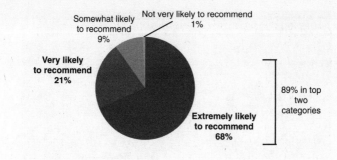

Figure 16.6   Creating Evangelists

Source: Virgin America.

Evidence of this contagious passion was apparent when talking to customers. When asked to rate the Virgin America experience as "better than or much better than I expected," 75 percent of respondents (the second highest score) assigned this score to "staff personality." By comparison, only 46 percent assigned that same mark to "food/beverage options available" (even with a revolutionary touch-screen ordering process whereby guests can select from an impressive array of meals from their seats).

Activating this brand passion or love was evident in the brand's secondary goal: to create and develop evangelists. When surveyed, 75 percent of guests indicated that their flight on Virgin America was either one of, or THE best flight they had experienced in a while, and 89 percent indicated they'd either be very or extremely likely to recommend the airline to a friend or colleague. (See Figure 16.6.)

With the help of technology—like Wi-Fi on every flight (Figure 16.7)—Virgin has helped put the "social" back into "media" or "marketing" by connecting the dots between guests and even team members, to foster a sense of belonging in the form of community.

Using conversational marketing tools such as Facebook, Twitter, and YouTube *in real time,* the brand has elicited the kind of responsiveness you only wish you could get from your spouse. Case in point: In one case, a guest who was overtly complaining in the air was met at the arrival gate by a Virgin representative who proceeded to solve the problem. How's that for turnaround?

Just being able to deliver a great product is probably 98 percent of the battle for most companies. For Virgin America, it's only one component of a total experience that is one part always on, one part real time, and one part

Figure 16.7   Wi-Fi, not "Why Fly?"

Source: Virgin America.

cost of entry in a market where customers *demand* an interactive relationship with the companies they patronize. It stems from both employees' and customers' rising expectation to take part in making decisions.

Feedback is continuous, and the loop that connects the brand with its guests and team members is endless, constant, and unbroken. The company also addresses this input, implements suggestions, and communicates their use back to those who initiated the contact. Virgin has since launched more diverse, healthier menus; videogame soundtracks; and premixed cocktails as the result of direct feedback from guests.

It's certainly a great start. However, it is a work in progress, even by Virgin's standards, and a learning curve that never quite straightens out. Virgin recognizes three challenges associated with this investment:

- It's resource-intensive.
- Success begets success. In other words, once customers experience a better way of doing business with open, accessible, and responsive companies, there's no going back—ever—to the old way of doing business.
- Strong stomachs are required for often brutally honest feedback.

And even Virgin is not immune to erring along the way (both normal and healthy). I noticed three mistakes the brand had made in an otherwise stellar performance:

- They were using interns for Twitter conversations ("twinterns")
- They still regard their customer-service department as slow-moving (one of the reasons why they opted for interns versus their existing customer-service agents)
- They admit that they haven't quite integrated all the real-time feedback from newer channels (especially in the social media realm) into their closed-loop learning process/knowledge base

And while Virgin is still learning and improving every day, spare a thought for the sluggish corporate behemoths that are struggling to turn *themselves* around or, at the very minimum, change course away from the turbulent seas of acquisition and toward the placid shores of retention.

What are they to do?

Vice President and Principal Analyst at Forrester Research Bruce Temkin puts forward what he calls the five stages of customer experience maturity (Figure 16.8).

For each stage, he defines a key focus and corresponding cultural imperative or directive.

	Interested	Invested	Committed	Engaged	Embedded
Key Focus	Explore opportunity	Fix problems	Redesign processes	Empower employees	Sustain customer-centric DNA
Culture	N/A	Get buy-in	Solidify beliefs	Align HR systems	Sustain customer-centric DNA

What's most interesting about Bruce's path is that the ultimate goal is to get to a point where customer-centricity is part of the company's DNA—pervasive, ubiquitous, ever-present, and all-encompassing—so much so that no one owns it because everyone owns it.

Did we just negotiate ourselves out of a job?

At the highest level, an experience chief, customer czar, or service ninja is not needed anymore. And why would they be, assuming customer experience is as horizontal, diagonal, and holistic as it is vertical?

Although I'd personally file that scenario under "things I probably won't see in my lifetime," that doesn't mean it can't or won't be achieved by a select group of forward-thinking companies, with the right mix of vision, determination, and execution.

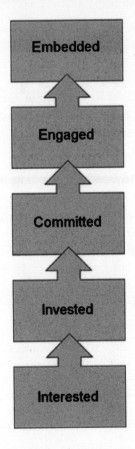

Figure 16.8   The Five Stages Towards Customer Experience Utopia

For everyone else, it's time to aggressively seek out a place where customer experience itself becomes the common thread uniting the old and new forms of acquisition. A chief is needed here, and part of his or her mandate is to obsess about and champion every aspect of the customer—both internal and external. To be successful, the chief must be able to foster a culture of access, collaboration, and responsiveness.

That mission includes restoring balance (proportion) between classic acquisition and retention—from strategic, budgeting, process, activation, and measurement perspectives. It requires that we move retention from the back office to the front office—even to the head of the table. The task itself is best suited to an internal change-agent that has clout, confidence, and conviction, or an external partner that can help "reorg the org" and realign it to relate better to the people it serves—and those who serve it.

17

Flip the Funnel for Your Personal Life

As I wrote this book, I kept on thinking about how a flipped-funnel mentality related to various industries, departments, processes, and consumer behavior. In Chapter 9, I showed how flipping the funnel can be equally effective for employees as well as customers.

But is this theory relevant to our personal lives as well? Perhaps it was the inspirational message of Barack Obama's presidential campaign and its transformative impact on people's personal lives that made me wonder whether a flipped-funnel approach could work for individuals as well. I came up with the following theories about how this book's central themes can translate from our professional lives to our personal lives.

On one level, it's about *balance.* It's about how we, too, operate at the wrong end of the 80:20 rule, and how it adversely affects our lives — either directly (through bad choices) or indirectly (based on the opportunity costs of *not* doing something more valuable).

In 2009, I lost 50 pounds. I flipped a funnel in terms of how I approached food. I used to live to eat; now I eat to live. Or perhaps I should say that I eat *better* to live *longer.* I turned the restrictive and unpleasant notion of dieting on its head and approached my shift as a lifestyle change.

When I existed at the wide end of the funnel, my life was a free-for-all. Everything went: no restrictions, boundaries, or framework. The end result at the narrow end of the funnel was probably proportionate to the wiggle room left in my arteries.

Now I have a singular objective in mind, and my focus is to act according to that goal. The narrow end of the funnel is my starting point. Perhaps it's literally portion size, or perhaps it's just the discipline to prioritize, based on what matters in life. My prize is a much wider funnel that represents an abundance of possibilities and choices (relative to what it once was) that affect me, my family, my friends, my health, and even my professional life. (Apparently I *don't* need the warm nuts every time I fly!)

By zeroing in on one directive (in this book, it's customer retention, service, and experience; in my particular case, it was health and wellness), I've discovered an entirely new suite of possibilities—from a one-hour run every weekend, to wearing my wedding suit for the second time in more than 10 years, to knowing that I've probably extended my life overall by a few more years.

The second insight is *commitment*. Throughout this book, I've shown how marketing, change, and customer experience are all about longevity, continuity, and commitment, as opposed to fleeting campaigns.

The same could be said about weight loss. My goal is no longer acquisition (in the form of pounds lost) but maintenance, in dieting terms. Keeping the weight off is a form of retention. The analogy also works in terms of diets or quick-hit remedies like herbal colonics that are essentially fads focused on instant gratification. The fundamentals of weight loss are simple: The longer it takes to lose, the longer it will take to put back on.

No more weight examples—I promise! Instead, I'll turn it over to you. How can you maximize the point of purchase; that is, extend the gratification you felt when you got married, had your first child, or closed on your home? It's so easy to take what we have for granted and move on to the next big thing—when in reality, it is staring you in the face. In *Flip the Funnel*, I talk about your customers—the sole reason you're in business at all. I challenge you to embrace these customers and figure out ways you can build lifelong, productive, and meaningful relationships with them. So when did you last flip the funnel for good with your marriage or your key personal relationships?

A third aspect of flipping the funnel is *quality*. Instead of continuing to woo scores of complete strangers who have zero affinity, loyalty, or history with the brand, why not focus on the people who have a reason to care, share, contribute, and support the business, and work with them to build even stronger bonds—internally and externally (through word of mouth). There's an old saying that if you can count your true friends on one hand, you are indeed a rich person. Quality trumps quantity; it always has, and it always will. Perhaps this is our chance to revisit the relationships that matter and invest a little bit more time, effort, and energy into nurturing them. From childhood friends to your work colleagues, they all count.

It's also a reminder that Facebook and Twitter popularity contests are rather juvenile and even pathetic.

Personal Branding Is Overrated

We're living in a world where anyone has the potential for 15 minutes or streams of fame; this is the rise and era of the weblebrity, as I call the elite few who get more views on YouTube than Nike or even Apple. It appears that anyone with a point of view, no matter how banal, is in the self-proclaimed-expert business. Like it or not, the democratization of opinion has completely leveled the playing fields and it's probably not going to change any time soon.

The new creative class is certainly embracing the tools at their disposal: YouTube, Twitter, Facebook, blogging, podcasting, Flickr, and the like. However, the flipped funnel warns all of us to avoid the lure of becoming just another broadcaster (read: spammer), turning an otherwise purely conversational platform into a one-way channel or vehicle that is no better — and probably is worse — than its predecessors.

I have more than 2,700 fake friends on Facebook; at least, I call them that. It's a term of endearment. I invite you all to become my fake friends as well. Use my vanity URL of www.facebook.com/jaffejuice to friend me. Here's the problem, though: I can't have a meaningful bond with my 14,000+ Twitter followers or 2,700+ Facebook friends. I've made the same mistake that most of us make in our personal and professional lives: We want to be popular, and we measure our success by tonnage as opposed to class.

It's the same mistake we make when we try to measure influence and authority in the "virtual" world. We employ a very limited method of trying to convert the number of blog posts or mentions into an apples-to-apples impression count and then assign an arbitrary media value to it by using size of audience and a traditional media benchmark equivalent.

A website called Twinfluence[1] claims that my circle of influence on Twitter is a lot more powerful than the raw number of 14,000 followers. It's actually a whopping 24 million, based on what would happen if each of my followers retweeted my message to *their* followers, and so on. According to graph theory, a twitterer's followers are the first-order network, and their followers count the same as their degree (as in degrees of separation), prestige, or popularity. Figure 17.1 illustrates the different neighborhoods in a network. The twitterer is the primary node

[1] http://twinfluence.com/.

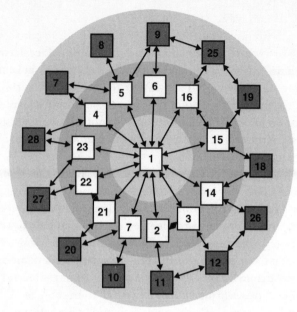

Figure 17.1   Degrees of Separation

Source: Twinfluence.

(in the middle), its first-order neighbors (the next ripple) surround it, and its second-order neighbors (the outer layer) circle on the outside.

The same ripple effect could be true for any social network in terms of its potential reach. Perhaps this is the real visualization of viral marketing in action, that is, what it takes to get an idea to tip in a networked world. It's really just a restatement of word of mouth itself—the megaphone—which, as discussed in Chapter 12, is one interpretation of what happens when you start small and grow big the right way.

There are incredible opportunities ahead to find true friendship and establish sublime connections by using a socially networked world. By focusing on intimate, authentic, human, and meaningful relationships with trustworthy, credible, and substantive REAL friends, anything is possible.

Next, there's *prioritization.* I was once flying back from a business trip and got to talking with a fellow road warrior about life, family, and goals. I'll never forget his words to me, which began with the exact words I used to open this book: "What if we got it all wrong?" He continued: "When we're in our mid-thirties to mid-forties, we work our butts off for our families, and all during this time, we're constantly on the road, away from our young children who literally hero-worship and idolize us. Then when we're in our late forties and fifties and finally have made it—thereby allowing us to take our foot off the gas and spend more time with our family—we look around and our teenaged kids don't want to know us anymore." These are such accurate words that challenge conventional wisdom about how we cultivate relationships with a different kind of customer—our family. The same might be true with respect to spouses, except in this case, failure results in the funnel ending up on our heads with a big *D* emblazoned on it.

Finally, there's *perspective*.

I've been fortunate enough to influence many people to change jobs or even careers. I've persuaded special folk to start blogs or podcasts, some of which have gone on to greatness and even overshadowed me in the process. When the student becomes the teacher, it is a beautiful thing indeed.

THE THIRD CUSTOMER

This book discusses two types of customers: the external customer and the internal customer (your employees). But there's a third kind: you. You are a customer too.

If I may, I'd like to encourage you to think about ways you can flip the funnel for *yourself*. You don't need to be dramatic or quit your day job. You can continue the path you're currently on, but perhaps you can accelerate your progress just a little by focusing on yourself as the customer. Take an existential position and put yourself at the center of the universe. You're in the middle, and everything ripples out from you. Only now, instead of all roads leading *away* from you, they're leading *to* you.

Just as we are nothing without our customers, the world is nothing without us. So how can we—and *you*—make a difference? How can you change the way business has always been done to leave your mark? How can you change a life or make this world a better place?

It *can* be done. Perhaps it's one YouTube video, like Jill Peterson and Kevin Heinz's incredible wedding procession (www.jkwedding-dance.com). Perhaps it's starting an inspirational blog that connects parents with other parents, cancer survivors with cancer sufferers, or fighters with lovers. (See www.blamedrewscancer.com)

Put the funnel to your eye. Use it as a spyglass or a telescope. See the world for what it is, but more important, for what it can become.

18

I Had a Great Experience—
How about You?

There's a lot of good in this world; hell, there's a lot of great in this world. Although it's easy to poke fun at, criticize, and berate the big dumb company, aloof brand, out-of-touch executive, or clueless customer-service agent, there's actually an increasingly inspirational set of best-in-class examples of unbelievable customer service and experience.

I've highlighted many of them in this book: from Steinway to CustomInk, Obama to Zappos, Cleveland Clinic to Virgin America, USAA to Smokey Bones, Best Buy to Umpqua Bank, and Enterprise to Comcast.

And there are countless others waiting to be celebrated. Won't you help me create a better sense of order and balance so we don't have to stew over the Domino's, Motrin, Delta, and Target cases at the expense of the really terrific examples of how business should—and, no doubt, *will*—be done from this moment forward?

Perhaps you created that experience for your own customers or encountered it yourself (you are, after all, a customer, too). Perhaps you read about it on a blog. Perhaps somebody told you about it at a cocktail party, online, or via a social network. Whichever way, leave your mark at www.ihadagreatexperience.com.

I don't mind if it's a personal moment between two individuals, an encounter at a mom-and-pop store, or an interaction with one of the world's mightiest corporations. We're all equal when customers dip into their wallets to reach for a hard-earned dollar. Who will they spend it with—you or your competitor? The choice ultimately depends on whom they care the most about—and who cares the most about them in return.

Submit stories with great customer experiences and examples of companies that flipped the funnel in terms of how they approach the people who keep them in business: their employees and, specifically, their customers. Who knows? Maybe I'll offer you an incentive along the way and feature your story on my video show, JaffeJuiceTV (www .jaffejuice.tv).

By the way, there's also www.ihadabadexperience.com, because there just had to be.

CLOSING REMARKS

Flip the Funnel is a book about the triangulation between future-focused vision, good old-fashioned business fundamentals and common sense, and turning convention on its head. However, as extreme as it might sound to walk away from the way things were always done—and, in this case, begin where you once ended—it's really not extreme at all. As Machiavelli or Richard III might have said, *the end justifies the means.* Except that there's nothing sinister or untoward here about either the journey or the destination.

This is about growing your business while shrinking your budget; about getting more from less at a time when business needs and even demands it. It's about eliminating waste and focusing dollars on the people who really matter: your customers. It's about harnessing the hidden potential of two incredibly underutilized constituencies: customer evangelists and employees.

Whether you use the funnel as a filter, megaphone, or spyglass, or to form a bowtie, rewarding and activating those who truly care about the brand—(without even remotely sacrificing trust and integrity in doing so)—the goal is to become completely self-sustaining: the not-so-silent *S* at the end of A.D.I.A. And when it does, self-sustaining becomes self-fulfilling, a *living, breathing, and thriving ecosystem that is powered by human beings with common goals, ideals, and beliefs.* How can you possibly argue with that?

THE BUTTERFLY EFFECT OF BUSINESS

Everything is connected and interconnected. So whatever happens in one of your stores (Domino's), one of your airplanes (United), or one of your written responses (Target)—even at the most junior, isolated, or granular level—can have long-term enduring effects on your business, reputation, image, and ultimately your sales.

In a world of connectivity, social networks, and social megaphones, the stakes have never been so high. The question is not WHETHER to flip the funnel, but WHEN. And the answer should not be WHERE to flip the funnel, but EVERYWHERE; not HOW, but HOW MUCH.

If customer experience is the sum total of all interactions, transactions, and encounters between a customer and a company, its brands, products, and services over a determined period of time, THEN it stands to reason that all of this will inevitably lead to materially impacting future sales—both repeat purchases from existing customers AND new business via existing customers.

You'll notice that nowhere in this revised equation have I focused on the traditional funnel's laborious quest for often-fleeting acquisition (new business from new customers). Do they go away? Not at all. But no longer are they the bullies that dominate the corporate conversation either.

Instead of dissecting how to incrementally tweak an already failing acquisition model in desperate search of new blood, we can shift our focus and momentum to rededicating ourselves to our customers with a renewed purpose and intensity. We begin with the end in mind: an economic boon in the form of more business. During trying times, our opportunity does not come from cutting costs, mitigating risk, or trading off quality (experience) for quantity (transactions). It instead comes from ramping up our investment and commitment.

So why don't you listen more, respond more, learn more, and do more—using a new CUSTOMER-behavior and activation model called the Flipped Funnel. This process guides a customer through a journey of discovery and a path to advocacy and, along the way, scatters various crumbs to help them find their way and to provide incentive to continue.

Everything we do that touches our customers—directly or indirectly— will have an effect on our future business. At times, it will be small and seemingly insignificant; at other times, it will be gargantuan and game-changing. What appears temporal today may well be permanent tomorrow.

If everything is indeed interconnected, then we need to act accordingly. This is the Activation of the model and the path to ensure the final S of sustainability, continuity, and success. Connect the dots. Fill in the blanks. Paint a masterpiece!

The COMPANY - CUSTOMER PACT

THE CHALLENGE

We, customers and companies alike, need to trust the people with whom we do business. Customers expect honest, straightforward interactions where their voices are heard. Companies work to inspire brand loyalty and deliver satisfaction while trying to understand their customers better. It is evident that we all have a crucial stake–and responsibility–in transforming the adversarial tone that too often dominates the customer experience.

A CALL FOR SHARED RESPONSIBILITY

Along with open, authentic communication comes the mutual responsibility to make it work. As each of us is both a customer *and* an employee, we share in the rewards and challenges of candor. By adopting these five practical measures, we can together realize a fundamental shift in our business relationships:

	COMPANIES	CUSTOMERS
1.	Be human. Use a respectful, conversational voice, avoid scripts and *never* use corporate doublespeak.	Be understanding. Show the respect and kindness to company reps that you'd like shown to you.
2.	Encourage employees to use their real names and use a personal touch.	Use your real identity, and foster your long-term reputation with the company.
3.	Anticipate that problems will occur, and set clear, public expectations in advance for how you will address (and redress) issues.	Recognize that problems will occur, and give companies the information and time required to competently address issues.
4.	Cultivate a public dialogue with customers so they feel they are being heard and to demonstrate your accountability.	Share issues directly, or through a forum where the company has an opportunity to respond, so it can work with you to solve problems.
5.	Demonstrate your good intentions by speaking plainly, earnestly, and candidly with customers about problems that arise.	Give companies the benefit of the doubt, and be open to what they have to say.

OUR PACT

By working together in these ways, people build long-term relationships that lead to trust, strong communities, and sustainable businesses. We, as companies and customers, support this call for change.

SUPPORT THE PACT AT HTTP://CCPACT.COM

Figure 18.1   The Company-Customer Pact

Source: Get Satisfaction.

WE'RE ALL IN THIS TOGETHER

Get Satisfaction came up with a company-customer pact. With permission, I've reprinted as in Figure 18.1 for you.

The company-customer pact imbues one particularly strong idea: partnership. It implies partnership with our employees and our customers and bonds the two.

As mentioned several times in this book, flipping the funnel isn't just common sense. It's good business sense. It's about continuing the conversation and building lasting relationships that are predicated on trust, humanity, and reciprocal value. That's the way to double your sales by halving your budget, and if you think it can't be done, that's just because you haven't tried.

If you enjoyed this book, let's continue the conversation. Here are a variety of channels or ways we can build our own relationship:

- My blog, Jaffe Juice, at www.jaffejuice.com, which encapsulates and extends many of the themes in this book on a fairly regular basis.
- My audio podcast, Jaffe Juice (www.jaffejuice.com, or you can subscribe via iTunes), which some say has been an instant cure for insomnia, and others who listen to it on the treadmill refer to it as a weight-loss panacea (due to its length).
- My video show, JaffeJuiceTV (www.youtube.com/jaffejuicetv). I'm Jim Cramer without the bad predictions, Lou Dobbs without the makeup, Larry King without the false teeth, and Jon Stewart without the pumps.
- My Facebook profile, www.facebook.com/jaffejuice.
- For those of you with serious concentration issues, there's Twitter. The microblogging platform built for generation huh? Follow me at www .twitter.com/jaffejuice (@jaffejuice) or www.twitter.com/flipthe funnel (@flipthefunnel) for exlusive book-related updates
- I guess there should also be a web site. There is: www.flipthefunnel now.com with a ton of "enhanced content".
- Good, old-fashioned e-mail: jaffe@getthejuice.com

(continued)

> (*continued*)
>
> Plus, if you'd like to take the dialogue from the virtual to the digital to the physical world, I'm available for speaking engagements (www.jaffejuice .com/speaking.html), and my company, crayon (www.crayonville.com), is available to help you and your company flip the funnel. Now.

In the spirit of A.D.I.A., I'm going to use my own philosophy to help market and promote this book. So ping me via Twitter or your platform of choice when you purchase the book and I'll ACKNOWLEDGE you accordingly. If you have questions along the way, reach out to me and I'd be delighted to answer your questions (DIALOGUE).

Don't forget to leave your mark by posting a review to Amazon.com, barnesandnoble.com, your blog, or virtual platform of choice. Add yourself to the "I reviewed the book" section on www.flipthefunnelnow.com.

As an INCENTIVE, I'll be surprising the occasional reviewer with a little experiential gift to recognize and reward your contribution. In addition, I'm also instituting a much more definitive and tangible reward system for my customers (readers) along the following lines: if you provide me with proof of purchase of varying levels or amounts of my book, I will respond in kind with the following:

- Phone calls of varying length
- In-person meetings
- Webinars
- Keynote presentations

Please refer to "Flip the Funnel Referral program" on www.flip thefunnelnow.com for specific details and minor "terms and conditions."

Finally, I invite you to join the Facebook page (www.facebook.com/ flipthefunnel), Twitter list (www.twitter.com/flipthefunnel) and become part of a growing community (ACTIVATION) dedicated to customer service, customer experience and retention as the new acquisition.

How's that for walking the talk? Now, let's see if it works . . .

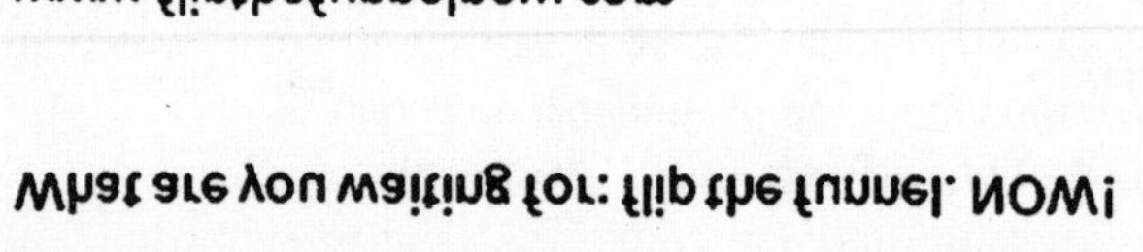

www.flipthefunnelnow.com

What Are You Waiting for? Flip the Funnel. NOW!

Figure 18.2 What Are You Waiting for? Flip the Funnel Now

Source: © Joseph Jaffe.

Resources

Chapter 7

How Better Marketing Elected Barack Obama
http://blogs.harvardbusiness.org/quelch/2008/11/how_better_market
  ing_elected_b.html

Slide Share: Case Study: The Barack Obama Strategy
http://www.slideshare.net/socialmedia8/case-study-the-barack-obama-
  strategy

Battle Plans: How Obama Won
http://www.newyorker.com/reporting/2008/11/17/081117fa_fact_lizza

The Social Pulpit: Barack Obama's Social Media Toolkit
http://www.edelman.com/image/insights/content/Social%20Pulpit%20-
  %20Barack%20Obamas%20Social%20Media%20Toolkit%201.09.
  pdf

Zappos.com Case Study: Why shoes are great for e-commerce . . . . . .
  yes, really
http://www.startup-review.com/blog/zapposcom-case-study-why-
  shoes-are-great-for-e-commerce-%E2%80%A6-yes-really.php

Focusing on Service — Nick Swinmurn's Key Move
http://www.startupnation.com/pages/keymoves/KM_NickSwinmurn
  .asp

Twitter: On Emerging Business Case Studies & Participatory Marketing
http://offthegrid-pr.com/socially-responsible-pr/2009/2/25/twitter-on-
  emerging-business-case-studies-participatory-mark.html

Slideshare: Zappos — – NPS Conference 1-26-09
http://www.slideshare.net/zappos/zappos-nps-conference-12609-
  presentation

How I Did It: Tony Hsieh, CEO, Zappos.com
http://www.inc.com/magazine/20060901/hidi-hsieh.html

Employee Innovator: USAA
http://www.fastcompany.com/magazine/99/open_customer-usaa.html

USAA Customer Service Is the Best in the Nation
http://www.mysanantonio.com/business/MYSA040807_1R_usaaser
  vice_2a75c75_html.html

USAA: Soldiering On In Insurance
http://www.businessweek.com/magazine/content/07_10/b4024003.htm

USAA Tops Insurers iIn Customer Experience
http://experiencematters.wordpress.com/2009/06/01/usaa-tops-insurers
  -in-customer-experience/

Forrester's 2008 Customer Experience Rankings
http://experiencematters.wordpress.com/2008/12/15/forrester%E2%
  80%99s-2008-customer-experience-rankings/

"BusinessWeek" Again Ranks USAA Among Top Customer Service
  Companies
https://www.usaa.com/inet/ent_blogs/Blogs?action=blogpost&blog-
  key=newsroom &postkey=businessweek_again_ranks_usaa_among

Business Week: The Customer Service Champs
http://bwnt.businessweek.com/interactive_reports/
  customer_service_2009/

Chapter 9

Brad Anderson, CEO of Best Buy at Zeitgeist '08
www.youtube.com/watch?v=n9cKXZBYapQ

Yellow Tag Interview — BlueShirtNation (Part 1/3)
www.youtube.com/watch?v=mFLIijjyKyU

Yellow Tag Interview — BlueShirtNation (Part 2/3)
www.youtube.com/watch?v=4UKGjqX2HGY

Yellow Tag Interview — BlueShirtNation (Part 3/3)
www.youtube.com/watch?v=ZIrQ41w-O9M

Index